Dedication

To Carolyn Thompson for her constant professional
and personal support.

Reviewers

Darla Castell, Ph.D.
Assistant Professor
University of Illinois at Urbana-Champaign
Urbana, IL

Tracy Gillespie
K-3 Physical Education teacher
Maypearl Elementary School
Maypearl, TX

Leanne O. Dennis
Physical Education Teacher
Florence Elementary School
High Point, NC

Scott Parker
Physical Education and Health Teacher
Marshall County Central High School
Newfolden, MN

Wilson Morales, M.A.
Elementary & Adapted Physical Education Teacher
Carmen Gómez Tejera School
Bayamón, PR

Using Technology in

Physical Education

**Books are to be returned on or before
the last date below.**

2 2 SEP 2006

WITHDRAWN

LIBREX —

I.M. MARSH LIBRARY LIVERPOOL L17 6BD
TEL. 0151 231 5216/5299

Bonnie's Fitware
Cerritos, California

Library of Congress Cataloging-in-Publication Data

Mohnsen, Bonnie S., 1955-
Using technology in physical education, 4th/
   Bonnie S. Mohnsen

ISBN 1-893166-97-X
1. Physical education and training–Computer-assisted instruction.
2. Educational technology. 3. Media programs (Education)

I. Title.
GV364.M64 2004

Library of Congress Control Number: 2003097382

Copyright © 2004 by Bonnie's Fitware, Inc.

Copyeditor: Carol A. Bruce

Printed in the United States of America

Bonnie's Fitware Inc.
18832 Stefani Avenue
Cerritos, California 90703
sales@pesoftware.com
http://www.pesoftware.com/

Table of Contents

Chapter 4

Chapter 5

Chapter 6

Chapter 7

Chapter 8

Chapter 9

Chapter 10

Chapter 11
Using Technology To Improve the

Chapter 12
The Future of Technology in Physical Education

Appendix A

Appendix B

Appendix C

Preface

U sing *Technology in Physical Education, Edition 4* is designed to keep you abreast of the ever changing landscape of technology and its uses in physical education. This book will help you accomplish your teaching responsibilities more efficiently and effectively. Technology can assist you with your paperwork and help you improve the quality of your instruction. Now is the time for you to benefit from the power of technology and this book will help you to get started. Here's what you'll find.

Chapter 1 describes the growth and variety of available technology and how to incorporate the most recent technological advances into your physical education program. Technology can be as commonplace as an overhead projector for enlarging visual aids or as futuristic as a hologram demonstration of the correct technique for a skill or game strategy. Chapters 2 and 3 introduce the many ways you can present information, including audio and video segments in physical education.

Chapter 4 focuses on devices that can assist in the learning process — especially in the area of fitness. You'll learn how to enhance a physical fitness unit with easy-to-operate blood pressure monitors, spirometers, and heart monitors.

Choosing the best computer and peripherals, such as printers and monitors, can seem overwhelming. Chapter 5 will show you how to identify your needs, consider your budget, and make those choices. This chapter also looks at notebook and handheld computers that make it easy to record grades, fitness test results, and data on teaching effectiveness when you are out in the field where a desktop computer is not readily accessible.

Chapter 6 looks at software for the teacher. It shows you how to manage fitness scores and grades effectively and efficiently. It also provides examples: using word processing software to create study guides, data base software to create a locker system, spreadsheet software to create an inventory and budget, and desktop publishing software to create your own newsletter to keep parents and community members informed about your programs.

In the classroom or the gymnasium, computers can help you instruct and improve your students' understanding of physical fitness, motor skills, and social skills. They can help you individualize instruction for your students, allowing them to progress at their own rates. Chapter 7 shows how computers can help students understand cognitive concepts, develop skills, and create their own fitness plans. Chapter 8 focuses on evaluating student learning using project-based assessment and electronic portfolios.

Chapters 9 and 10 introduce telecommunications and the Internet in physical education. Whether you're sharing information with colleagues or reviewing lesson plans with a student teacher, electronic mail can help you make more efficient use of your time and abilities. Chapter 9 targets selecting an Internet Service Provider (ISP), electronic mail, listservs, chats, telephony, and video conferencing. Chapter 10 focuses on the many uses of the World Wide Web—the world's largest library.

Chapter 11 focuses on you and how you can become an even more effective teacher. For example, you can use video technology and special software to watch yourself teach, analyze your own performance, and enhance your teaching skills.

The final chapter takes a look at the future of technology and provides possible scenarios that will help you keep your students motivated and physically educated.

A companion web site is located at http://www.pesoftware.com/ Support/techbk.html. Here you will find links to additional web resources, updates on this book, and additional learning opportunities. In addition, for those using this as a course textbook, you will find sample syllabi and course outlines, along with additional reflection questions and projects.

I hope this book will help you find the justification and leverage you may need to begin or increase your use of technology in physical education. It's a wide open field with continuous innovations. Our challenge is to learn to use these innovations to best meet our needs and the needs of our students.

Let us begin our journey...

Other Books by Bonnie Mohnsen

Teaching Middle School Physical Education

Concepts and Principles of Physical Education:
What Every Student Needs to Know (editor)

The New Leadership Paradigm in
Physical Education (editor)

Integrating Technology and Physical Education

Chapter 1

Introducing Technology in Physical Education

The year is 2013. The place is the gymnasium of Middle School USA, where a group of students is about to begin physical education class. The teacher, speaking into a microphone attached to a wearable computer, quickly takes attendance and begins the warm-up/fitness phase of the lesson. The students perform flexibility, muscular strength, and muscular endurance exercises in their cooperative learning groups. They have been in the tumbling unit for the past three weeks, and most have already met the performance criteria for a variety of forward and backward rolls, headstands, cartwheels, and handstands. Today they will learn the roundoff, review the skills already covered, and create a routine that combines all the skills. There are eight stations, or learning centers, set up around the room for tumbling and cardiorespiratory endurance activities. Each group rotates from one station to the next.

At Learning Center 1, a DVD player shows sample floor exercise routines from the 2012 Olympics. Learning Center 2 is a review station, where the more skilled students help others in their group who have not yet met the minimum performance standards or who wish to strive for higher marks. When a student achieves a higher standard during the period, another student

1

alerts the teacher, who verifies and records the accomplishment. Learning Center 3 is an aerobic station where students choose an activity (e.g., virtual reality rowing, jump rope, interactive dance routines following a robot that provides feedback) that will improve cardiorespiratory endurance. The students wear devices to record their physiological data (e.g., heart rate, energy expenditure, breathing rate) and gauge the intensity of their workouts. Learning Center 4 focuses on the new motor skill—the roundoff. Students take turns capturing one another's attempts to perform the skill and then view their attempts on a large flat screen monitor attached to the gymnasium wall for immediate feedback. Learning Center 5 is where the students create their own routines. Using handheld computers, they input the names of their stunts in the order they wish to perform them, and the routines are demonstrated by a 3D hologram. The students edit and fine tune their routines, then perform them at Learning Center 6, where the performances are captured for immediate playback and review.

Learning Center 7 is a fitness station. Once a month, the students measure their blood pressure, percent of body fat, muscular strength and endurance, and aerobic capacity. A body composition analyzer, an electronic blood pressure device, a max VO2 device, and a strength/endurance machine measure the students and store the data. At Learning Center 8, a virtual human provides students with information on the biomechanical principles of a roundoff. It speaks the native language of each student in the class.

The data collected at each station are entered into a networked computer. All networked computers in the school are wirelessly connected to a server where student work is stored in a separate folder for each student. The teacher or the student can check that folder at any time from a personal handheld or worn (e.g., wrist watch, glasses, belt, ring) computer.

Some of what I've just described can be seen in some physical education classes today, although generally not to the extent described in the scenario. However, once a school acquires the technology, its applications for physical education are limited only by the imagination of the user. Some skeptics may say that the promise of technology has been around for decades and, as yet in many schools, is still a mere promise. However, one has only to remember that television did not catch on until 29 years after its invention. The zipper required 32 years, and the ball point pen was around for 50 years before it was mass produced (Thornburg, 1992). The lesson here is that many innovations develop slowly. However, it is a certainty that the future holds many new ideas and innovations for our daily lives as well as for instruction in physical education.

Growth of Technology

Webster defines technology as "a scientific method of achieving a practical purpose." The inventions noted in the highlight box below, which have advanced the enjoyment and safety of various sporting events, can be included in that definition. The 19th century chalkboard and the 20th century computer, videocassette recorder/player, digital camera, and personal digital assistant

Technological Developments

1860	Heel bindings added to skis. The bindings added comfort and speed.
1876	First spoke tension wheel for a bicycle developed by Archibald Sharp. It improved the bicycle's stability and balance.
1895	First bicycle derailleur patented by Huret. It assisted with uphill cycling (gears did not become popular until the 1950s).
1928	Invention of the wet suit. It made cold water swimming bearable.
1960	First steel tennis rackets became commercially available.
1975	The original Nordic Track was created. It consisted of a simple flywheel and a few cables and pulleys.

also fit the definition. Of course, no one can be entirely certain about the tools of the twenty-first century. However, in order to gain insight into where we are going, it is important to know where we have been.

History

The first "computer revolution" in education occurred in the 1960s, when school districts installed computer terminals in special rooms in their schools. The computers were linked to a mainframe system (master computer) located at the district office or some other central location. Teachers signed up for times when they could take their classes to the computer room. This first effort didn't last long, because the machines were too expensive and they often broke down. Few physical educators were involved in the first computer revolution.

The second "computer revolution" in education began in the late 1970s. It coincided with the appearance of the personal computer. Personal computers made it possible to bring computers into classrooms, gymnasiums, and even our homes. During the early 1980s, some physical educators at the university level began to experiment with the computer and to develop software for various specialty areas such as exercise physiology. In the K-12 public education setting, the first computers were used primarily for fitness reports. Then, physical educators began to see the need for other types of application software. Eventually, some of us began to use the few available computer-assisted instruction programs with our classes.

Current Status

Today, there are computers, wireless networks, DVDs, and other new technologies everywhere we look. The use of the Internet has literally exploded. Virtually all physical educators now have e-mail addresses, and they have moved beyond using a computer only for fitness reports. Elementary, middle school, and high school physical educators in pockets across the United States—and around the world—are exploring the effects of instructional software, the Internet, heart monitors, video analysis of performance, electronic portfolios, and multimedia development on student learning. For physical educators, the 20th century was an era of exploration and of promises to come.

Studies show that when computer programs are used learning $\cdot \not{\tau}\, \mathcal{U}\ell$ time can be shortened by 50 percent, retention can be increased by 80 percent, and costs can be cut in half (Levin & Meister, 1986; Niemiec, Blackwell, & Walberg, 1986; Gu, 1996). And, the costs continue to decline and the number of components in an integrated circuit doubles every 18 months (see highlight box below). The federal government and many states have earmarked funding to help bring new technologies into K-12 classrooms. Physical educators need only desire, know how, and vision to bring these technologies into their gymnasiums.

Future of Technology

In this century, the true power of technology will become a reality. Futurists are predicting that we will no longer have to worry about finding a computer to use, since we will actually be wearing one. Voice input will replace keyboarding, glasses will replace monitors, storage will become so compact that everything we can read in a lifetime will fit into an object the size of a pen, and smart machines will learn from their interactions with us (i.e., the coffee machine will learn how we like our coffee and continue to improve the coffee it produces based on our preferences).

Emerging technologies will continue to have an impact on education. Management theorist Peter Drucker has predicted that traditional universities as we know them will become a big wasteland in the next 25 years. The Association of Governing Boards predicts that one-third of the existing independent

The Growth of Technology

	1986	1996	2000	2009
RAM	1MB	8MB	51MB	3,251MB
Storage	40MB	500MB	3.2GB	36GB
Speed	15mhz	100mhz	36ghz	203ghz
Cost	$2,500	$1,500	$240	$10
Power		1x	6x	665x

colleges and universities in the United States will close in the next 10 years. Some predict that 10 percent of existing public colleges and 50 percent of independent colleges will close in the next 25 years. Almost all colleges will be radically reshaped by the digital revolution; students will come to the colleges for their social, artistic, athletic, and spiritual programs.

Virtual reality will have the greatest impact on instruction in physical education. Virtual reality technology allows the user to transcend the barriers of keyboard and screen and to have an immersive interactive *physical* experience. As an early example, consider the experience of the programmer who, in 1985, developed a virtual reality system so that he could learn to juggle. With virtual goggles over his eyes and virtual gloves on his hands (both goggles and gloves were connected to the computer), the programmer picked up the virtual balls and began to practice juggling. He altered the physics of his new artificial world so the balls moved in slow motion, giving him more time to react. Because the computer responded to the force and release angle of each throw, however, each of his tosses and catches needed to be accurate. The more proficient the programmer got, the more he speeded up the balls until the speed matched that of reality. Eventually, he removed the virtual equipment and began juggling three "real" balls.

In the next decade, we will see students using virtual reality to learn motor skills and prosocial skills. They may even have their own personal trainer in the form of a hologram or a robot. Technology has the potential to increase physical activity and improve learning in physical education if used in conjunction with high-quality instruction. For this to occur, technology must be seen as more than hardware and software, it must be viewed as a term for processes in which human beings engage themselves in order to increase their control of the material environment and to solve problems (Anglin, 1995).

Types of Technology

Technology is defined as anything that achieves a practical purpose. In physical education, then, technology is anything that helps students improve their physical performance, social interaction, or cognitive understanding of physical education concepts. It is well known that people learn through three modalities—visual, aural, and kinesthetic. The greater the number of learning modalities that are engaged, the greater the learning that can occur. The types of technology used in physical education, therefore, can be organized into the following categories: auditory, visual, manipulative, and multi-modal devices.

What To Expect in the Next 10 Years

1. Virtual reality in education.
2. Three-dimension fax (objects will have depth).
3. Personal robots.
4. A 500 "phone number" that tracks you for life.
5. Cellular phones in the form of earrings, watches, and glasses.
6. Smart machines (capable of learning).
7. Affordable flat screen high definition television.
8. Six-language instantaneous translators.
9. Holograms.
10. Wearable computers (clothing, jewelry).

Auditory Devices

Auditory devices include tape players, radios, MP3 players, and compact disc players. The content for these devices includes classical music for relaxation, a variety of music to accompany different movement experiences (e.g., exercising or tumbling routines), and recordings that explain specific concepts, such as those published by SyberVision. It is important to have a good sound system when using auditory devices. Be sure to purchase or select one with the capability of playing cassettes, compact discs, and MP3 digital files. Good speakers also are a must, so that all students can hear clearly. In addition, a remote microphone can save your voice when you must talk over music or give instructions to large groups. Chapter 2 addresses the use of auditory devices.

Visual Devices

Visual devices (text, pictures, and video) provide learners with additional information to help them better understand the concepts of a lesson. Pictures, charts, graphs, and diagrams are fairly common in physical education, but have you ever used models? Models are three-dimensional representations of real-life events. For example, playing fields can be made from plywood or particle board, and small dolls can be used to depict players. Models also can be manipulated by the students, thus including a second modality. Today, 3D software can bring 3D models to a computer screen. Whether the models are made up of real-life objects or digital images, they show students how players move during a real game. Chapters 2 and 3 focus on the selection and use of visual aids.

Manipulative Devices

A manipulative device is one that students can handle and control. In the K-12 school system, these devices tend to be low-end models of sophisticated machinery. Digital blood

Considering Instructional Strategies for a Variety of Learning Outcomes

Learning Outcome	Instructional Strategies
Organization Skills	Brainstorming Outlines Overviews Prior reading
Attention	Familiar music Novelty Size of print Use of color Volume of audio
Comprehension	Collecting data Examples Connection with prior knowledge Modeling Organization of content
Creativity	Independent projects Interactive multimedia Problem-solving Virtual reality
Mastery	Making presentations Problem solving activities Projects
Motivation	Challenging Encouraging Intrinsic value Related to real world
Transfer	Application Simulations Solving "real" problems

pressure machines, body composition analyzers, heart monitors, and printout stopwatches are examples of devices that provide students with hands-on opportunities to learn the scientific side of fitness and exercise physiology. Although these instruments don't compare with the more sophisticated (and expensive) models in terms of accuracy, they do serve to motivate students and to teach them about the relationship between bodily functions and exercise. Chapter 4 addresses manipulatives.

Multi-Modal Devices

Video and audio technology—television, cable television, satellite dish, videotape, laser disc, computer software, DVD, or the Internet—can bring model performances of trained athletes along with accurate explanations to your students during the initial stages of learning new motor skills. Students also can use video cameras to record and replay their performances for feedback and to monitor their own progress. The rest of this book addresses different aspects of multi-modal devices and software, including those found on the Internet.

Incorporating Technology

It has taken time for all new technologies, including the chalkboard, to be accepted by teachers and to become integral parts of the education environment. If a new technology gets in our way, we won't use it. The technology must support what we are already doing, and we must have access to it where we work and live.

Making Technology Happen for You

The first step to integrating technology into the physical education environment is to learn how to use it to deal with the paperwork (e.g., attendance, grades, locker assignments, inventories, budgets) that we face daily. You will need to read,

What You Need to Know:

National Educational Technology Standards

for Teachers

Standard I: Technology operations and concepts
Performance Indicators:
A. Teachers demonstrate introductory knowledge, skills, and understanding of concepts related to technology.
B. Teachers demonstrate continual growth in technology knowledge and skills to stay abreast of current and emerging technologies.

Standard II: Planning and designing learning environments and experiences
Performance Indicators:
A. Teachers design developmentally appropriate learning opportunities that apply technology-enhanced instructional strategies to support the diverse needs of learners.
B. Teachers apply current research on teaching and learning with technology when planning learning environments and experiences.
C. Teachers identify and locate technology resources and evaluate them for accuracy and suitability.
D. Teachers plan for the management of technology resources within the context of learning activities.
E. Teachers plan strategies to manage student learning in a technology-enhanced environment.

Standard III: Teaching, learning, and the curriculum
Performance Indicators:
A. Teachers facilitate technology-enhanced experiences that address content standards and student technology standards.
B. Teachers use technology to support learner-centered strategies that address the diverse needs of students.
C. Teachers apply technology to develop students' higher-order skills and creativity.

D. Teachers manage student learning activities in a technology-enhanced environment.

Standard IV: Assessment and evaluation

Performance Indicators:

A. Teachers apply technology in assessing student learning of subject matter using a variety of assessment techniques.
B. Teachers use technology resources to collect and analyze data, interpret results, and communicate findings to improve instructional practice and maximize student learning.
C. Teachers apply multiple methods of evaluation to determine students' appropriate use of technology resources for learning, communication, and productivity.

Standard V: Productivity and Professional Practice

Performance Indicators:

A. Teachers use technology resources to engage in ongoing professional development and lifelong learning.
B. Teachers continually evaluate and reflect on professional practice to make informed decisions regarding the use of technology in support of student learning.
C. Teachers apply technology to increase productivity.
D. Teachers use technology to communicate and collaborate with peers, parents, and the larger community in order to nurture student learning.

Standard VI: Social, Ethical, Legal, and Human Issue

Performance Indicators:

A. Teachers model and teach legal and ethical practice related to technology use.
B. Teachers apply technology resources to enable and empower learners with diverse backgrounds, characteristics, and abilities.
C. Teachers identify and use technology resources that affirm diversity.
D. Teachers promote safe and healthy use of technology resources.
E. Teachers facilitate equitable access to technology resources for all students.

International Society for Technology in Education (2000). *National education technology standards for teachers*. Eugene, OR: ISTE.

Suggested Computer Book Series

Dummie Series (Dummie Press)

Visual Quick Start Series (Peachpit Press)

take classes, or complete tutorials on using your operating system, word processing, data base, and spreadsheet programs. No matter which method you use to learn a software program, be prepared to invest some time in it. The time invested up front will pay dividends in the time you save once you start using the computer to complete your daily tasks. Many software programs come with on-screen tutorials or manuals that explain how to use them. For software packages that don't include either of these types of assistance, support can usually be purchased separately.

Obviously, you must have access to a computer for practice if you are to truly benefit from any of these learning experiences. Many districts allow educators to borrow computers on weekends and during vacations. You also should consider purchasing your own computer, especially as prices continue to drop and discounts for educators continue to improve.

Once you have learned to use the computer for yourself, the next step is to learn how to use the computer, videos, the Internet, and other technologies for teaching and assessing students. You can do this by reading (this book is a great start), attending inservices (whether or not they are specifically designed for physical education), taking classes through the local college or adult education program, and participating in online courses at your leisure. Once you have learned to use these technologies, you must determine the roles they will play in helping you to be more productive in the physical education of your students. You will need to determine these roles for yourself, but this book will describe a wide variety of possible applications.

Finding Funds for Buying Equipment

Regardless of which technology you would like for your department, you will need money to purchase it. Many state departments of education allocate money specifically for the purchase of technology. Private grants also are available. For example, in 1989, IBM formed a partnership program with the State of California and gave $20 million to provide IBM computers to schools in the state. Some of the money was used for competitive grants, which were awarded to 42 educational programs throughout the state. One of these was in the area of physical education.

As of the writing of this textbook, thousands of schools across the country are benefiting from Physical Education for Progress (PEP) grant funds (also known as Carol M. White grant). PEP provides funds for local educational agencies (LEAs) to initiate, expand, and improve physical education programs and assist LEAs in meeting State standards for physical education. Fifty to 60 million dollars are being distributed yearly to approximately 200 LEAs. The money may be spent only on equipment, supplies, and training for physical education.

Grant information can be found on the World Wide Web, in computer magazines, and through your school administrators. However, more important than finding money is having the vision to creatively use and implement technology in physical education. New and innovative ideas have the greatest potential of being funded through competitive grants.

Justifying Technology to Administrators

Administrators evaluate teachers in four different areas: environment, curriculum, instruction, and assessment. To justify technology, physical educators must demonstrate how it will make them better teachers in each of these areas. For example, computer-generated newsletters that provide parents with up-

Sample Grant Proposal # 1

The Problem

Cardiovascular disease is the number one killer in the United States. Lack of exercise is noted by the Surgeon General's report on physical activity as one of the major risk factors for heart disease—it clearly states, "physical inactivity is hazardous to your health." About 25 percent of adults report no physical activity at all in their leisure time. Only about one-half of our young people (ages 12-21 years) regularly participate in vigorous physical activity. One-fourth report no vigorous physical activity. In addition, research shows that 90 percent of children who fail to exercise adequately in their teenage years also do not exercise adequately when they become adults. The result is that in the United States, cardiorespiratory fitness continues to decline, percent body fat continues to increase, and risk factors for heart disease are now known to exist in nearly half of the elementary children in this country. It is no wonder it is costing this country nearly $130 billion a year to treat cardiovascular disease!

The Solution

This proposal strives to improve the quality of life for students, staff, parents, and community members through a life long practice of physical activity. Our students will work and live in the 21st century—maybe! It is up to schools and community programs to keep our students fit. In order to educate and motivate people to be concerned about their health and fitness, I will use a high-tech fitness and wellness system. This state-of-the-art technology provides clients with valuable data (text, charts graphs) about their personal well being, suggests options for improving their quality of life, teaches them the importance of activity, provides them with the opportunity to design their own exercise program, and monitors their implementation of the program and their improvement.

Objectives

1. Participants (specify a number) assess their personal fitness using the wellness system.
2. Participants (specify a number) design their own personal exercise programs.
3. Participants (specify a number) implement their exercise programs.
4. Participants (specify a number) improve their physical fitness.
5. Students (specify a number) provide community service as "technicians" for the wellness system.

Budget
Wellness System: $xxxx.xx
Wellness Software: $xxxx.xx
Freight and Handling: $xxxx.xx
Total: $xxxxx.xx

Activities
XYZ High School will offer its students, staff, parents, and community members a free "high tech" fitness/wellness evaluation along with free access to its Fitness/Wellness Center. The Fitness/Wellness Center and wellness system will be available before and after school, at lunch, and on the weekends. During the school day, the center and system will be used by ninth grade students during a fitness unit in their physical education classes. The students will not only utilize the center and system for fitness assessment and implementation of a personal fitness program, but they also will learn how to set up the system and assist with the administration of the assessment and monitoring protocols for others.

During an individual's first visit to the Fitness/Wellness Center, he or she will participate in the fitness/wellness evaluation using the wellness system. The data collected will include health risks, resting heart rate, muscular flexibility, muscular strength and endurance, blood pressure, percent body fat, lung capacity, nutritional needs, and cardiorespiratory endurance. Based on the results, the participant will be provided with individualized guidance for setting up a personalized exercise/wellness/ nutrition program.

During subsequent visits to the Fitness/Wellness Center, the participants will implement and monitor their personalized exercise/ wellness programs. Periodical assessments, using the wellness system, will be conducted to document each participant's improvement and to serve as a personal source of motivation. The wellness system will be supervised at all times by students under the direction of a certificated physical educator.

Evaluation
1. A log listing all participants who utilize the wellness system will be maintained.
2. Copies of each personal exercise/wellness/nutritional program will be maintained.
3. Participation logs will be maintained to document implementation of exercise/wellness programs.
4. Before and after data will be collected and analyzed to document changes in participants' fitness levels.
5. A log listing student participation as technicians will be maintained.

Sample Grant Proposal # 2

Abstract

This project has three phases — development, training, and implementation. The developmental phase will occur during the 20xx-20xx school year, the training phase during the summer of 20xx, and implementation during the fall of 20xx. The first phase will include the development of lesson plans to accompany the Biomechanics Made Easy software (Bonnie's Fitware). This program will allow students to learn and apply the biomechanical principles of movement, which is a basic concept listed in the National Physical Education Standards.

During the training phase, the high school physical education teachers from XYZ Unified School District and QRS Unified School District will attend a workshop put on by the AB County Office of Education using the training module developed by CD University. During the implementation phase, these same high school physical education teachers will use the multimedia system and fitness labs with their students in half of their classes. The other half of their classes will not use technology. This will establish an experimental group and a control group. In addition, the teachers will share lesson plans and information using their modems, and the Internet.

During the implementation phase, the university will begin using the teacher training module with its student teachers.

Anticipated Products

Development of lesson plans and student materials that meet the requirements and philosophy of the State Physical Education Standards. In addition, a training module for the professional preparation and professional development of physical education teachers will be produced.

Field Test/Evaluation Strategies

The effectiveness of this project will be evaluated using a variety of tests and projects that will comprise a student portfolio.

Project Objectives

1. Students in the experimental group will score significantly (.05 level) higher than students in the control group on each of the skills tests.
2. Students in the experimental group will score significantly (.05 level) higher than students in the control group on the cognitive tests.
3. A physical education teacher training module will be produced for the professional preparation and inservicing of teachers using technology in the physical education setting.

Associated Partners

The associated partners of this project will be the AB County Office of Education, the XYZ School District, the QRS School District, and CD University. The AB County Office of Education will assume the leadership role in this project. CD University will assist with teacher training using the technologies acquired through this project and assist with the development of lesson plans and student materials. The two school districts, XYZ Unified School District and QRS Unified School District, will assist with lesson plans and students materials, but their major contribution will be during the implementation phase.

Timeline

The project will begin on July 1, 20xx or as of notification date if later than July 1. The developmental phase will be completed during the 20xx-20xx school year with the implementation phase occurring during the fall of 20xx.

Do's and Don'ts of Grant Writing

Do:

Start with a real need.
Develop an innovative project idea that is fundable.
Be realistic and honest about what you put in writing.
Review copies of funded proposals.
Search the Internet for potential funders.
Read Requests for Proposals (RFPs) very carefully.
Follow the directions in each RFP.
Make sure that you fit the eligibility criteria noted in the RFP.
Develop a timeline to assemble the grant application.
Allow time for review and final editing before submission.
Double check everything—especially spelling.
Include a table of contents.

Don't:

Contact a funding source without reviewing all information.
Invent a need.
Exaggerate your objectives.
Inflate the value of in-kind contributions.
Use creative writing skills—stick to the facts and be concise.
Submit incomplete applications or poorly assembled applications.
Turn a proposal in late.

to-date information on the physical education program, and computer-generated bulletin boards that create an energizing and engaging instructional climate can help to establish a positive learning environment. The use of a data base during the curriculum development process can ensure that all standards for both scope and sequence are addressed. Computer-assisted instructional software, heart monitors, and video feedback are but a few of the technology-based instructional resources that can help improve student learning. Grading programs and electronic portfolios are technology's answer to assessment. Chapters 3 through 12 will provide you with additional examples of how you can justify technology to your administrators.

Ergonomics

As we begin to use technology, we also must be aware of the potential hazards associated with it. Ergonomics is the study of the effects of technology use on humans. According to Walter J. Zinn, O. D., at least half of the people working with video display terminals (VDTs) experience vision and physical side effects. Similarly, almost two decades ago, a panel of vision experts assembled by the Research Council of the National Academy of Science estimated that more than 50 percent of VDT users experienced visual discomfort. Headaches, eye strain, back pain, and shoulder or arm pain all are common complaints of VDT users. As physical educators interested in the health and well-being of our students, we can play an important role in modeling healthy behaviors when using technology.

Position of Monitor

The monitor and any documents should be placed so that the user's head is in a comfortable and relaxed position to reduce the chance of neck and shoulder pain. Current thinking places the monitor directly in front of the user and at least 20 inches from his or her eyes. The top of the monitor should be at or just below eye level.

Posture

In addition to proper positioning of the monitor, the user also must have the appropriate posture. Place your chair so that you can sit directly facing the monitor and make sure the chair is adjusted so your feet rest flat on the floor with your knees at a ninety degree angle to help your circulation. When you sit against the back of your chair, make sure there is clearance between the seat and the back of your legs. Adjust your back rest to support the small of your back. If possible, occasionally lean back in your chair to relax your back. Also, stand up and stretch periodically.

When you're seated at your desk and are in the typing position, your hands and wrists should be straight and your elbows should not be lower than your wrists. Desk height should be adjustable between 20 inches and 28 inches for seated tasks. The keyboard should be positioned so that a 90-degree angle is formed between the upper arms and the forearms. Keep your elbows close to your sides with the forearms parallel to the floor. Keep the mouse close to the keyboard. When typing, use a light touch—don't arch fingers up to hit the keys, don't type with wrists resting on the desktop, and don't pound the keyboard. The use of palm or wrist rests (foam or rubber devices placed in front of the keyboard) and an angled keyboard can eliminate pain and stress, and can help prevent Carpal Tunnel Syndrome, a soreness caused when muscles rub against each other in a small wrist passage called the Carpal Tunnel.

Preventing Eye Strain

The number one VDT-related health complaint is eyestrain. Red, sore, and dry eyes, blurred vision, headaches, and more develop with extended use of computers. Overly bright lighting

Do's and Don'ts of Computer Set Ups

Do:

Maintain a good rest position.

Take two "minute-long" breaks per hour and, at least, look away from the screen.

Blink more often.

Consider computer glasses.

Use a chair with arm rests that support your elbows.

Reduce monitor glare.

Keep your arms and hands suspended above the keyboard.

Purchase adjustable chairs.

Keep your feet flat on the floor.

Keep knees bent at just over a 90-degree angle.

Press your back against the backrest so the chair's lumbar support fits snugly into the small of your back.

Maintain forearms parallel to floor.

Use a wrist rest to help keep wrists straight.

Purchase keyboards that are simple, colorful, and smaller for children.

Lower background light.

Don't:

Overextend your reach.

Strain your shoulders.

Let the seat press into the back of your knees.

Lay your wrists flat on the desk in front of the keyboard.

Let your wrists absorb the weight of the arms.

Overdo it.

or windows can cause glare on the screen and can increase eye strain. This occurs because your optic system is confused— your pupils are shrinking to accommodate the bright room or window light while you are simultaneously trying to focus on the relatively dim screen.

The best solution is to move the monitor away from the window in order to minimize or eliminate the bright light and glare. In overly bright areas, one solution is to remove half of the florescent bulbs in the overhead fixtures. Other solutions include lowering background lighting, adjusting the position of the monitor, and checking your posture. You should look away from the screen every few minutes and blink more often than normal in order to lubricate your eyes. Computer glasses, specially designed for the working distance from the eyes to the monitor based on desk setup and posture, also can help to eliminate tired, red eyes and blurry vision.

Summary

Technology is changing the way we teach physical education— from its early uses in creating fitness reports to the future use of holograms as personal trainers. Technology, however, is not a means unto itself. It is a process and a tool for increasing student learning and teacher productivity. It can provide visual, aural, and kinesthetic input. As physical educators, we must access it, learn it, and use it. We also must be cautious of the potentially negative side effects of technology and counter those elements under our control: We must ensure that our students practice the proper ergonomics when using computers.

Reflection Questions

1. What technologies have you heard about that you would like to try?
2. Can you demonstrate each skill listed on pages 11-12? If not, what can you do to acquire these skills?
3. Is your personal computer setup ergonomically correct? Why/why not?

Projects

1. Write your own one-page scenario describing a physical education class in 2013.

2. Investigate grant opportunities in your district and community. Make a list of potential grant opportunities including: name of grant source, contact information, amount of money, deadline for proposal, name of grant, and description of grant. In Chapter 6 you will enter this information into a data base.

3. Write a one-page letter to an administrator describing why you need a computer for your work as a physical education professional. You will update this letter in Chapter 12.

Chapter 2

Using Audio and Visual Technology in Physical Education

Today you start a new unit in physical education, a game called "Takraw." Many students have never heard of this activity, and they wonder why they should learn to play it. Some wonder why they should play anything except basketball. You play a "Takraw" video (e.g., "Just for Kicks") set to popular music. Immediately, the students are drawn into the video and the game. After viewing the video, the students are eager to begin the new activity. The first skill to learn is the kick, and you use a video clip to demonstrate it. With the remote control, you access the starting frame for the segment on kicking and a model demonstration of the skill appears. In 10 minutes you have successfully introduced your new sport unit and provided a model demonstration of the primary motor skill used in the game.

Human brains are programmed to learn through a combination of motion and sound. Seventy percent of the information reaching our brains comes through the eyes. Studies (Kulik, 1994; Kromhout & Butzin, 1993) show that significantly greater learning results when audiovisual media are integrated into traditional teaching programs. The use of sound and motion increases understanding by 30 percent over other presentation methods; and interest, motivation, and retention remain 33 percent higher for up to one year after viewing.

In addition, most students enjoy learning and participating in an activity more once they are somewhat familiar with it. Several technologies are available for familiarizing your students with new activities. Visual, audio, and video presentations can teach rules, illustrate game concepts, and demonstrate different offensive and defensive strategies. Showing model demonstrations in slow and regular motion can enhance explanations of motor skills and strategies, and allow students to focus on specific aspects of skills and plays. Watching video clips at the beginning of class can generate interest in the new activity.

This chapter introduces you to static visuals, audio and video technologies, and audio and video cables and plugs. It will help you identify appropriate hardware and software, and it will suggest specific ways to use these technologies in physical education classes.

Static Visuals

Static visuals include texts, pictures, graphics, and three-dimensional models. Text conveys information while pictures attract attention, provide realistic images of objects, document events, and speak to those who are hearing-impaired, non-English speaking, or unable to read. In physical education, pictures are especially good for illustrating sport skill techniques and strategies.

Graphics contain pictures, words, and, frequently, symbols. They come in many forms, such as maps, diagrams, charts, tables, graphs, and cartoons. They are designed to communicate information clearly, precisely, and efficiently. In physical education, charts are good for calendars that can show frequency, intensity, time, and type of exercise over a week or month. Cartoons are ideal for conveying information and concepts through humor. Graphs can be used to show average heart rate before, during, and after exercise. Maps are great for orienteering experiences. Tables can be used for summarizing information, such as fitness competencies by age, while diagrams are perfect for offensive and defensive strategy formations. Chapters 3 and 6 provide additional information on creating your own visual images.

Three-dimensional models are representations of real-life events. They can be made with boards that depict playing fields and toy people that portray players. They can be positioned on the board to demonstrate offensive and defensive strategies, along with rule situations. When selecting static visuals, look for presentation style, text, technical quality, and effectiveness. Most static visuals can be held up, posted on bulletin boards, drawn on chalkboards or markerboards, and attached to walls or cones. Three especially effective static visual applications are textbooks, worksheets, and task cards.

Textbooks

Textbooks are fairly new to physical education, but they are excellent resources for students, especially those who are visual learners. However, we do need to be careful how we use them in physical education, since using limited instructional time to have students read a chapter in a book is not consistent with physical education goals. Ideally, you have access to one class set of textbooks for every class you teach, plus one extra class set. This allows you to assign reading as homework. The extra class set of textbooks can be used in a number of different ways: Students who are excused from an activity can do a reading and writing assignment. Reading station(s) can be established as part of a circuit that includes more traditional physical activities (skill practice, exercises).

If, like many physical educators, you have limited equipment/ facilities for practice, the reading station can serve those students who might otherwise be waiting to practice a skill. During inclement weather, shortened instructional periods, and other special situations, you may assign a reading activity—reading and answering questions, researching a specific topic, or participating in a jigsaw activity (each student in a group of four is assigned one reading assignment, which he or she reads and learns in order to share with teammates). For teachers on more limited textbook budgets, one class set or only a few books can be purchased and reading can be done in a circuit approach, on special occasions, or for special projects.

When selecting textbooks you need to note the reading level of the textbook. Some publishers advertise the reading level at which the book was written; others do not. The highlight box on this page provides you with a formula for estimating the reading level of any textbook using a short passage. For a more accurate estimate, examine text content and style. Watch for profound thoughts expressed in simple terms, ambiguities, figures of speech, and complex grammatical constructions.

Estimating Reading Level

$$RGL = 0.4(wps + \%hw)$$

• RGL is the grade level of students who, on the average, should have no difficulty reading and understanding the text.

• wps is the total number of words in a selected passage (at least 100 words) divided by the number of sentences in that passage.

• %hw is 100 times the number of hard words divided by the total number of words in the passage. Hard words are those with three or more syllables, excluding: (a) proper nouns; (b) combinations of short, easy words such as "forevermore"; and (c) verbs made into three syllables by the addition of a suffix (e.g., "studying").

There are basically three types of physical education textbooks on the market for kindergarten through twelfth grade: sport activity textbooks, fitness-specific textbooks, and conceptually based textbooks. *Australian Physical Education, Book 1* (Blackall, 1992) and *Australian Physical Education, Book 2* (Blackall & Davis, 1992) are examples of sport activity textbooks. Designed for grades five through eight, they contain information on a variety of traditional activities (e.g., basketball, volleyball). Each chapter contains a description of one activity and its rules, skills, and safety issues. Short-answer questions, word searches, and crossword puzzles are available at the end of each chapter. A similar book for the high school level is *Physical Activity and Sport for the Secondary School Student* (Dougherty, 2002). It also is organized by activity, with sections on skills and techniques, safety, scoring, rules, etiquette, strategies, equipment, and related terminology.

Fitness books have become increasingly popular especially at the secondary level. *Fitness for Life* (Corbin & Lindsey, 2002) is in its fourth edition. The package includes a student textbook, annotated teacher's edition, and teacher's resource book. Support materials include: a series of 10 videos entitled *Teaching Lifetime Fitness*, a *Fit Fun Audio CD* that contains music and timed sounds for activities, *Fitness for Life Presentation Program* (CD-ROM) that includes electronic presentations on each chapter, and *Fitness for Life Fitness Profile Software* (Macintosh and Windows) that allows students to enter fitness self-assessment scores and then print a complete personalized fitness profile. *Fitness for Life* provides a conceptual approach to fitness, covering both health-related and skill-related topics.

The *Fitness for Life* student textbook, available in English and Spanish, includes fitness activities that help students relate concepts to their personal fitness. Specific information on principles of fitness, cardiorespiratory fitness, strength, muscular endurance, flexibility, body composition, warm-ups, nutrition, stress, consumer issues, and planning and evaluating exercise programs is included. The teacher's resource book provides transparency masters, information sheets that include answers for the worksheets and tests, fitness focus instruction sheets, student questionnaires, self-assessment and activity record sheets, application worksheets, reinforcement worksheets, activity cards, and chapter tests. The annotated teacher's edition of the textbook includes background notes, teaching strategies, safety concerns, research data, professional articles, flexible management schedules, vocabulary lists, and suggestions for individualizing instruction. Written at an eighth grade reading level, it is best used with eighth or ninth grade students.

Roberta Stokes has written three textbooks for middle/high school physical education. *Lifetime Personal Fitness* (Stokes, Schultz, & Polansky, 1997) targets the Texas standards and can be used at either the middle school or high school level. *Personal Fitness and You* (Stokes & Schultz, 2002) comes in two editions. The first edition targets high school physical education in Florida, while the second book is more generic, addressing standards in states such as Georgia, Tennessee, and South Carolina. Both books cover an introduction to fitness, fitness evaluation, principles of training, flexibility, cardiorespiratory fitness, muscular strength and endurance, nutrition, weight control, stress, exercising safely, planning an exercise program, and consumer awareness. The laboratory activities are especially effective for reinforcing the information in the textbook. Ancillary materials include a teacher edition, teacher resource manual, four CD's, color transparencies, and a video.

Personal Fitness: Looking Good/Feeling Good (Williams, Harageones, Johnson, & Smith, 2000) also falls into the fitness category. The student text covers an introduction to fitness, components of fitness, goal setting, guidelines for exercise, principles of training, flexibility, cardiovascular fitness, muscular fitness, nutrition, body composition and weight control, stress, consumer issues, evaluation of activities, and designing a fitness program for high school students. The student text is accompanied by a hands-on activity handbook that includes 51 different activities to reinforce and apply the fitness concepts.

The annotated teacher's edition for *Personal Fitness* includes a guide that addresses the following: features of the program; implementing the program; planning the program; fitness assessment; helping students set goals and develop exercise prescriptions; students with special needs; grading procedures; health, environmental, and safety considerations; and planning for emergencies. Annotations include teacher objectives, teaching notes and strategies, and answers to study questions. The teacher's resource book includes the following for each chapter: bulletin board ideas, transparency blackline masters, learning activities to reinforce fitness concepts, and chapter tests and answers. Also available are videos on fitness, an electronic (Macintosh and Windows) version of *MicroTest* for test development, and a CD-ROM containing materials for presentations, posters, and handouts. This book best serves the needs of tenth, eleventh, and twelfth grade students.

Foundations of Personal Fitness (Rainey & Murray, 1997) rounds out the fitness category with another textbook geared for high school students. Covering much of the same information as the previous textbooks, this textbook highlights the idea that "any body can be fit." The teacher's wraparound edition is an especially strong component with lesson plans, strategies for working with special populations, ideas for student evaluation, and tips for fitness testing. The teacher resource package also contains vocabulary worksheets, reteaching worksheets, transparency masters, color transparencies of key figures, chapter tests, and additional handouts. There is a video series entitled *Foundations of Personal Fitness* that addresses and reinforces many of the different topics covered in the book, such as muscular strength and endurance, weight training, and aerobics. On the software side, an informational nutrition laser disc/CD-ROM, diet analysis program, and computerized test bank complete the package. A new edition is scheduled for release in 2005 from McGraw-Hill.

Kendall/Hunt's *Essentials of Physical Education* series is in the conceptually-based category of books. The high school textbook (Spindt, Monti, & Hennessy, 1991) and middle school textbook series (Spindt, Monti, Hennessy, Holyoak, & Weinberg, 2002) comprise the first comprehensive textbook series for students in physical education. The sixth grade book is entitled *Moving with Confidence*, the seventh grade book is *Moving with Skill*, the eighth grade book is *Moving as a Team*, and the high school book is *Moving for Life*. This series covers motor skills, movement patterns, biomechanics, motor learning, fitness, social skills, self-esteem concepts, pursuing lifelong movement activities, and promoting individual excellence. The teacher's edition for each level includes margin notes that direct teacher actions. The student portfolio for each grade level contains classroom, laboratory, and field activities for students to complete in and outside of class. There also are teacher resource books.

Physical Education: Theory and Practice (Davis, Kimmet, & Auty, 1986) is another conceptually-based textbook for students. Designed for high school students, it is divided into six parts and covers each of the subdisciplines of physical education— anatomy and physiology, exercise physiology, biomechanics, motor learning, history, and sociology. Each chapter contains information, worksheets, and laboratories.

A more recent addition to the conceptually-based textbook category is *Senior Physical Education: An Integrated Approach* (Kirk, Burgess-Limerick, Kiss, Lahey, & Penney, 2004). Written for juniors and seniors in high school, it is divided into three parts: Learning Physical Activity, Physiological Dimensions of Physical Activity, and Sociocultural Dimensions of Physical Activity. Test-yourself questions are found at the end of each chapter; answers are located in the back of the book. Focus activities and extension activities are located throughout the book to help reinforce concepts.

In order to determine the textbook that best meets your needs and those of your students, contact the publishers listed in the Appendix. The publishers will either send you a complimentary copy or a review copy to keep for an established length of time. Either way, read through the book, have your students try several of the activities, and then approach the individual on your campus in charge of textbook purchases with your purchase request.

Worksheets

Worksheets (see Figure 2.1) provide students with directions for a physical or cognitive activity and a set format for written responses. Worksheets can be created by the teacher on a word processing program (see Chapter 6) or purchased in workbook form or as part of a textbook package. Cognitive worksheets include steps for calculating personal target heart rate range, identifying muscles worked during different exercises, and

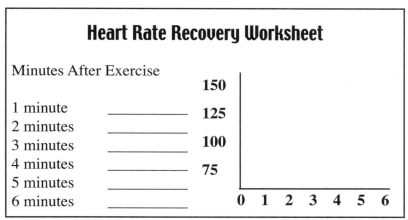

Figure 2.1 Sample worksheet where a student records and then charts his or her heart rate one minute, two minutes, three minutes, four minutes, five minutes, and six minutes after completing an exercise period.

Practice Backhand Grip

Shake hands with base of racket.
Form "v" with thumb and index finger.
Rotate racket so "v" is on top.
Spread fingers slightly.

©2003 Bonnie's Fitware

Figure 2.2 Sample task card with critical features for the backhand grip.

matching biomechanic principles with their motor skill applications. Physical worksheets, sometimes referred to as data collection sheets, include recording sheets for fitness tests as well as checklists for motor skill performance, heart rate data collection during different situations, and distance, time, and accuracy data collected while performing motor skills. Many teachers find that worksheets help keep students on task, making movement purposeful and meaningful. Even though the teacher may not necessarily need or want the data collected, the worksheet holds the student accountable for performing the instructional task.

Task Cards

Task cards (see Figure 2.2) typically are used in circuit teaching. Each task card includes a series of directions for students to follow. Teachers can either purchase preprinted cards (from Sportime or Bonnie's Fitware) or create their own using a word processing or desktop publishing program (see Chapter 6). Each task is printed on a separate sheet and posted at a station in the circuit. Students, working in groups of four, follow the directions on the task cards as they rotate through the stations in the circuit.

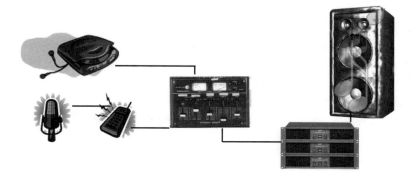

Figure 2.3 The wireless microphone sends a signal to the receiver that is connected to the mixer. The CD player sends a signal to the mixer. The mixer sends both signals to the amplifier and on to the speakers.

To make your task cards do double duty, incorporate peer feedback: List the critical elements for each skill on the card so students can check one another's performance. When making your own task cards, be sure to include color and graphics, and laminate them so they will withstand the harsh physical education environment.

Audio

Watching a movie with no sound helps you understand the importance of sound in multimedia tutorials and presentations. Effective uses for sound include providing a speech synthesis of the text for visually impaired students, a language translation of the text for bilingual settings, directions that explain specific concepts for auditory learners, and music for rhythms, tumbling, dance, exercising, and other appropriate activities. Audio should be clear, engaging, accurate, and accented with special effects and music when appropriate. And, most importantly, you should have a good sound system.

Sound systems are made up of audio components from a single manufacturer that are grouped together to offer optimum value and performance. You can be assured that the matched components will work well together and that little wiring will be required. In the past few years, mini- and microsystems have surpassed full-size systems in popularity. Many of these small systems reproduce sound faithfully, with output comparable to that of the bigger systems. It is important to have at least the following components in your system: amplifier, mixer, microphone, speakers, headphones, and CD player.

The amplifier adjusts the sound volume so that it can be heard clearly. The power output is stated in wattage. Two hundred watts are a minimum for indoor needs, while outdoor areas require higher wattage. Keep in mind that most professional amplifiers do not have tone controls (bass and treble) since the mixer controls the tone in most professional workstations. So, if you don't plan to use a mixer, look for an amplifier that has tone controls. Also, be sure that the power of the amplifier matches the power of the speakers; otherwise, damage can occur to one or both components.

Mixers are an important feature if you are going to combine sounds (i.e., voice and music). They give you the capability to adjust the microphone and the music independently of each other. A good mixer will help you compensate for poor room acoustics and feedback. Purchase a mixer with independent tone controls (bass, treble, and mid-frequency adjustments) for each channel.

A microphone is essential for teachers who must project their voices in a noisy gymnasium or over music. The signal strength of your voice is reduced by six decibels every time you double the distance from the teacher to the students. A wireless headband microphone is lightweight and durable. Most have a flexible gooseneck design that allows you to adjust the position of the mike. The microphone is attached to a small wireless transmitter. The teacher's voice is fed to the receiver, mixer, and amplifier, and then projected out into the gymnasium through the speaker.

Wireless microphone systems transmit sound using VHF (very high frequency) or UHF (ultra high frequency) bands. The VHF band of frequencies is more crowded and therefore makes VHF wireless microphone systems more susceptible to interference. The UHF wireless microphone systems, although slightly more expensive, will give you more reliable performance.

When it come to speakers, the first consideration is the quality of sound reproduction. Some speaker systems contain one full-range speaker cone designed to handle the entire frequency spectrum, while others contain two or three drivers for each channel. While a two-way system is almost always better than a single full-range speaker, a three-way system isn't necessarily better than a two-way system. The most important specification is frequency response. This indicates the highest and lowest frequencies of sound that a speaker is physically capable of reproducing. The ideal range is 20Hz to 20Khz, the range of an average ear. Other useful features include a separate volume and tone control for each speaker.

Headphones are a must if individual students will be listening to audio. Full base response with accurate tonal definition and balance from the mid-range frequencies up to the highest frequencies is best. The headphone must be lightweight and comfortable. Circumaural phones—headphones that cover the entire outer ear—block out all external sound and provide the best base sound.

Compact Discs (CDs) have revolutionized sound reproduction, producing the first commercially accepted digital sound format. CDs store sound as a string of numbers by sampling the sound thousands of times each second and assigning each sample a numeric value based on a binary code of zero or one. The CD stores its digital information as a series of microscopic pits arranged in a continuous spiral pattern below the disc's clear plastic surface. The CD player reads the reflection of a laser beam that tracks these pits. Nothing but the beam of light touches the CD while it plays, so there is no wear and tear on the disc. CDs usually surpass the sound quality of LPs and analog tapes because there is virtually no distortion. A programmable CD player can play specific tracks in ascending sequence or randomly, while most players also let you program the order in which the tracks will be heard. Be sure that the CD player you purchased has pitch control so that you can control the playback speed. This will, for example, allow you to slow down the speed of the music when students are first learning a new dance.

Due to the rapid expansion of the Internet, MP3 audio is the new "popular" audio product. MP3 is a method of compressing audio files into one-tenth of their normal size while still keeping near CD-quality sound. Five thousand songs, four minutes each, can be stored on a 20 GB drive. MP3 files can be downloaded from the Internet on a song-by-song basis and stored on a computer or separate MP3 player. MP3 players can assume many different shapes and sizes and can be integrated into stereo systems.

Two-Way Communication

Two-way communication has become increasingly popular with new small, lightweight, easy-to-carry radios or cell phones. Two-way communication devices are especially beneficial in the physical education environment where physical educators and their classes are often thousands of yards away from other people. In an emergency situation, the radio or cell phone can be used to call for medical or security assistance. The qualities to look for when purchasing two-way radios include: rechargeable batteries, several frequency channel, and a maximum range equivalent to the campus size.

Video

Dynamic images (hereafter referred to as video) are created by the rapid showing of still images—typically shown at 30 frames (60 fields) per second. Students often concentrate better with video because the moving images hold their attention. Presenting information through video technology can speed up learning.

There are two types of video: analog and digital. Analog video refers to video stored as motion ("television" language). Digital video refers to video stored in a series of zeros and ones ("computer" language). Currently, most televisions and videotapes are distributed as analog video. However, the trend is toward digital video in the form of satellite dish systems, digital cable boxes, high-definition televisions, and DVDs (digital versatile discs). Digital video has the advantages of image quality and ease of manipulation. Digital video can be cut, copied, and pasted just like text and graphics.

Regardless of the source, video images require a display system. At the high end, there are presentation systems that display images on a screen of any size. The images are bright (and getting brighter with each new generation) and are of high resolution. At the low end is the basic monitor or television set. When going this route, be sure to purchase a 25-inch screen, and perhaps more than one, depending on the size of your class or group. Also, make sure the monitor can accept connections from your sources (see cables and plugs later in this chapter). Other output devices include:

- Flat-panel displays that offer lower voltage and fewer emissions than monitors of the same size (these can fit in smaller spaces and are generally much lighter).
- High-density television (HDTV) that provides greater visual detail (higher resolution) and wider screens. HDTV does require special broadcasts.

Now, let's take a closer look at the various sources of video, including broadcasts, videocassettes, and DVD.

Broadcast Video

Broadcasts include televised (air waves), cable, and satellite-delivered video. Instructional television began in the mid-1950s, when many school districts bought television equipment and produced their own programs. PBS has distributed instructional videos on a large scale for many years. Many of the PBS programs are accompanied by study guides that summarize content, provide questions, make suggestions for preparatory and follow-up activities, and list supplementary readings.

Cable television systems tend to use fiber optic and coaxial cable to distribute video materials, whereas satellites, parked in orbits about 22,300 miles above the equator, function as aerial relay stations. As few as three satellites are needed to provide telecommunication services around the globe. A transmission is sent up (uplinked) from a ground-based television station, received by the satellite, and then retransmitted (downlinked) back to earth, where it is received by a satellite dish. The signal from the satellite can be received by any dish in the satellite's coverage area that is pointed at that satellite and turned to the appropriate channel (transponder).

Instructional broadcasts for physical education and health have included *Slim Goodbody Presents All Fit* (Slim Goodbody Corp.), *PE-TV* (PE-TV), *More than Human* (Cable in the Classroom), and *SportsFigures* (ESPN). *SportsFigures* is presented weekly throughout the school year on ESPN2. It uses sports and professional athletes to demonstrate math and physics concepts to high school students. Each lesson includes background, discussion, step-by-step explanations of equations, activities, answers, and suggestions for extending the lesson in the classroom. ESPN recently launched a companion web site, http://sportsfigures.espn.com/sportsfigures/. The site is designed for teachers, students, and parents. It contains interactive components such as educational games and contests, chats and trivia, as well as audio and video clips and curriculum information.

Fair Use Guidelines

Material	Copy for Teacher	Copies for Class
Books	1 chapter	1,000 words (10 percent)
Encyclopedias	1 story	2,500 words (1 story)
Poems	1 poem	250 words (1 poem)
Periodicals	1 article	2,500 words (1 article)
Charts	1 per book	1 per book
Lectures	1 per book	1 per book
Multimedia	no more than three minutes or 10 percent	
Illustrations/Photos	no more than five by one artist/photographer	

Note: Videotapes of TV (noneducational) programs may be shown twice to students within 10 days of broadcast and retained for a maximum of 45 days for evaluation purposes. Educational television may be recorded and used for educational purposes for a maximum of seven days.

Source: Kenneth T. Murray, "Copyright and the Educator," *Phi Delta Kappan*, March 1994, p. 555.

Physical educators also use broadcasts such as professional sports, college/university sports, and the Olympics to illustrate excellence in sports. In addition, programs like *The Wonder Years*, *Boston Public*, and *After-School Specials* focus on social and self-esteem issues related to physical activity.

Videocassettes

Videocassette players play back video, whereas videocassette recorders can play and record. When you shop for a videocassette player/recorder, consider durability, ease of operation, reliability and quality, ease of repair and maintenance, and cost. Critical features include:

- •Three-prong UL safety plug
- • Front loading

Tape Storage

- Store tapes upright
- Store tapes fully wound
- Store tapes at room temperature (65 degrees Fahrenheit is best)
- Store tapes in cases
- Store tapes away from any magnetic field
- Store tapes in a dust-free and debris-free environment
- Transfer your footage every seven years

- Front panel AV inputs (for easy plug-in of other video components)
- Real time readout in hours, minutes, and seconds
- Slow motion (including frame-by-frame action) using jog-shuttle dial
- Freeze frame
- Fast forward viewing
- Reverse viewing
- Automatic tracking control

The ability to operate these features by remote control is important in a class setting. A combination videocassette recorder and television is convenient for avoiding excess cable connections; however, the combination will cost the same as if the items were purchased separately, and combination sets often lack a variety of features.

Videocassette recorders come with two, four, or six heads. The actual recording and playback of information to and from tape occurs at the location of the heads. Two heads work fine for off-air recording and playback. In a physical education instructional setting, however, it is better to use four heads, with two for speed and two for slow motion. Six-head VCRs use the two extra heads for a high-fidelity (hi fi) audio track, which improves the sound quality.

If you are interested in making recordings from live broadcasts, you should purchase a machine you can program in advance.

The ease of programming the machine, including either on-screen prompts or VCR Plus (which uses a short numeric code for programming), also should be considered. Try experimenting with the programming features before you make your purchase.

If you will be analyzing sports skills, a VCR that can encode the video will provide quicker access to different video segments. The encoder places a time code on the videotape, so that individual frames can be called up by number. This is more precise than the counter feature available on most videocassette recorders. Other access options include:

- Repeat playback, which designates a recorded tape segment for automatic replay.
- Index search, which places an electronic marker at selected locations.

Suggested Videos

Juggling for Success: Grades 3-8 (Human Kinetics)
Jump Rope Primer: Grades 3-8 (Human Kinetics)
Finding Your Way in the Wild: Grades 6-12 (Quality Video)
Fitness for Life Series: Grades 8-12 (Human Kinetics)
Multimedia Folk Dance: Grades 4-12 (Human Kinetics)
Personal Fitness: Grades 8-12 (Kendall/Hunt)
SportsFigures: Grades 4-12 (ESPN)
Science and Myths of Tennis: Grades 7-12 (Human Kinetics)
Conflict Resolution: Grades 5-8 (Pyramid)
AIDS—One Teenager's Story: Grades 7-12 (Sunburst Communications)
Crack: Grades 6-12 (Media)
Fire Fighters and Fire Safety for Kids: Grades K-6 (AIMS Multimedia)
Food: Keep it Safe to Eat: Grades 7-12 (Alfred Higgins Productions)
Lots of Kids Like Us: Grades 4-12 (AGC Educational Media)
Respect: The Real Deal: Grades 5-9 (Sunburst Communications)
Smokers and the People Who Smell Them: Grades 4-11 (Pyramid)
Stop the Violence!: Grades 9-12 (Sunburst Communications)
What's Wrong with Marijuana: Grades 3-6 (Human Relations Media)

- Real time search, which lets the user enter the length of tape that is to be skipped in minutes.
- Search and skip, which advances the tape in 30-second increments.

The counter is the least effective, the search and skip button is a little more effective, and the time encoder is the most effective.

It is important to consider the grade of videotape you purchase. Premium and high grades are more expensive, but they tend to stand up to repeated use and have better quality color and sound. However, there are no industry standards for the grades. So, consider using shorter tapes since longer tapes tend to be thinner and thus stretch and sag more. Also, consider the tape's coercivity and retentivity ratings. A higher coercivity rating means greater detail and a higher retentivity rating means it is longer lasting.

Video copies made from the master (original tape) will look almost as good as the master. These are referred to as first-generation copies. A copy made from a first-generation copy is referred to as a second-generation copy, and the quality of the image is greatly reduced. By the third generation, the image is unacceptable. When videos are copied, horizontal lines, called noise, may be recorded onto the new tape. The tracking control on the videocassette recorder has two adjust buttons that can be manipulated to eliminate much of this noise distortion.

Each videocassette tape is equipped with a safety tab on its edge. By breaking off the tab you can protect a cassette from accidentally being erased. Once the tab is removed you will not be able to record onto the tape again unless you cover (i.e., place masking tape over) the hole.

DVD

Digital versatile discs (DVDs) are replacing videotapes, CD-ROMs, CD-Rs, and CD-RWs. These CD-sized storage devices hold gigabytes of information, including audio and visual data. Like audio CD players, only a beam of laser light ever touches the playing surface, so it is virtually indestructible. Its higher resolution means that DVD picture quality is very clean. DVD audio is noise free at digital quality. Key features include: multiple aspect ratios, slow motion (1/2, 1/8, and 1/16 regular speed), eight audio tracks (i.e., eight languages), and 32 subtitles. Interactive menus provide the user with random access to any scene on the disc, along with pan and scan options. Stand alone DVD recorders function like VCR recorders, allowing for the capture of broadcasts directly to DVD. Some even have FireWire input allowing for very high quality video capture.

Audio and Video Cables and Plugs

Cables connect one piece of equipment to another. Cables that are short, heavy, shielded, and require the fewest connectors are best. Just as there are different types and sizes of light bulbs, there are different types of cables and plugs. Read the manual that comes with your equipment to find out which ones you need. Then, go to an electronics store (i.e., Radio Shack) and ask for that cable and/or plug.

The most common types of audio plugs are XLR, 1/4-inch connectors (called stereo mini-plugs), extended (longer) mini-plugs, and RCA connectors (see Figure 2.4). The XLR provides for the best quality of analog sound. The XLR cable has two inner conductors to carry the signal and a third which serves as the ground. It is typically used with high-quality microphones, mixers, and other audio equipment. The stereo mini-plugs are typically used for musical instruments, stereo headphones, and camcorders. The extended mini-plugs, which are slightly longer, are found on voice-quality microphones and typically work in

Mini Stereo   RCA   XLR

Figure 2.4 Sample audio connectors.

BNC   F-connector   S-video

Figure 2.5 Sample video connectors.

your computer's sound input port. The mini-stereo connectors tend to be fragile and are notorious for failing. RCA connectors are used with consumer electronic equipment—typically to connect the audio from the videocassette recorder/player to the television or monitor. The ports and plugs are color coded—red is for the right port and black or white is for the left port.

The four most common types of video plugs are the F-connector, BNC connector, RCA connector, and S-video (see Figure 2.5). The cable that brings cable television into your home is probably a coaxial cable with F-connectors. Coaxial cables are commonly used with video to shield the signal from airwave interference.

The most common connection between a VCR player and monitor is composite video input. It uses one yellow RCA jack with a single pin to pass video signals. It is cheap and very simple to use, but there is some signal loss, image degradation, and color bleeding. BNC connectors also can be used to transmit composite video and the locking connector works well in the school setting.

The S-video (compatible with both seven-pin and four-pin S-video plugs) connector is a round plug with several small metal pins. It accepts better quality signals since the signal is separated into two parts, color and brightness. S-video is typically used to carry high-quality analog video between camcorders, VCRs, and video monitors.

Component video input uses three RCA or BNC jacks. It splits the video signal into three separate signals—two color and one brightness. Component video is typically found on higher end professional grade equipment, new high-end televisions, and DVD players and recorders.

Firewire/1394 communication protocol is fairly new for video devices, but can be used to carry digital audio and video information. It provides a fully digital pathway with a perfect reproduction. Firewire typically is used to transfer digital video (DV) from a mini DV camcorder.

Using Video in Physical Education

Broadcasts, video cassettes, and--in the future--DVDs have many uses in physical education. But they also can be misused—for example, showing videos that you have not previewed, showing videos for an entire instructional period,

National Standards for Physical Education

1. Demonstrates competency in motor skills and movement patterns needed to perform a variety of physical activities.
2. Demonstrates understanding of movement concepts, principles, strategies, and tactics as they apply to the learning and performance of physical activities.
3. Participates regularly in physical activity.
4. Achieves and maintains a health enhancing level of physical fitness.
5. Exhibits responsible personal and social behavior that respects self and others in physical activity settings.
6. Values physical activity for health, enjoyment, challenge, self-expression, and/or social interaction.

National Association for Sport and Physical Education, 2004. *Moving into the Future,* 2nd ed. Reston, VA: Author.

or providing no interaction with students regarding the video. We will now turn our attention to several appropriate uses of video, including its use in providing an anticipatory set, demonstrating a concept, modeling a skill, leading a routine, demonstrating strategies, illustrating movement patterns, setting up scenarios, analyzing movement, providing stimuli for mental imaging, assessing student learning, and providing raw material for student projects.

Providing an Anticipatory Set

In exemplary lessons, the teacher begins with an anticipatory set. This serves to motivate students and makes a connection between prior instruction and the new learning that is about to take place. The use of video is very appropriate for this task, as the example of the Takraw video from the vignette at the beginning of this chapter demonstrates—using the video on Takraw serves as a quick and effective way to jump start students' curiosity about the activity.

Demonstrating Concepts

Video has long been used to demonstrate concepts. As you review videos for use in your physical education program, consider how well each video addresses the National Standards for Physical Education. For example, *PE-TV* (PE-TV), available via instructional television and regular television, provides middle and high school students with fitness concepts related to National Standards 3 and 4 in a visually engaging format. Each segment is 12 minutes long, and there are more than 50 episodes.

Visual images are especially valuable for visual learners. One segment of *PE-TV* can be shown each week throughout the year, or one segment can be shown each day during a fitness unit. For the elementary level, *All Fit* (Slim Goodbody) provides a nice introduction to fitness areas and concepts.

National Standard 6 includes the subdiscipline of aesthetics. When teaching to this standard, video can be used to show professionals in activities, such as dance, figure skating, tumbling, and skiing. Students who view the tapes are asked to identify aesthetic features and note the elements they find especially meaningful. Videos can be shown in normal and slow motion so students have the opportunity to study each movement.

Two aspects of National Standard 2 deal with student understanding of biomechanic and motor learning concepts. Vic Braden has produced two videos that address these areas at a

Using Video Successfully

1. Preview every program to ensure that the pace, language, and presentation are appropriate. Previewing allows you to identify, in advance, places where the program can be paused for student reflection, discussion, writing, or questions.
2. Have the videotape ready to start at the appropriate spot. Having to spend time searching through the videotape for the correct counter number will cause students to lose interest.
3. Show only the section of a videotape that adds to what is being taught. A well-focused three-minute segment will have far more impact than a rambling 15-minute segment.
4. Video can be shown to large groups, or to small groups at one station in a circuit.
5. When you show a video to a large class, use a video projector and a large screen.
6. Do not turn out the lights. Students can see the video image clearly with the lights on, and they will be less likely to drift off, get restless, or fall asleep.
7. If you want to use more than one section on a tape, use the tape counter to assign a number to each section so you can fast forward when necessary.
8. Use the pause button when you need time to explain a term or concept.
9. Show some segments twice.
10. Lead a pre-video and post-video discussion.

friendly level. The first is *The Science and Myths of Tennis* (B Ventures). This video poses 20 commonly asked questions about tennis and then analyzes the answers using statistics, timed experiments, and slow motion graphics. The second video is *Motor Learning: Secrets to Learning New Sports Skills* (VB Ventures). This video addresses the science of learning new motor skills in tennis. Both videos target the recreational and amateur player and are very appropriate for middle and high school students.

The historical perspective related to sports is addressed in National Standard 6. There are numerous videos on the Olympics—including highlights and historical events. There also are videos on the history of specific sports such as baseball, and athletes such as Michael Jordan, Wilma Rudolph, Jackie Robinson, and Roberto Clemente. Students learn not only the who, what, where, and when; they also learn the how and the why related to the event.

Showing Model Performances

Model demonstrations can improve learning, especially for those students who are visual learners or who have limited English proficiency. It is difficult for teachers to be proficient in all motor skills (Standard 1); a few minutes of video can demonstrate the technique students are to learn—especially if shown from a number of different angles. The image not only serves as a substitute for teacher demonstration, but it lets students view the skill in both normal motion and slow motion as many times as they wish. And, you can pause at various points to comment on the critical features (Standard 2) of the skill. This is especially important in less traditional activities such as karate, in-line skating, gymnastics, hockey, and mountain biking. Social skills (Standard 5) also may be demonstrated using videos.

Leading Dance and Aerobic Routines

There are a number of videos on the market that lead students through dance and aerobic routines. Although it is tempting to simply turn these videos on and let the on-screen instructor do the work, it is important to preview the video and select the appropriate pieces for each lesson. It also is important to pause when students are having difficulty with a step, or in order to emphasize a particular step or concept. Physical educators also should be alert for contraindicated exercises, especially during aerobic routines. If these exercises are on the video, you will need to pause, explain the problem, and then proceed.

Demonstrating Game Strategies

Video clips of game situations can demonstrate offensive and defensive strategies. By showing a volleyball game in slow motion you can point out how effectively the offensive team fakes a spike or chooses to dink, depending on the defensive setup. There also are special video pens (such as those that come with the Smart Board) with a writing pad so that you can write on the pad and superimpose diagrams of plays and formations over a video image. This is especially effective for sports such as football and basketball.

Identifying Movement Patterns

National Standard 2 addresses student understanding of various movement patterns, including foot patterns, pivot patterns, turning patterns, kicking patterns, throwing patterns, and absorption of force. Students must learn to identify movements and categorize them into appropriate patterns. Teachers use video technology to show teams playing a game, pausing to point out different movement patterns. As the students become more familiar with the patterns, they watch the game and categorize the movements for themselves. This activity allows students to construct their own meaning from movement and see that learning a new sport is easy, since they have executed the same movement patterns in other sports. This activity also can be used to assess student understanding.

Using Scenarios

In specialty classes such as sports medicine and athletic injuries, videos are used to demonstrate athletic taping methods and injury analysis. Once students begin to understand injury analysis they are shown a variety of injuries on video and asked to assess the situation and determine the appropriate action steps to take. Showing the initial accident scene from television shows such as *911* and asking students to assess the situation before showing them the actions of the paramedic can be an effective way to teach problem-solving skills and to assess student understanding.

Analyzing Movement

Viewing video performances takes on a new dimension when the goal is to learn about the science of movement. Analysis of movement requires that motor skills be viewed in slow motion or through the more scientific method of recording displacement (amount of change in movement from one frame to the next). Converting displacement to real world units by having an object of known length in the picture allows the viewer to determine the acceleration, velocity, etc., of any object or body part. This provides the viewer with the data necessary to analyze performances and to determine the critical features and biomechanic principles that make certain performances more successful than others. Students can use this method to analyze their own movement and compare it to the model to determine where they need to improve.

Providing Stimuli for Mental Imagery

The use of mental imagery (visualization) can help improve motor skills. Your mind doesn't know the difference between vividly imaged pictures and reality—it sends one-third of a neuromuscular contraction with either image. Students can observe an expert golfer's perfect form again and again as he or she hits a drive. The students then close their eyes and visualize themselves performing the skill before actually going out to practice it. Companies such as SyberVision produce videos that demonstrate a model execution of a skill again and again at various speeds and from various angles for just this purpose.

Administering Tests and Quizzes

Video clips can be used during testing periods. Play a sequence of a motor skill and ask students to identify the critical features, errors, and/or biomechanic principles. If a computer is placed near the VCR/monitor, students can rotate in groups of three or four to the testing station and register their responses on the computer. Or, wireless audience response keypads can be used to collect responses from all students.

Creating a Medium for Student Projects

Students can use video clips to create their own projects. By selecting appropriate clips, they communicate their understanding of the critical features or biomechanic principles. For example, a group of students preparing a report on the biomechanical principles of stability can search through a videocassette to find examples from a variety of physical activities. They can develop a presentation for the rest of the class, accessing the appropriate frames to emphasize certain points. Students also can develop presentations using video images they have captured themselves or download from the Internet. These images also can be used in multimedia projects.

Summary

Although technology is often thought of only as computers, it also includes visuals, audio, and video. Used appropriately, these technologies can add much to the learning process. In addition, they often are more readily available to the physical educator. Remember, the bottom line is the learning process, not the use of technology in and of itself.

Reflection Questions

1. Which of the uses for video presented in this chapter would you like to try? Why did you select them?
2. Think about the last time you showed a video in your class. Which National Standard for Physical Education were you targeting? How did you prepare your students for the video? What kind of follow-up activity did you schedule?

Projects

1. Investigate the sound systems currently available in your school and determine the additional components required to use one of these systems in your teaching. Create a proposal requesting these components for your principal.
2. Contact the publishers of physical education textbooks for review copies. Read, compare, and select one textbook for use with your classes. Provide a rationale for the book selected.

Chapter 3

Capturing Audio and Visual Images for Use in Physical Education

Before class, John Washington sets up 10 learning stations to help his students learn the correct technique for bowling. When class begins, John divides the students into groups of four and has them move from one learning station to the next. In addition to the six skill-practice stations, one cognitive activity station, and one computer station, there also is a station where the students can video one another performing the bowling approach and release, and a station where students can review their performance. This last station allows the students to immediately see and analyze their performance.

You will find many uses for captured audio data and visual images for use in physical education. Digital cameras and camcorders allow you to capture still and moving visual images. They provide students with the opportunity to see themselves in a physical activity, compare their performances to model performances, and create their own visual projects. As schools continue their restructuring efforts and place increasing emphasis on process learning, student projects will play an even greater role while sound and visual images will be a key element in these efforts.

This chapter will help you decide which digital camera and camcorder is right for you. I will describe the different types, basic features, and optional features (for those with additional funds). I also will suggest ways to use the images captured with these devices in your physical education classes and will offer tips for successful recording and reproducing of sounds and images. The integration of visual images and computers will be addressed in greater detail in Chapters 6 and 10.

Selecting a Digital Camera

Digital cameras differ from traditional cameras in that they don't record images on film. Instead, the images are stored in digital files. The advantages of a digital camera are that you will never have to purchase film again, pictures are immediately available for use, and the images can be manipulated on your computer. The disadvantages include a slight reduction in the clarity of the photograph and a delay after each shot while the camera records and compresses the image. The criteria for selecting a digital camera include cost, durability, ease of operation, reliability and quality, and ease of repair and maintenance along with the selection of specific features including resolution, storage, viewfinder/LCD size, lens features, shutter features, and type of batteries. The top of the line is the D-SLR (digital single lens reflex) that comes close in quality to a 35mm film camera and includes manual features that professionals appreciate. Physical educators should be happy selecting a lower-level digital camera with the features described in the following sections.

Resolution

Digital camera resolution determines the size of the photo. If you want a 4x6-inch print, then two, three, or more megapixels will produce the same image. In fact, a two-megapixel camera provides excellent 4x6 and 5x7-inch prints. A three-megapixel camera provides excellent 8x10-inch prints, while a four-megapixel camera provides excellent 11x14-inch prints, and a five-megapixel camera provides excellent 16x20-inch prints.

Storage

Most digital cameras use memory cards for storage, including CompactFlash, MemoryStick, SecureDigital (SD), SmartMedia, and xD. While it is important to have a memory card reader that matches your camera's memory card; don't let storage be the deciding factor when selecting a camera, since they all are very similar. Be aware that most cameras come with a small amount of memory space, so you will probably want to purchase an additional memory card. See Chapter 5 for more information on each media.

Viewfinders/LCDs

You will have a choice of viewfinders when you purchase a digital camera. Some cameras have small glass viewfinders, while must have a color Liquid Crystal Display (LCD) screen that shows you what the lens sees. The LCD screen also lets you review your pictures while still in the field—if you don't like the picture you can immediately erase it. Be aware that small increases in the size of the LCD can increase the cost of the camera, since the LCD is one of the most expensive parts on the camera. Also, check the LCD outside before purchasing to verify that the screen is viewable in direct sunlight.

Lens

There are two variables related to the lens to consider when selecting a camera. The first is the composition of the lens—glass is better than plastic and will produce much clearer images. The second, is the zoom feature. A zoom lens allows you to change the focal length to see a wider view of a large area or a smaller view of a close up. An optical zoom of 3x is good for general purpose pictures. You can basically ignore the

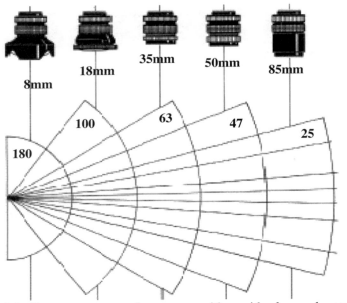

Figure 3.1 You can capture a larger area with a wider lens, whereas a telephoto lens captures a much smaller area. This illustration reflects 35mm cameras.

digital zoom, which uses a part of the charged couple device (CCD) to capture a section and enlarge it as would a magnifying glass, since it results in poor quality.

Be aware that most digital camera image sensors are about two-thirds the size of a 35mm film frame—so the sensor can "see" only the center part of the lens image circle. This effectively multiplies the focal length of attached lens by a factor of 1.6, so that an 18- to 55-mm lens offers a field of view roughly equivalent to that of a 28- to 90-mm lens on a 35mm camera.

Shutter Features

Digital cameras experience a shutter lag—a split second from the time you press the shutter before the shutter fires. This is time that the camera needs to charge the sensor, perform exposure, and focus operations. The actual shutter speed varies from camera to camera, and the information can be found in the specifications listed for each camera.

If you are fairly new to photography, you will want a camera with programmed screen modes. These modes provide pre-set settings for specific situations, such as night exposure, landscape shots, portrait shots, close-ups, and athletic shots. This feature takes the guess work out of proper camera exposure.

Batteries

Nickel metal hydride (NiMH) or lithium ion (LiOn) batteries are the best choices for a digital camera. They can be charged at any time and will last longer. However, if you use your camera infrequently, then a better choice for you is alkaline batteries.

Digital Imaging Software

Digital imaging software (e.g., Adobe Photoshop Lite) is frequently bundled with the digital camera. Imaging software can greatly improve digital photos by changing colors, increasing sharpness, and replacing unwanted items in a photo. A few keystrokes can crop a photo, remove the red flash spots from someone's eyes, change the brightness, or switch a picture from left to right. The imaging software also can reduce the resolution and color depth for smaller images when posting to the web. Digital imaging software is addressed in Chapter 6.

Selecting a Camcorder

The criteria for purchasing camcorders include cost, durability, ease of operation, reliability and quality, ease of repair and maintenance, and compatibility between camcorder and videocassette player or computer. Camcorders fall into four major categories: VHS, VHS-C (compact form), 8mm, and digital. VHS camcorders are usually larger (bulkier and heavier)

Figure 3.2 A camcorder is ideal for physical education.

and record onto VHS-formatted videocassettes that are played on a VHS videocassette recorder (VCR). The VHS-C model is a compact version of the VHS format. Both the camcorder and the tape are smaller (about a third the size of regular VHS) and lighter than the VHS, but there is some loss of quality. In addition, tape length is 40 minutes in standard play (SP) speed, and two hours at lower quality extended play (EP) speed. The VHS-C tape fits into a special adapter for playback on a VHS player. Generally, 8mm camcorders are much lighter (many models weigh less than 1.5 pounds), more compact, easier to use while traveling, and can record 150 minutes in standard play (SP) speed. The cassette is the size of an audio cassette, although it is slightly thicker. The quality of the 8mm picture is almost as good as VHS, and the audio is superior, except for VHS hi-fi models. However, the 8mm cassette cannot play on a VHS videocassette recorder, and therefore most be connected to the VCR via a cable or played in a special 8mm videocassette player.

The VHS, VHS-C, and 8mm recorders are available in a superior quality (S-VHS, S-VHS-C, and Hi8) format that enhances picture sharpness—especially in slow motion—and reduces the false color effects and wavy edges often seen on regular VHS recordings. The super VHS (S-VHS) uses a specially formulated, more expensive tape and superior electronics. The tape records up to 400 lines of resolution, compared to 240 lines of resolution on the conventional VHS tape. Hi8 (Hi-Band 8mm) offers the same resolution as S-VHS, but Hi8 records with slightly less color noise (unwanted electrical signal that interferes with sound or image), making the picture quality better than the S-VHS.

Hi 8 camcorders, like the S-VHS, include S-video jacks for maximum signal transfer quality to a television or an S-VHS VCR. However, most of the Hi8 advantages can be realized through ordinary cables. Analog cameras are coming to an end in terms of production, but we will continue to find them in schools for years to come and they still function for many of the tasks we perform in physical education.

Digital camcorders offer superior audio and video quality compared to their analog counterparts. These camcorders record and process information in much the same way as a digital camera. This means there is no film and virtually no loss of picture quality when you transfer the images to your computer. In addition to high-quality recording, most digital camcorders come with an IEEE1394 (i.link/FireWire) connection that can send a digital signal directly to your computer.

Digital camcorders come in two basic models. The first, the DV camcorder, uses cassettes (digital video cassettes) that are slightly larger than a matchbox. These cassette tapes hold up to 60 minutes of video and audio. The second digital option is the DVD-CAM. It writes MPEG-2 video directly to DVD rewritable or recordable discs. These discs may then be played in the computer or set-top DVD player.

Combination cameras also are available and include the ability to take both still and video images. As of the writing of this book, there are combination cameras that provide 3.3-megapixel still images and two-megapixel video images. This makes the combination camera a viable choice for the physical educator. When selecting a combination camera be sure that it provides true digital still frames, since these images are of much higher quality when compared to camcorders with just a freeze frame feature. The freeze frame image is simply recorded on the tape. With true digital still frame capability, a JPEG or TIFF image is captured on a separate memory module, such as a MemoryStick. Many combinations cameras, as well as some still cameras and some camcorders, have a burst or continuous shoot mode that allows you the option of taking thirty shots at three frames per second (fps).

Parts and Features

The features to consider when purchasing a digital camcorder include weight, good picture quality, good viewfinder placement, power zoom lens, automatic focus, automatic white balance, low-light use, wireless microphone, shutter speed, rechargeable battery, and tripod. There also are optional features to consider, depending on your budget and needs. Once you have selected the features that are important to you, the purchasing department in your school district can provide you with assistance in selecting the specific camcorder.

Weight and picture quality. Determine the acceptable weight and picture quality by experimenting with several camcorders in the store. The camera that feels light enough to carry around for a class period and whose picture looks good enough for the price is the one to buy. The quality of the image is often dependent on the quality of the CCD—a sensor that records light passing through the lens and captures the video. Physical educators typically choose a single CCD; however, as three CCDs come down in price, it might be a feature to consider. Three CCDs improve color accuracy and contrast while reducing the signal noise that shows up as interference in the image. A third alternative is a special filter that actually mimics the three CCD system; while not quite as good as a real three CCD system, it does provide a step up from the single CCD.

Be sure to purchase a camcorder with an electronic image stabilization feature. It keeps track of the image, so it doesn't move—even if the camera does. The dual gyro digital image stabilization adjusts for both up-and-down and side-to-side movement. Be aware that image stabilization works best for distant subjects, and won't compensate for really wild gyrations.

Also, select optical stabilization, since it is better than digital stabilization, which simply reduces the size of the image to compensate for any distortion.

Viewfinder/LCD. The viewfinder is the part of the camcorder that you look through when recording. It is a tiny television screen that also allows for instant review. A viewfinder that is adjustable for different angles, and that gives users a choice between using the left eye or the right eye is preferred. However, two, three, or four-inch LCD screens are ideal for physical education, since students can replay the video in the camera and still see the images clearly. Some of these LCDs are built in, while other models have pivoting attachments that allow the monitor to swivel out for viewing. As with the digital camera, be sure to try the LCD screen outside to verify that you can see the image in direct sunlight. Also, be aware that the LCD screen causes an increase demand for power, so use it infrequently or be sure to have additional batteries available.

Zoom lens. The lens should have a motorized, variable-speed zoom feature that moves in and out smoothly. The variable speed allows the user to press hard for a quick zoom in or out and to reduce the zoom speed to a third by using less pressure. Focus only on the optical zoom ratio (e.g., 4:1, 6:1, 10:1) and not the digital zoom when making a purchasing decision, since the digital zoom electronically enlarges the central portion of the image by increasing the pixilation, which results in a loss of clarity. A wide-angle lens is used for distance shots and a telephoto lens for close-up details (see Figure 3.1). This combination provides you with the capability to capture a full-body shot of an individual performing a skill like a golf swing and then focus in on only the hands.

Automatic focus. The automatic focus feature helps to ensure good photography. However, there are times when the automatic focus may not function properly and should not be used—for example:

-When you are shooting through dirty glass,

-The subject has a shiny surface,

-Part of the subject is near and another part is farther away,

-The subject has distinct horizontal stripes,

-You are shooting flat subjects such as white walls,

-No part of the subject is within the focusing zone frame,

-You are using the macro close-up function,

-You are shooting fast-moving action, or

-The lighting is poor.

Under these conditions, you will want to switch to manual focus. Look for a camera that has small thumb wheels or rotating lens barrels that let you make subtle adjustments. Some models offer only tiny push buttons that are difficult to tweak accurately.

Automatic white balance. Picture quality and color are controlled by the white balance, which helps to keep colors true under different lighting conditions. An inaccurate white balance can produce a picture that is too pink or too blue. True white will differ, depending on whether you are shooting under regular (incandescent) bulbs, fluorescent light fixtures, outdoors in bright sun, or in some combination of these lighting conditions. White balance can be set automatically (shoot at something white and press "white balance") for easy and accurate use under varying light conditions. However, in certain circumstances the white balance should be set manually for indoor or outdoor use. These include situations where there are different illuminations on the subject and the camera, the subject or camera is in the shade, it is sunrise or sunset, or you are using the macro lens to videotape images at very close range.

Low-light use. The amount of light received by the camera is measured in lux and is determined by a combination of shutter speed and aperture opening. A camcorder with a lux rating of three to five (the average indoor room provides 20-40 lux) provides adequate illumination in all but the worst situations.

Of course, many older gymnasiums and weight rooms do have very poor lighting, so you may want a lower lux rating. The auto-iris feature, which is found on almost all video cameras, automatically adjusts the lens aperture to optimize the exposure, even when you move from bright to dim areas. Built-in video lights are typically more than adequate to enhance colors and lift shadows in dim areas. Some video lights are programmed to turn on automatically if the available light isn't adequate, making it even more convenient for the user. More lighting can be added by attaching an external light to the camera's hot shoe extension, holding a portable light, or positioning free standing lights. If the sun is behind your object, be sure to use the backlight control, which can improve exposure when dark subjects are shot against brighter backgrounds.

Wireless microphone. Most camcorders come with a built-in omnidirectional mike. Although mikes that are built in to the front of the camera are better than the ones on the top, both make it difficult to hear what is being said. This is especially true in gymnasiums and indoor swimming areas where there are echoes. The addition of a wireless camcorder microphone system allows for cable-free audio recording at distances of up to 200 feet.

There are three parts to the microphone system: receiver, transmitter, and microphone. The receiver is mounted on the camcorder's accessory shoe and plugged into the microphone input jack. An earphone or headphone jack on the receiver lets the user monitor the input. A single directional lapel microphone, headset microphone, or hand held microphone is attached to the transmitter and used by the person who is being videotaped. An in-use indicator light tells the user when the transmitter and receiver are turned on and ready to go. In addition, I would recommend selecting a wireless microphone with multiple channels, since at times two microphones are used in the gymnasium, and one camera may pick up the other microphone unless they are on separate channels.

Shutter speed. The normal shutter speed on a camcorder is 30 frames (60 fields) per second; however, cameras can be purchased with variable shutter speeds. High-speed shutters from 2,000 to 10,000 frames per second are great for shooting sporting events and analyzing motor skills, since even small changes in movement can be captured. Be sure you have extra light when using high-speed shutters, as exposure times are very small.

Be aware that some camcorders are described as high-speed cameras; however, this refers to the exposure time (e.g., 1/500th of a second) and not the number of frames per second. Capturing a field in 1/500 of a second ensures that moving objects do not move much as the image is being captured, so there is little or no blurring. But this does not make the camera "high-speed."

Batteries. Portable microphones and cameras use large amounts of electricity (especially if you are using the built-in light), so it is wise to have several rechargeable batteries on hand. Lithium-ion or NiMH batteries provide excellent performance and can be recharged hundreds of times. The camera will have some type of low-battery indicator that alerts you when batteries should be changed or an AC adapter used. Some cameras allow for the simultaneous use of the AC adapter while batteries are being charged.

Tripod. A tripod is important because it provides a stable base of support for the camera. Several adjustments on the tripod control the movement: pan control allows the camera to be rotated in 360-degrees; tilt control allows the camera to move up and down; and elevation controls allow the tripod's legs to be extended. A level on the tripod is beneficial, since it quickly shows if the tripod is tilted.

Optional features. If your budget allows, you will want to purchase such additional features as a fade button and a character generator. A fade button allows for a gradual transition from one image to black, and then back to the next image. Character generators superimpose titles, times, and dates on the video. These are easy to attach and come with directions for composing titles and other character lines. Some camcorders offer "titlers" that have built-in titles ready to go. When selecting optional features, be sure you understand their purpose. Consider whether you will really use the feature before investing additional money in your purchase. Remember too, that video editing software can add these features once the footage is transferred to the computer.

Successful Recording

When recording, the background ideally should be plain, uncluttered, and in contrast to the subject. Be sure to avoid shiny surfaces, which tend to create reflections. At the start of any shoot, assemble the tripod and set it to the correct height by adjusting the elevation controls. Then, connect the camera to the tripod and practice movements using the pan and tilt locks. Always place a blank label on the media (e.g., videotape, DV tape, DVD) before placing it in the camcorder, and title it immediately after recording.

Tips for Still and Video Success

1. Use a tripod.
2. Capture different angles for variety.
3. Get close to subject (use wide-angle lens setting).
4. Keep subjects' eyes high in the frame.
5. For macro shots - put glass on blocks to hold objects and put backgrounds under glass.
6. Be sure to have sufficient light.

Tips for Video Success

1. Reframe from zooming in and out quickly.
2. Record for a minimum of 10 seconds.

Additional Tips for Videotaping

When You Start
Press the play and record button, and let the tape run for five seconds to ensure that you are past the lead and into the film.

When You Are Finished
Film for an additional five seconds—the next time you videotape, the camera will rewind the tape slightly before recording, and you don't want to lose anything.

After you place the blank media in the camcorder, set the standby switch on the camera to on, the white balance switch to automatic, and the focus to automatic. Zoom in on the subject. When you are ready to record, press the standby switch again to start the recording.

During playback, the fast forward switch advances the media forward quickly, the rewind switch moves to previous images, the play switch shows what has been taped, and the stop switch literally stops the showing.

The camera must be held steady when recording, which is why a tripod is recommended. If you must hand hold the camera, you should lean against something, or even sit down. Use smooth and slow movements as you follow the action. For the best results, move your whole body. To make an object larger, move closer rather than zooming, if possible.

Reproducing Analog Videotapes

To copy or edit a tape, connect the camcorder to a videocassette recorder or connect two videocassette recorders together. At a more sophisticated level, two videocassette recorders can be connected and controlled by an editing controller or a computer. To connect a camcorder to a videocassette recorder or a videocassette recorder to another videocassette recorder, use two lines of cable with appropriate plugs for your machines. Plug one end of the cable into the camcorder's video output and the other end of the same cable into the videocassette's video input. Then, plug one end of the other cable into the camcorder's audio output and the other end into the videocassette's audio input. Another cable may be used to connect the videocassette recorder to a television or monitor, so that you can watch the video as you record or edit.

To make a copy, place a blank tape in the videocassette recorder and the original tape in the camcorder or the second videocassette recorder. Rewind both tapes to their beginning and set both tape counters to zero. Press the record and play buttons on the videocassette recorder simultaneously and allow it to run for five seconds before pressing the play button on the camcorder (or second videocassette recorder). Once the entire tape has been played and recorded onto the new tape, press the stop button on the camcorder (or second videocassette recorder) and then press the stop button on the videocassette recorder.

In many cases you will want to edit a video presentation. The manual editing process, which is similar to the copying process, allows you to copy certain portions of the tape into a new sequence. Rewind the original tape to its beginning, and set the counter to zero. As you watch the original tape, record the starting and ending number of each scene you wish to copy, and write a brief description. Then, note the sequence in which you want the scenes organized on the final tape.

Place a new tape in the videocassette recorder and press the play and record buttons simultaneously, letting the tape run five seconds before pressing the pause button. Advance the original tape to the first scene to be recorded and press the pause button. Pressing both pause buttons simultaneously starts the recording. The pause buttons—not the stop and record buttons—are used because pressing the stop button usually rewinds the tape a short distance. Pressing the pause button, on the other hand, holds the tape in front of the recording heads. A synchro cable can be used to connect the two machines and control the pause function on both machines. This cable eliminates the chance of inadvertently starting one machine before the other.

For some video projects, you may want to add music or change the original audio portion. This can be accomplished easily if your camcorder has an audio dubbing button. Advance the videotape to the location where the audio dubbing will begin and press the pause button. Connect your new audio source and press the audio dubbing button and play button simultaneously to record. Similarly, video dubbing records video without disturbing the existing soundtrack. It allows you to cleanly replace a segment of videotape with a new one, without any lines of distortion. If you plan to do a lot of editing, video and audio dubbing should be two of the most important items you look for when deciding which camcorder to purchase.

Editing machines—either computer-based or stand alone boxes—are available. These devices allow for more professional transitions (fades, wipes, dissolves) between scenes, special effects, and audio/video mixing (fading the sound with the picture or switching in separate audio and video sources). Many editing machines also are capable of placing characters on the screen for titles, dates, and descriptions—replacing machines whose only function is to generate characters. If these devices are available on your campus, they will typically be located in your audiovisual department. Availability of these devices for use in physical education will be determined by your interest in learning to use them, your educational goals for their use, and your rapport with the video instructor.

Reproducing Digital Video

The process for reproducing digital videotapes and DVD is similar to reproducing analog videotape. Simply connect one DVD player or digital camcorder to a DVD recorder. Typically, you will use a fire wire cable, which will transfer the audio and video simultaneously. Chapter 6 covers transferring analog and digital video to a computer and computer-based editing.

Camera Care

Cameras require protection from the elements—especially rain, dust, and condensation. Keep a lens cap on the camera when it is not in use and don't leave the camera in the trunk of your car. Condensation can be avoided by not breathing on the lens and by keeping the camcorder in a constant temperature. When you are recording around a swimming pool, place the camcorder in a tightly closed plastic bag until it warms up. If the camcorder's indicator reads DEW, it means that so much condensation has built up inside the camcorder that it will shut itself off in minutes. The camcorder should not be used for at least an hour after this occurs.

Videotapes also require some special care. Store tapes by standing them on their spine. Never lay a videocassette down on its tape side, since the pull of gravity will cause the tape to stretch. Break off the erasure prevention tab to prevent anyone from inadvertently taping over a previously recorded tape. If you later decide to rerecord on that tape, cover the tab area with a piece of tape.

Uses in Physical Education

You and your students can use digital cameras and camcorders to improve the overall learning environment and process. Student use includes replay of performances, biomechanical analysis, special projects, and documentation of learning. Teacher use includes the development of instructional aids, assistance for substitute teachers, demonstrations of model lessons, and monitoring student behavior. These devices also can help you analyze instructional effectiveness and create professional portfolios.

Replaying Performance

Video and still image replay have been shown to be most effective when used with students of at least an advanced beginner skill level. Students need some knowledge of the skill and a viable mental image of it in order to use the information these images provide. Video and still images are especially effective when replayed immediately after the performance, when the teacher provides verbal feedback and cues while replaying the images, and when the performance is shown from at least five different angles (front, back, top, left, and right) including close-up shots that focus on specific aspects of a performance (Rothstein, 1981; Darden & Shimon, 2000; Lee, Swinnen, & Serrien, 1994; Darden, 1999; Doering, 2000). For students with advanced skills, replay also is useful for strategy and tactics. Because advanced movement is so fast and sometimes difficult to analyze at normal speed, slow motion replay and freeze frame capabilities are essential.

After students have had an opportunity to view replays with the teacher, they can capture and review their performances by themselves. Students can use the images to guide changes in their own internal imagery and improve their performance. Be sure to provide task analysis sheets listing the critical features for the skill, so students can evaluate their performances against a set of criteria. They should focus on one aspect of the skill and, after viewing their performance, spend more time practicing before videotaping themselves again.

To provide for student self-analysis, place the digital camera/ camcorder at one station on a learning circuit. Begin by modeling each phase of the skill while students work in pairs to identify critical features, patterns, and concepts associated with the skill. Students also might draw stick figures to illustrate the different phases of the skill. Then, students should rotate through the stations in groups of four. For example, in a tennis circuit, one group would begin at the digital camera/camcorder station. One person tosses the tennis balls, the second person executes a forehand stroke, the third person acts as the coach, and the fourth person videos the skill performance. Each group member is shot executing several forehand strokes. The student-coach uses the first set of columns on the criteria sheet to provide specific feedback. On the rotation after shooting, the students review the images while the next team shags the tennis balls and gets set up for its turn.

The instant replay provides immediate feedback for the performer, who uses the second set of columns on the criteria sheet to assess his or her own performance. The team then moves to the next court, where students practice the forehand stroke while the images of themselves executing the skill are still fresh in their minds. Self-analysis is even more beneficial to the student than visual replay, since he or she is actively involved in both the performance and feedback stages. The images also can be used by the teacher at the end of class to assess student progress.

Sample Checklist
Basketball Set Shot

_____ Place feet apart with dominant foot forward.
_____ Hold ball with back of dominant hand toward face.
_____ Place non-dominant hand on side of ball to support it.
_____ Keep elbows close to body.
_____ Bend knees and lower ball slightly.
_____ Straighten knees and thrust arms forward and upward.
_____ Push ball toward basket.
_____ Release ball off ends of fingers with wrist snap.
_____ Follow through toward target.

Parent Permission Form for Videotaping

Dear Mr. Garcia,

This year I am participating in the Orange County Physical Education Leadership Academy. This learning experience is sponsored by the Orange County Department of Education and the California Technology Assistance Project. The goal of the project is to enhance the teaching of physical education through the use of technology.

As part of my professional portfolio, I will be preparing short videotapes of the lessons I teach in your child's class. Although the videotape will involve both myself and students, the primary focus is on my teaching. In the course of taping however, your child may be filmed. These videotapes will be shared with other physical educators, both within and outside the Orange County Physical Education Leadership Academy setting. If, for any reason, you do not wish your child to be involved, please let me know by October 15.

Sincerely,

Mrs. Washington
Physical Educator

Please sign and return this form to indicate your wishes regarding your child's participation in this project.

____ I give my permission for my child to be videotaped.

____ I do not wish to have my child videotaped.

Name of student_____

Signature of parent _____

Date: _____

Analyzing Movement

When students capture images of themselves and others practicing a skill, they gain a better understanding of the "why" behind the correct technique. Students compare the performance displayed on a monitor to a model performance displayed on a second monitor in terms of a particular biomechanical principle. Or, using software such as *DartTrainer*, both images can be seen on the same computer screen--either side-by-side or one on top of the other. For example, while comparing performances on the shot put, students might compare the angle of release or speed of approach. Software programs are available that allow for more detailed biomechanical analysis (see Chapter 7 for more details).

Project-Based Learning

Students can participate in project-based learning by planning, shooting, and editing their own video. However, this is time consuming. So, although project-based learning can be done solely in physical education, you will find collaboration with the media specialists or other teachers helpful.

Projects allow students to demonstrate what they have learned about a particular concept. For example, after a unit on movement patterns, assign students to work in groups of four to develop an in-depth video on one particular movement pattern (overhand throw, underhand throw, catch, kick, etc.) The students record a description and demonstration of the correct technique for the pattern, explain the reasons for the technique, and then record different examples of the pattern. They might go from one physical education class to another, recording different skills to demonstrate their particular movement pattern. Students recording the overhand movement pattern might video the overhand serve or spike in volleyball, the overhand clear in badminton, and the overhand throw in softball. The students then show their completed projects to the rest of the class.

Another video project involves having students demonstrate their understanding of biomechanical principles. Students select one motor skill and record each person in their group as he or she performs it. The students then review the video to determine what was correct or incorrect about their performances, using biomechanical principles to justify their findings. The students then create and record an audio script that summarizes their findings to accompany their video performances, and share their work with the rest of the class.

Other project ideas include recording fitness plans developed by students, games created by the students, or demonstrations of rule situations for established sports. For example, cut up the rule sheet for any sport and tape each rule, description, and violation or foul onto a three-by-five-inch card. Again, the students should work in groups of four. One person from each group draws a rule card from the teacher's hand. The instructions for the video project are given verbally as well as posted on a portable dry board for reference. These include:

1. Re-enact the foul or violation (create it in a game-like situation).
2. Explain the foul or violation.
3. Demonstrate the penalty for the foul or violation.
4. Explain the penalty and its advantages and disadvantages.

Each group creates its scenario and prepares for the recording. The entire class watches each completed video and reviews all the rules.

In specialty classes dealing with such subjects as sports medicine and athletic injuries, students are recorded while reenacting situations that resulted in injuries. Students work in groups of four to plan and perform their scenes. One student is the opponent, the second student is the athlete who is injured, the third student is the trainer, and the fourth student records the event. The entire class views the video, discussing the following items: injury procedure, cause of injury, location, signs, assessment questions, and care/taping.

In still another video project, students might design a rehabilitation program for an athletic injury in a sport of their choice. After learning about the therapeutic modalities and the therapeutic process of sport rehabilitation, groups of four use the following criteria to design their rehabilitation program: one of the three injury phases (acute, subacute, or chronic), warm-up exercises, stretching exercises, cardiorespiratory activities, strength training, sport-specific drills, and cool down. Again, the students critique each group's video using a criteria sheet based on the elements listed above.

Documenting Learning

Students can capture images of themselves performing selected skills at the beginning of an instructional unit, midway through the unit, and at the end of the unit. These images may be e-mailed home for review or sharing with parents, or simply posted into an electronic portfolio (see Chapter 10 for more details). At the end of the unit, students observe their performances and growth. Instructors asks the students to write a reflection piece about their progress.

Developing Instructional Materials

Many of the preceding examples used either visual images or video images to meet the learning objectives. However, still images may be used exclusively to model performance for task cards or reciprocal feedback sheets. Several companies, such as Sportime and Bonnie's Fitware Inc., develop and sell task cards. However, you can use your students as models and create your own task cards. In fact, using instructional materials that include images of students' peers is a great motivator!

These same images can be included in testing materials or in newsletters that are distributed throughout the community or sent home to parents.

Assisting Substitute Teachers

You can prepare video lessons of yourself for use when you are absent. State your expectations for the class, give a lecture, provide students with motivation, and give specific directions. The substitute teacher plays the video, and there is little question what the lesson involves because you have given the directions yourself. (You might even provide your substitute teacher with a list of student names accompanied by photos.) You may, at times, also choose to use the video to explain a series of steps to the students when you are in the classroom. This protocol allows you to rotate from student to student to ensure that they are following the directions correctly.

Demonstrating Model Lessons

While you may be unable to leave your classes to view outstanding teachers demonstrating model lessons, you might persuade them to have their lessons recorded by a student or another teacher. You can start and stop the video as needed, or replay particular portions to better grasp how outstanding teachers handle certain situations.

Monitoring Student Behavior

Using videos to monitor student behavior allows teachers, parents, and students to see what actually occurred during class. This eliminates unnecessary discussion about what students did or did not do during the lesson. It is a good idea to get parental permission before using this particular strategy. In addition, be sure to secure written parental permission before showing a video of a student outside the class. A sample letter is provided for your use (see page 74). Be sure to check with your school or district for additional requirements regarding parent permission for recording of students.

Summary

Digital cameras and camcorders are technologies that can be used on a daily basis. They are effective for both instruction and assessment. They provide feedback and allow for analysis of movement and documentation of student learning. Digital cameras allow teachers to create instructional materials, and camcorders can help improve teacher effectiveness. Teachers can view tapes of effective teachers, they can create videos to assist substitute teachers, and they can use videos to monitor student behavior. The quality of still and video images continues to improve, and equipment availability on school campuses continues to increase. As "technology money" funnels its way into schools, consider purchasing digital cameras and video technology as well as computer technology for use in your physical education program.

Reflection Questions

1. Envision the last time you used a camera or camcorder in your teaching. Which of the standards were you addressing? What was your strategy? What was the impact on student learning?
2. Several ideas were presented on how to use video technology in physical education. What other ways can you think of to use video technology in your classes?

Projects

1. Make a list of the features you would like on your next digital camcorder. Then, peruse a catalog for camcorders that fit your criteria. Finally, go on the Internet and compare reviews of these camcorders. Select a camera and write a brief explanation of why you selected it.

2. Design a video-based learning project for your students. Identify the standard(s) you are addressing, the instructional strategies you will utilize, and how you will assess your students. Write up the project in a format that will make sense to your students.

Chapter 4

Devices

The physical education department at Montebello Intermediate School has developed a fitness/wellness lab in an effort to motivate its students to assume a physically active lifestyle. It contains a cardiorespiratory circuit (consisting of rowing machines, stair steppers, ergometers, recumbent cycles, an elliptical, and treadmills), a strength circuit, and a small computer lab. Staff members schedule the facility so that all classes can take advantage of it. During their time in the lab, students rotate from the cardiorespiratory circuit, where they wear heart monitors, to the strength circuit where they work on muscular strength and endurance. In the computer lab area, students can upload their heart monitor data and update their electronic portfolios. In another area of the physical education facility, tables and chairs are set up to serve as a classroom where students learn cognitive health and fitness concepts, read, write, develop projects, and work on creating week-long fitness plans.

In the subdisciplines of exercise physiology, motor learning, and biomechanics, several low-end models of sophisticated machinery have brought a new dimension to the K-12 setting. Aerobic equipment, timing devices, measuring devices, positioning devices, spirometers and peak flow meters, electronic blood pressure devices, body composition analyzers, and heart

How To Grow a Fitness Lab
Contributed by Scott Bowman

Step 1: Answer these questions
Is the lab going to be a portable or permanent facility?
Is the lab going to be used daily, weekly, or monthly?
What fitness program(s) do you want to provide for your students?
What resources do you need?
How many phases will it take to build the lab?

Step 2: Secure funding
Contact local exercise clubs, tell them your goal, and ask for their support in the form of dumbbells, free weights, and exercise machine donations.
Contact local business groups that might be involved in fitness and ask for their support.
Put together a parent newsletter and tell parents of your goal and ask for their support.
Look for grants that are offered in any area that would fit with lifelong fitness, at-risk students, or technology.

Step 3: Choose equipment
Purchase equipment that can be used by a large number of students.
Purchase equipment that is sized for your students.
Develop your lab around a circuit program.
Purchase equipment with as few moving pieces as possible.
Save top-end items for your second or third phase.

Step 4: Implement your program
Develop a three-year plan that will allow you to grow slowly.
Do not let "No" bother you; it is just an invitation to try somewhere else.
Get your entire school population involved.
Ask for media coverage for your program.
Do not give up!

monitors provide students with hands-on learning opportunities. Although these devices aren't always as sophisticated or expensive as models used in university and research settings, they do help students learn about the relationship between bodily functions, movement patterns, exercise, and success in physical activities.

Aerobic Equipment

The range of aerobic equipment available to schools continues to expand. Today we see treadmills, ergometers, rowers, stair climbers, cross-country ski simulators, striders, treadwalls, and downhill skiers in secondary school settings. Treadmills require the highest rate of energy expenditure, followed by cross-country skiers, rowers, and stair steppers (Zeni, Hoffman, & Clifford, 1996). However, most physical education departments purchase a variety of devices in order to motivate students to participate in aerobic activity.

When purchasing equipment, look for durability and safety features. For example, the more gadgets there are on a piece of equipment, the greater the possibility for breakdowns. In addition, all flywheels should be enclosed to prevent harm to fingers or damage from pencils or other foreign objects.

Videos provide a sense of realism for some pieces of exercise equipment. For example, cross-country ski videos place the user right on the trail, gliding over the snow with the real motion of cross-country skiing. Hiking videos provide added realism for steppers and stair climbing machines. A pleasant ride in the country along with comments on the scenic route provide the stationary bike user with a feeling of being an active participant in a cross-country bicycling tour. Rowing videos put the user in the bow, with Olympic team members in the front seats.

Exercise equipment with a serial, USB, or RJ45 interface provides users with the option of connecting to a personal computer. *UltraCoach*™--a popular Windows-based interface software for running, swimming, and bicycling--records, analyzes, and manages all of the user's workout information, including heart rate, time, speed, and grade changes. It generates a detailed report that includes three-dimensional graphs showing heart rate distribution curves. Using an analysis feature, the software can prescribe new workouts based on past performance.

NetAthlon™ enables users of fitness machines to train alone, in groups, or against virtual competitors on lifelike 3D real-time virtual reality courses. Using a network (e.g., LAN) or the Internet, NetAthlon™ permits fitness machines users to compete against other users or fitness machines around the world.

Before selecting any equipment, develop a layout plan for your fitness center. Consider good ventilation for the machines, adequate on-off access space, pathways for rotation from one piece of equipment to another, and safety considerations. It also is a good idea to visit schools where fitness centers already exist. Find out which pieces of equipment and which brands hold up best with daily use by teenagers. Or, go online and research various types of equipment. Busy Body Online (see Appendix A) is especially helpful at assessing various types of exercise equipment.

Aerobic exercise equipment can be used in several ways:

1. The equipment is set up in a circuit and students rotate from one apparatus to another, maintaining their target heart rate for a period of time.
2. Students select one piece of equipment and exercise exclusively on that apparatus while maintaining their target heart rates.
3. Several circuits (computer, aerobic equipment, strength equipment) are set up and students rotate through each circuit, maintaining their target heart rate while in the aerobic circuit.
4. Students collect heart rate data while exercising on different pieces of aerobic equipment. They write a comparison essay for homework.

The most important advice regarding exercise equipment is to keep it clean Dust and dirt are attracted to the internal electronic motors, tracks, and cables in the machines. This dust and dirt causes the machines to wear out quickly. Therefore, consider cleaning the machines on a daily basis. Now, let's take a look at some special requirements for each type of equipment.

Treadmills

A treadmill (see Figure 4.1) is a wide belt stretched over a flat bed and around two or more rollers. Some units are powered by the users, others are motor driven. Treadmills are specifically designed for walking, jogging, or running, so it is important to purchase the one best suited for the needs of your students. When selecting a treadmill for educational purposes, pick one that is simple and easy to use, with a solid (welded) carbon or steel frame and all steel rollers for easy rolling, less slippage, and fewer maintenance problems. Be sure to select a treadmill with handrails and an automatic shut off device for safety. For the preferred motor-driven treadmills, 1.75-2.0 horsepower, for a maximum speed of 11 miles per hour, with a maximum elevation of 15 percent with five increments is recommended. When considering horsepower, check whether it is a peak horsepower rating or a continuous horsepower rating. Neither one is better, but they can't be compared. In other words, a 2.0 horsepower peak duty motor may or may not be better than 1.5 horsepower continuous duty motor. As a general rule, as you go up in price you will get a larger, more sturdy treadmill, a maintenance free deck, and more preprogrammed interactive features.

Features to look for when purchasing a treadmill, include: a wide belt that is long enough for each student's stride, good shock absorption, adjustable elevation and speed, handgrips in front or on the sides, and low noise. Most treadmills come with easy-to-reach control panels that display heart rate, speed, and distance covered. Optional display features include exercise time, aerobic points, incline controls, and a variety of exercise modes (i.e.,

Figure 4.1 Treadmill   Figure 4.2 Exercise bicycle

warm up, cool down, endurance, interval, cardiovascular, fat burn) that cause the treadmill to automatically adjust its incline and speed. A flat bed with more cushioning will reduce the impact shock to bones, joints, and muscles. Treadmills that incorporate upper body workouts also are available, but most users find the arm motion to be uncomfortable.

Treadwalls

Treadwalls are essentially vertical treadmills. They are rock climbing simulations, and there typically are no electrical motors or parts that will need to be replaced. Treadwalls typically feature a 20-foot climbing surface that moves by body weight alone. As climbers move "up," the wall moves down along a continuous track. When the climbers stop, the wall stops as well. The braking system ensures that climbers are always in control, keeping them no more than 2 1/2 feet off the floor. Movable hand and foot holds and incline-adjustable wall angles accommodate varied fitness levels. The climbometer displays pertinent workout data such as distance climbed, time elapsed, and calories burned. Treadwalls provide the added feature of climbing practice for students.

Exercise Bicycles

Exercise bicycles (see Figure 4.2) come in a variety of models, including upright ergometer, recumbent ergometer, semi-recumbent ergometer, and gravity bikes. True ergometers are unique in that they accurately measure the true power in watts being produced by the user. Recumbent bikes place the user in a position to maximize cardiorespiratory benefits while preventing lower back pain; they are ideal for those recovering from injuries. Gravity bikes — also known as riders — provide both upper body and lower body aerobic workouts. To use a gravity bike, you push with both feet as you pull on the handlebars. Resistance is controlled by adjusting a shock absorber-like cylinder, adding weights, repositioning feet to higher foot pegs, or adjusting the height of the handlebars.

Special features to look for in exercise bicycles include comfortable, wide, and adjustable seats, galvanized steel construction to prevent rusting, adjustable resistance, and smooth turning flywheel or resistance fan. Optional features to consider, include an LCD (liquid crystal display) readout display showing pulse, revolutions per minute (RPM), calories burned, time elapsed, speed, and/or distance. Some models come with a variety of programs that include flat paths, hill-climbing challenges, and assessments of users' Max VO2 and fitness levels. The ergometer automatically adjusts the pedal resistance depending on the incline of the path and the user's heart rate.

Rowing Machines

Rowing machines simulate the action of rowing, providing a workout for both the abdominals and the back. When selecting a rowing machine, look for a smooth gliding seat and a sturdy glide rail that adjusts to the length of the user's legs. Silent magnetic resistance adds to the cost but is worth it if you prefer a quieter workout environment.

Special options include monitors that display elapsed time, strokes, workload, distance, calories burned, heart rate, and a fitness score at the end of each workout. Preset programs are included in several models that adjust the resistance based on the user's heart rate and the course selected. Rowers equipped with an RS 232 interface can be connected to a personal computer to keep performance records or for racing. The Concept II Rower provides racing options for up to 128 rowers configured as singles, doubles, fours, or eights. The monitor displays the position of 10 different boats simultaneously. Races can be conducted over distance or time. The software (e-row) detects false starts and displays average pace, current pace, and projected finish. Using an optional attachment, rowers also can be connected to the Internet for races with other rowers across the country. Like treadwalls, rowers provide the added feature of rowing practice for students.

Steppers

Steppers are designed to simulate hiking. Resistance options include air, electromagnetic, and friction brake cable drive. Air resistance, which increases as the speed increases, makes the workout more efficient. However, electromagnetic resistance provide users with the option of selecting a preset program or designing their own programs. Pedal resistance can be adjusted to simulate various inclines or to keep the heart rate in a specific zone.

Features to look for when purchasing include: pedals that move smoothly and independently, adjustable resistance, handgrips on the front or sides, and sturdiness. Optional features include oversized pedals and an advanced display. The oversized pedals provide comfort and safer motion. The advanced display includes elapsed time with alarm, bar graph showing steps per minute, total calorie consumption, and a scan feature.

Customized Data Cards

Designed to work with fitness equipment, a user inserts his or her personal data card into a machine and it instantly inputs a personal profile and desired workout.

Stair Climbers

Stair climbers go one step farther than steppers by providing for an upper body workout as well as a lower body workout. The best climbers keep your feet on an even plane with the floor at all times, maintaining a totally natural foot articulation. Some machines prevent extreme foot flexion without keeping their steps completely horizontal. When purchasing a climber, look for sturdy handrails to aid balance, easy-to-use resistance settings, and optional electronic programs that fit your needs.

Ski Machines

Ski machines offer all the benefits of cross-country skiing—the poling motion builds upper body strength, the leg motion builds leg and lower back strength, and the combined motions provide a cardiorespiratory workout. NordicTrack introduced the first ski simulators in the mid '70s, and now many other companies also offer ski machines. There are basically two types of ski machines: independent leg motion and dependent leg motion. The former is harder to master but offers a better workout; dependent models typically cost more. Worthwhile features on ski machines include an easy-to-use LCD monitor that performs a number of functions, a variety incline feature to increase front thigh workout, and preset resistance settings. Most ski machines fold for easy storage, and some have wheels for easy movement.

Downhill Skiers

A relatively new piece of exercise equipment, the Skier's Edge simulates downhill skiing. It strengthens the exact muscles used when skiing and provides a cardiorespiratory workout. Burning 800 calories per hour while improving rhythm, timing, balance, stance, and edging for skiing as well as tennis, racquetball, running, cycling, basketball, football, soccer, hockey, golf, and water skiing makes this device attractive for many users. With 13 different resistance settings, it is designed to accommodate skiers of all ages and skill levels. In 20 minutes, the user can make 1,800 turns simulating five to 10 challenging downhill runs. Optional features include the Black Diamond™ one-foot carriage that provides an intense workout for one leg at a time and the *Assistant Coach*™, a bar to hold onto instead of ski poles.

Striders

Striders are an offshoot of the ski simulators that move legs in a scissors-like motion. This provides for a lower body workout but does little for the upper body, since the hands grasp a stationary rail. Nevertheless, striders do provide a zero-impact aerobic workout when used on a regular basis.

Elliptical Machines

Elliptical exercise machines are the result of a marriage between stair climbers and cross-country ski machines. One's hands grasp handlebars that move back and forth while one's feet are placed on pedals that move in a flattened circle (elliptical) motion. The machine resists the motion of the arms and legs with a flywheel that is braked in one of two ways. Many health club ellipticals have magnetic resistance, which gives the pedaling a smoother feel. Features to look for include: adjustable resistance, nonslip pedals, stability and quiet and smooth performance.

Timing/Speed Devices

Print-out stopwatches that store times and numbers for 100 to 10,000 runners (depending on the model) are used by most cross-country coaches. They also can benefit the physical educator during the mile run assessment, because they print out completion times and give split times, lap times, accumulated elapsed times, and split-lap numbers to 99 places. These types of data can be very motivational for students. Several models have computer interfaces so that lane, place, and time data can be transferred to a computer. Other models have a 10-lane feature that allows for simultaneous timing of up to 10 lanes.

Sports radar guns are affordable and portable speed measuring devices that can be used with individuals and with manipulatives (balls, bats, racquets). The continuous-on or trigger activation lets you select the data you want to collect. A beeper sounds with every new speed measured, and a large digital readout clock shows you the speed in one-mile-per-hour increments. You and your students can use the sports radar gun in many ways, including the following:

1. Compare running speed to jumping distance as students participate in the running long jump.
2. Compare running speed to throwing distance as students participate in the softball throw.
3. Compare running speed to vertical jumping height.
4. Compare running speed to high jump score.
5. Compare throwing speed to upper body strength.

Stop Watch Features

Lap time - the interval or segment of time from the previous recording.
Split time - measures the accumulation of time from the start.
Dual split - stopwatch simultaneously displays lap and split times.
Lap counter - keeps track of the number of readings taken.
Memory recall - ability to retrieve earlier time readings.

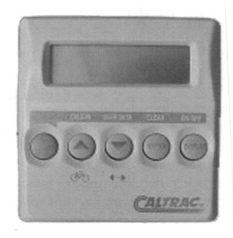

Figure 4.3 CalTrac®

Measuring Devices

Measuring devices consist of accelerometers, pedometers, and cyclometers (for bicycle use). These devices measure distance, steps, and time and attempt to correlate these variables with energy expenditure. The International Consensus Conference on Physical Activity Guidelines for Adolescents (Sallis et al., 1993) recommend that all adolescents should be physically active daily, or nearly every day, as part of play, games, sports, work, transportation, recreation, physical education, or planned exercise, in the context of family, school, and community activities. In addition, adolescents should engage in three or more sessions per week of activities that last 20 minutes or more at a time and that require moderate to vigorous levels of exertion. The Council for Physical Education for Children (COPEC) recommends that elementary school children should accumulate at least 30-60 minutes of age appropriate physical activity on all, or most, days of the week (COPEC, 1998). The devices discussed in this section attempt to verify that students are in fact meeting recommended guidelines for physical activity.

Accelerometer

Accelerometers are electronic devices used to measure the quantity and intensity of movement in one or more dimensions. They provide information on the intensity of acceleration or movement at user-specified intervals and some can be downloaded to a computer for data reporting and analysis. Research (Ernst, 2000; Welk & Corbin, 1995; Epstein et al., 1996; Sallis et al., 1993; Janz, Witt, & Mahoney, 1995; Simons-Morton, Taylor, & Huang, 1994; Janz, 1994; Freedson, 1991; Trost, Ward, & Burke, 1998; Eston et al., 1998; Freedson & Miller, 2000) has shown that, "accelerometers provide a valid indicator of overall physical activity, but a less accurate prediction of energy expenditure" (Welk, 2002b). Researchers have found both over and underpredictions of energy expenditure during different activities when using an accelerometer (Bassett et al, 2000; Hendlemen, et al., 2000; Campbell, Crocker, & McKenzie, 2002).

Accelerometers are typically attached at the hip of the user; although Bouten, Sauren et al. (1997) concluded that monitor placement position does not influence the prediction of energy expenditure. The devices contain a motion sensor and a very small computer programmed to convert acceleration to activity counts or energy expenditure (kcal). Depending on its design, the sensor can measure acceleration in one, two, or three planes. Although most accelerometers are based on the same design, they differ in the amount of memory, software capability, size, and sensitivity of the sensor. It is well known that accelerometers are more accurate for walking and running activities than for biking and other physical activities. It also is well known that the accelerometer cannot account for the increased energy expenditure of going uphill or carrying a load.

The CalTrac® (Muscle Dynamics Fitness Network) is considered one of the more popular accelerometers for use in the K-12 setting. Its reliability and validity have been reported in several studies (Meijer et al., 1989; Simons-Morton, Taylor & Huang, 1994; Sallis, et al., 1990; Pambianco, Wing, & Robertson, 1990). The CalTrac fits on your waistband and calculates the number of calories that you expend throughout the day. You also can program it for basal metabolic rate and calorie input. Although the CalTrac is primarily designed for recording horizontal movement, it has a feature that allows the user to program it for a pedaling (bicycling) or a weight lifting mode. At the conclusion of a collection period, the user can access a visual display of information in a number of ways, including total calories expended, activity calories expended, and net calories. The CalTrac is not used in research because it does not allow data to be stored on a minute-by-minute basis.

The Computer Science and Applications (CSA) model used to be the most widely used uniaxial (horizontal motion) accelerometer in physical activity research. In August 2001 it was acquired by MTI and renamed the ActiGraph product line. It functions much like the Cal Trac, except it is smaller and has a time sampling capability (e.g., minute-by-minute collection of data) at 5-, 10-, or 60-second intervals over a 22-day period of time. These additional data provide a chronological record of frequency, duration, and intensity of movement. The monitor has been validated for children performing activities including treadmill, walking, jogging, catching a ball, playing hopscotch, and sitting (Eston, Rowlands, & Ingledew, 1998; Dale, Corbin, & Dale, 2000; Nichols, et al., 2000; Melanson & Freedson, 1995; Janz, 1994; Janz et al., 1995).

The BioTrainer is a consumer model available from IM (imsystems.net). It is considered to be bidirectional, since it is positioned at a 45-degree angle to vertical in the sagittal plane. It uses Windows-based software and connects to the computer, so that the activity data can be downloaded to a PC for display and analysis. The BioTrainer Pro is smaller and has been designed as more of a true research instrument. It allows for user-defined recordings ranging from 15 seconds to two minutes for 28 days as well as various user-defined sensitivity settings that allow for maximizing the range of scores for monitoring (Welk, 2002b).

The Tracmor (Welk & Corbin, 1995; Freedson, 1991) is an example of an accelerometer that collects movement data in three planes (side-to-side, vertical, and horizontal) instead of one. It performs this task by collecting data from three separate accelerometers, positioned internally at 90-degree angles to one another. It calculates a composite score based on the movement from all three planes. This device also has the capability of storing movement information on a minute-by-minute basis. However, most researchers conclude that the triaxial accelerometer is no more accurate than the uniaxial in field settings.

Accelerometers come factory calibrated. There is little mention in most of the manuals from the manufacturers about the need for calibration. However, anecdotal observations from various researchers indicate that monitors do go out of calibration and that failure to correct the calibration can result in inaccurate data. Therefore, researchers are encouraged to incorporate some type of quality control into their measurement protocol to ensure that the monitors function consistently over time. A specific calibration tool is available for use with the Actigraph monitor, and calibration procedures also are available from IM Systems for the Biotrainer and Actitrac. A second possible source of error is weak batteries, so they should be checked and replaced regularly.

In conclusion, accelerometers provide an objective indicator of body movement, store data, detect intermittent activity, provide data at specific times of day in order to assess physical activity patterns, are noninvasive, and can be used in both the lab and the field. The disadvantages include high cost, time required to transfer data to the computer, and inaccuracy in estimating precise energy expenditure—especially in the field.

Pedometers

The first pedometer was designed more than 500 years ago by Leonardo DaVinci (Montoye et al., 1996). Pedometers provide an objective (the industry standard is less than a three percent error) indicator of step counts that can be converted into distance and calorie expenditure. The advantages of a pedometer include: inexpensive, noninvasive, and easy to use. The disadvantages include loss of accuracy when jogging, since they were designed for walking.

There are three types of pedometers. The first type uses a spring-suspended horizontal lever arm that moves up and down with each step. This movement opens and closes an electrical circuit, the lever arm makes an electrical contact (metal-on-metal contact), and the accumulated number of steps is displayed on a digital monitor. The second type is a magnetic reed proximity switch. With this type, a magnet connected to a spring-suspended horizontal lever arm moves up and down with each step. The magnetic field triggers a proximity switch encased in a glass cylinder and a step is counted. The third type uses an accelerometer-type mechanism consisting of a horizontal beam and a piezoelectric crystal. The third type offers the advantage of distinguishing between differing intensities of exercise. Pedometers also can differ in their sensitivity and overall quality. Several research studies have shown the Walk4Life (specifically model LS2525) and the Yamax pedometers (DigiWalker) to be most accurate (Bassett et al., 1996; Welk & Wood, 2000; Crouter, et al., 2003)

Figure 4.4 Pedometers

When purchasing a pedometer, you will see a variety of features: stopwatch function for recording exercise time, distance covered using stride length, calories expended using height and weight, and the ability to differentiate between walking and running.

There are even models that interface with a personal computer via a cable to download data from the workout. The personal computer software then creates detailed reports and graphs showing distance, speed, calories expended, and pulse rate. However, most experts agree that the simple step counter is the most accurate, useful, and least expensive device.

Pedometers may be stored in shoe holders, hanging jewelry holders, or buckets. It is important to have a distribution system to ensure that all pedometers are returned at the end of class. Pedometers should be worn on the waistband, positioned directly above the midline of the thigh on either side of the body (Bassett et al., 1996). Be aware that batteries can last anywhere from one and a half to five years. As the battery starts to die it becomes less accurate; therefore, it is important to perform a yearly accuracy test on the pedometers. The easiest accuracy test is to have students wear the pedometers and walk 100 steps. The pedometers should record between 97 and 103 steps. If not, try replacing the battery and repeating the test.

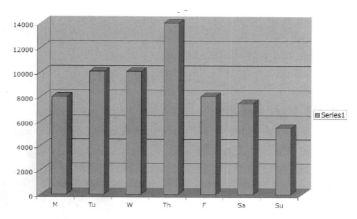

Figure 4.5 Pedometer steps chart

Vincent and Pangrazi (2001) found in one study that boys (6–12 years of age) who walked 13,000 steps and girls (6–12 years of age) who walked 11,000 steps met the recommended daily requirement for physical activity. Activity monitors and pedometers provide feedback and motivation to the students as they move. Students can record the number of steps taken during physical education, during a specified time period, during a specified activity, outside of school, or on a daily basis. The data recorded also can be graphed (see figure 4.5) for comparison. Students, after wearing the pedometers, may be asked reflection questions including:

What do the data tell you?

What did you learn?

Why are these data important?

Cyclometers

Cyclometers are similar to pedometers, but are used in conjunction with bicycles to display current speed, average speed, maximum speed, time, and distance ridden. A liquid crystal display shows the information in an easily readable format. A sending unit mounted on one of the spokes of the wheel and wired to the mounting bracket on the handlebar keeps track of wheel rotations. Cyclometers are used in physical education to monitor physical activity levels of student who choose bicycling as their physical activity or during a bicycling unit to teach students how to monitor their workouts.

Positioning Devices

Global Positioning System (GPS) shows your approximate position on the Earth. The GPS has three parts: the space segment, the user segment, and the control segment. The space segment consists of 24 satellites, each in its own orbit 11,000 nautical miles above the Earth. The user segment consists of ground stations (five of them, located around the world) that make sure the satellites are working properly. The GPS satellites each take 12 hours to orbit the Earth. Each satellite is equipped with an accurate clock that allows it to broadcast signals coupled with a precise time message. The ground unit receives the satellite signal, which travels at the speed of light. Even at this speed, the signal takes a measurable amount of time to reach the receiver. The difference between the time the signal is sent and the time it is received, multiplied by the speed of light, enables the receiver to calculate the distance to the satellite. To measure precise latitude, longitude, and altitude, the receiver measures the time it takes for the signals from four separate satellites to get to the receiver. The GPS system tells you your location anywhere on or above the Earth to within about 10 feet. Even greater accuracy, usually within less than three feet, can be obtained with corrections calculated by a GPS receiver at a known fixed location.

There are basically two types of GPS—a self-contained unit (see Figure 4.6) and a device that attaches to a laptop or handheld computer. Even several self-contained units are capable of downloading and uploading data to a personal computer. A GPS is an excellent device for orienteering, camping, and hiking units. Possible future applications include calculating running speeds, object trajectories, and energy expenditure. These data are then used for analysis of movement or physical activity.

Figure 4.6 GPS

Spirometers and Peak Flow Meters

Spirometers are instruments that measure forced vital capacity (FVC). This is the total amount of air an individual is capable of exhaling at one time. Spirometers are used to help estimate an individual's cardiorespiratory fitness. (Some evidence suggests that endurance training may have an effect on altering lung structure, volume, and capacity.) In physical education, students can monitor their FVC over the course of a semester.

A peak flow meter is a device that measures the force with which you expel air from your lungs. The measurement it gives is called a peak expiratory flow rate (PEFR). It helps determine the degree of airflow obstruction present. Most models come in two sizes—regular for adults and low range for children. The PEFR is important because it can detect subtle changes in lung function before you are aware of them.

Medical studies have shown that asthma patients, who use peak flow meters regularly and correctly, tend to need less medication and enjoy a more active lifestyle. It is important for students with asthma to keep a daily record of PEFR scores. Most peak flow meters come with a daily record chart to help you do this. For greatest accuracy, the measurement should be taken at the same time each day. In fact, the usual recommendation is twice daily at about 7:00 a.m. and 7:00 p.m. This is because PEFR rates can vary widely from morning to night. Decreases (below 80 percent of normal) in peak flow meter readings can alert both the student and the teacher to pending asthma attacks.

Both the peak flow meter and the spirometer use disposable paper or plastic mouthpieces. The plastic mouthpieces are recommended, since they can be cleaned with bleach and water for reuse and thus are more cost efficient in the long run.

We have discussed the use of the peak flow meter for students with asthma. There also are educational benefits to using both the spirometer and the peak flow meter. Students can be asked

Spirometer Directions

Step 1: Put a new mouthpiece on the nozzle. Hold spirometer by one hand and confirm that the indicator points at zero.

Step 2: Adjust indicator to point at the zero if necessary by turning the upper outer ring to the right or left.

Step 3: Inhale deeply, stretching the body upward. When the lungs are full, pinch your nose and set mouthpiece between lips.

Figure 4.7 Spirometer

Step 4: Breathe out strongly in one motion for five or six seconds.

Step 5: After breathing out, read measurement on indicator.

Step 6: Repeat three times. The maximum value of the three measurements is your lung capacity.

Peak Flow Meter Directions

Step 1: Place one of the white mouthpieces on the peak flow meter.

Step 2: Make sure that the blue indicator is at the bottom of the scale.

Step 3: Hold the peak flow meter vertically, being careful that your fingers don't block the opening.

Figure 4.8 Peak Flow Meter

Step 4: Inhale as deeply as possible and place your mouth firmly around the mouth piece, making sure your lips form a tight seal.

Step 5: Blow out as hard and fast as you can. The final position of the blue indicator is your peak flow.

Step 6: Take three readings and record the highest value, along with the date of the test.

PEFR value 80-100% of Normal - pursue regular activities.
PEFR value 50-80% of Normal - use caution in your daily activities.
PEFR value 0-50% of Normal - requires immediate medical attention.

to compare their personal scores to those recommended for their age and gender; chart their scores over the course of the semester; compare their scores to other data such as mile times and resting heart rate; and research questions such as can either score be improve through exercise, and what exactly does each score mean.

Electronic Blood Pressure Devices

Electronic blood pressure devices help students learn about blood pressure. They also can screen students to help identify those who may have blood pressure problems. Many models allow students to take one another's blood pressure with very little training. The machines run on batteries, and are quite affordable ($60 to $200, depending on the model). Some machines take readings on the index finger or wrist; the preferred models employ a cuff around the upper arm and come with an automatic inflation device. The cuff is inflated until the screen displays a reading of 180. The machine then automatically deflates the cuff, reading systolic and diastolic blood pressure as well as pulse rate. The results are held in memory, with blood pressure and pulse readings displayed alternately. A quick release valve purges pressure after measurement for greater comfort when using the manual inflation model.

For accuracy, it is important to use the correct cuff size for each participant. Different sizes may be purchased from the vendors. Measurements should be taken at least 30 minutes after eating, drinking caffeinated beverages, or exercising.

Teaching students to take their own blood pressure has educational value in and of itself. However, other learning activities include: comparing one's blood pressure to the recommended pressure for age and gender; monitoring blood pressure over the course of the semester; and researching the meaning of blood pressure and recommendations for lowering blood pressure, if necessary.

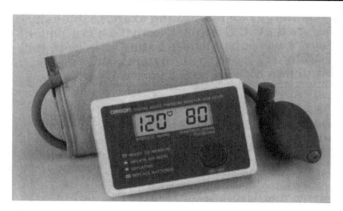

Figure 4.9 Electronic Blood Pressure Device

Electronic Blood Pressure Device Directions

Step 1: Rest arm on waist-high table and keep both feet flat on the floor.

Step 2: Wrap cuff around left upper arm (bottom edge of cuff should be one inch above elbow).

Step 3: Inflate the cuff until the screen shows "180" on the display.

Step 4: Wait for the down arrow symbol to appear on the display.

Step 5: Press air release button to complete the process.

Step 6: Watch unit alternately display blood pressure and pulse readings.

Body Composition Analyzers

Body composition analyzers allow students to determine their percent body fat. Simply weighing themselves on a scale won't tell them their body composition—for instance, many athletes are heavy because they tend to be muscular (muscle weighs more than fat) even though their percent body fat is within an acceptable range. There are a variety of devices available that measure body composition—underwater weighing, skinfold, automatic skinfold, infrared technology, and bioelectrical impedance.

The most accurate method of body composition measurement is underwater weighing. Individuals are placed on a scale in a tank of water, asked to exhale to expel the air in their lungs, and submerge. All other methods compare their validity to this standard. However, underwater weighing requires that participants fast for two hours, disrobe, refrain from exercising prior to the measurement, and void within 30 minutes of the test.

Skinfold calipers are the next best method for determining body composition. For people in the 15 to 45 percent body fat range, skinfold calipers are actually as accurate as underwater weighing. For people with less than 15 percent body fat, skinfold measurements are more accurate. Skinfold calipers require no fasting and can be used after exercise. However, taking skinfold measurements requires training and practice on the part of the examiner, and participants may need to disrobe, depending on the measurement sites. When selecting skinfold calipers, consider ease of use, durability, and cost. The Slim Guide, a relatively inexpensive, easy to use, durable, plastic pistol grip and trigger device for the K-12 environment, produces results that are almost as accurate as those of more expensive professional models such as the Lange caliper. The primary disadvantage is that the Slim Guide does not look professional, high tech, or sophisticated.

AccuMeasure calipers have an unique click and slide feature. This ensures that you pinch the skinfold with a consistent and uniform pressure each time you measure. The slide apparatus gives you an automatic measurement reading by stopping at the correct measurement reading once the right amount of pressure has been reached.

Automatic skinfold calipers have built-in computers that calculate percent body fat, so you don't have to add up the skinfold measurements and do the calculations. Skinfold caliper computers are preprogrammed, using one of the popular conversion formulas, to automatically display percent body fat after taking a few skinfold readings.

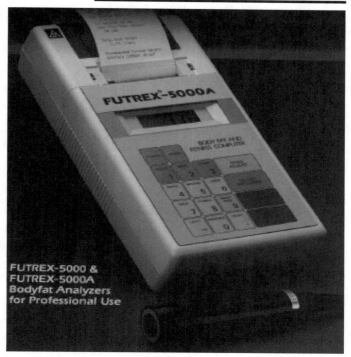

Figure 4.10 Futrex 5000 A, Body Composition Analyzer

Infrared technology for determining body composition has demonstrated its accuracy (+-two percent compared to hydrostatic weighing) in determining percent body fat (Cassady, et al., 1993). Infrared devices do not require fasting or disrobing, and they can be used immediately following an exercise period. The Futrex 5000A Body Composition Analyzer is an example of an infrared technology device. It requests the student's age, gender, current weight, body frame, height, and exercise level. Its wand is placed on the biceps, where it beams a harmless infrared light into the arm. An optical sensor measures the intensity of the re-emitted light. After two measurements, the built-in microcomputer converts the measurement into percent body fat and shows it on the LCD display. Using a built-in printer, the Futrex prints out the student's percent body fat and percent lean body weight. The printout compares the student's current data (percent body fat, age, height, weight, gender) to the National Institutes of Health reference data and generates diet and activity suggestions aimed at improving fitness and reducing health risks. Model 5000A/ZL is the model appropriate for students from age five and above and adults; Model 5000A/WL is for high school athletes, students age five and above, and adults; and Model 5000/XL is only for adults age 18 and older.

The final category of devices use the bioelectrical impedance method. Bioelectrical impedance measures the flow of electrical current through the body. Measurements are taken between the leg and arm, one foot and the other, or one hand and the other. These devices operate on the principle that lean tissue conducts electricity better (i.e., faster) than fat does. Leg to arm measurements have a .97 correlation with hydrostatic weighing. In children, arm to leg bioelectrical impedance has been validated against the criteria of skinfolds (Eston et al., 1993), hydrodensitometry (Houtkooper et al, 1989), and total body water (Houtkooper et al., 1989; Goran et al., 1993). Burkett (1994) concluded that, "Bioelectrical impedance analyzers produced values for percent body fat that were acceptable for field testing subjects." However, there tends to be an overprediction of body fat in lean and athletic types.

Bioelectrical impedance devices require a four to six-hour fast, a two-hour wait after exercise, the removal of stockings, and voiding within 30 minutes of the test. Women cannot be measured prior to or during their menstrual period. Adhesive sensors are applied to the student's hand, wrist, foot, and ankle, or to the wrist and ankle. The internal computer requests the student's gender, age, weight, and height, and then makes 256 measurements, calculates the average, and displays the results in 3-10 seconds. The data include percent body fat, lean weight, fat weight, basal metabolic rate, and total body water.

Tanita is the primary manufacturer of foot-to-foot bioelectrical impedance devices. Looking much like a scale, this battery-operated device estimates body fat by sending a minute electric current up one leg, through the torso, and down the other leg, measuring differences in the body's electrical resistance and displaying the percent body fat. Users stand on the device in bare feet and enter their height, gender, and age. After sending the signal through the body, the built-in computer analyzes the signal, determines percent body fat, and displays the result on the digital readout.

Tanita makes several different models, both for home and institutional use. Since this is one of the newer devices on the market, more refinements and research are needed to confirm its viability in the educational setting. When compared to underwater weighing, the Tanita consistently has been inaccurate—readings have averaged three percentage points high for men and eight points high for women. However, in one study, the leg-to-leg bioelectrical device demonstrated an overall performance similar to the conventional arm-to-leg devices (Nunez et al., 1997).

Body Composition Analyzers

	Infrared	Bioimpedance
Fasting	No	Yes, 4-6 hrs
Disrobing	No	Yes, no stockings
Following Exercise	Yes	No, 2 hrs
Voiding	No	Yes, 30 minutes
Restrictions	No	Yes, menstrual cycle
Accuracy	Excellent	Excellent
Repeatability	Excellent	Excellent
Possible risks	None	Yes, defibrillator

Omron is the primary manufacturer in the area of hand-to-hand bioelectrical impedance devices. Its Body Logic™ is a one-pound battery operated device that estimates body fat by sending a minute electrical current up one arm, through the torso, and down the other arm, measuring differences in the body's electrical resistance. Users enter their height, weight, age, and gender. They then press start and hold onto the two handles. Within seven seconds, the built-in computer estimates and displays the percent body fat and body fat weight on its digital readout. Again, this is a newer device and more refinements and research are needed. However, for both the foot-to-foot impedance devices and the hand-to-hand impedance devices, the advantages are their ease of use and speed—two important considerations in the school setting.

Some type of body composition device should be used during fitness testing at the beginning, middle, and end of the year. At the beginning of the year, students should set goals and develop plans for reducing, maintaining, or increasing their percent body fat. Throughout the school year, they should monitor their body composition, noting changes along with changes in eating and exercise behaviors. At the end of the year, students should be tested to determine whether they met their goals and to set goals for the summer.

Heart Rate Monitors

The goal of any cardiorespiratory workout is to maintain the heart rate in the target range. It is difficult, even for athletes, to count a heart rate that is up to 150 to 160 beats per minute. Pulse meters and heart monitors record heart rate, allowing students to concentrate on their workout while receiving constant updates on their pulse rates. Some monitors can be programmed to beep if the heart rate falls below or rises above the target range. All heart monitors record the heart rate while updating the display every eight seconds. This allows for the irregular rhythm of the human heart.

Heart rates are measured in beats per minute (bpm). Resting heart rate is measured when the student is sitting and relaxed, and it should be around 70 bpm—the lower the number the better. Ideally, the resting heart rate is measured when you first wake up in the morning, before getting out of bed. Maximum heart rate (Max HR) is the fastest your heart can beat for one minute. Maximum heart rate is used when calculating target heart rate. Target heart rate is the beats per minute your heart should be pumping when you are exercising. Historically, the following two calculations have been used to determine target heart rate ranges:

1. (220-age) X .65 and .90 --- corresponds with 50-85 percent of VO2 reserve

2. ((220-age) — resting heart rate) X.50/.80 + resting heart rate

In these two calculations (220-age) is used to determine the maximum heart rate. However, there is evidence that maximum heart rate doesn't decrease with age if you exercise regularly. Therefore, some experts use the following formula:

210 - (1/2 age) — (1% body weight) + 4 [for males]

Figure 4.11 Heart monitors provide visual feedback of students' heart rates during exercise periods.

Maximum Heart Rate Assessment – Educational Setting Method

I. Select level of fitness

Poor shape—has not exercised regularly during the last two months.

Fair shape—pursues any aerobic activity for 20 minutes at least three times per week.

Good shape—exercises regularly more than an hour a week, or walks or runs at least five miles a week.

II. Take the one-mile walk test

The first three laps increase heart rate to a plateau.

During the fourth lap hold the heart rate steady.

Determine average heart rate for final lap.

III. Predict maximum heart rate

Poor shape— add 40 beats per minute.

Fair shape— add 50 beats per minute.

Good shape— add 60 beats per minute.

The preferred method of determining maximum heart rate is to participate in a maximum heart rate assessment. Although this is usually not possible in a school setting, the Maximum Heart Rate Assessment - Educational Setting Method box shows an example of one assessment that can be done in a school setting using heart rate monitors.

Be aware that resting heart rates and exercise heart rates in children are higher than in adult populations, and the prescribed methods for calculating target heart rate zones were developed for adult populations. There is evidence to suggest that the maximal heart rate for youth should range from 195-200 bpm (Buck, 2002). Corbin, Pangrazi, and Welk (1994) used 140 bpm as the point above which the student is considered to be engaged at moderate intensity, and 160 bpm as the point above which the student is considered to be engaged at vigorous intensity.

The .70, .85, .60, and .80 numbers in the calculations refer to percentages of maximum heart rate. Different percentages of maximum heart rate result in different benefits for the body. The Heart Rate Zones Chart shows the benefits at each of the various percentages (otherwise known as heart rate zones).

Now that you have an idea about maximum heart rate and target heart rate, we can explore the different types of devices that monitor beats per minute. There are three basic types of pulse meters or heart monitors, depending on the body site where the monitor attaches. The first type attaches to the hand, the second type attaches to the index finger or earlobe, and the third type attaches to the chest. The first and second types—pulse meters—are inexpensive and use small infrared sensors to detect tiny changes that result from the pulsing of the blood through the

Heart Rate Zones Chart

50-60% of your individual Max HR—here you strengthen your heart and improve muscle mass while you reduce body fat, cholesterol, blood pressure, and your risk for degenerative disease. Your endurance or strength will not improve, but your health will improve. This also is the zone for warming up and cooling down before and after more vigorous zones.

60-70% of your individual Max HR—while still a relatively low level of effort, this zone starts training your body to increase the rate of fat released from the cells to the muscles for fuel. Up to 85 percent of the total calories burned in this zone are fat calories. To burn more total calories, you'll need to exercise for more time in this zone.

70-80% of your individual Max HR—the number and size of your blood vessels actually increase, you step up your lung capacity and respiratory rate, and your heart increases in size and strength so you can exercise longer before becoming fatigued. You're still metabolizing fats and carbohydrates at about a 50-50 rate.

80-90% of your individual Max HR—here you get faster and fitter, increasing your heart rate as you cross from aerobic to anaerobic training.

capillaries. However, head motion and changing light conditions can cause errors in readings, and these devices are uncomfortable and sometimes interfere with movement.

Even though it is more expensive and requires a little more time to adjust, the third type — the actual heart monitor — is the model of choice for both comfort and accuracy. A strap goes around the chest (directly below the chest muscle/breast tissue) and holds the transmitter in place that picks up the ECG signal (see Figure 4.11). The ECG signal is then transmitted to the receiver, which is located in a watch worn on the wrist. The receiver then processes the values by calculating a moving heart rate average for short periods of time (five to 15 seconds). This is updated and displayed as beats per minute (Karvonen et al., 1984). Because the number of heart rate values determines the average time, the calculation period is shortened during vigorous physical activity and the averaged heart rate value nearly approximates real-time heart rate (Karvonen et al., 1984; Montoye et al., 1996). The receiver must be one meter or less from the transmitter in order to pick up the signal. Within the receiver, a timing circuit measures the interval between heartbeats and provides a very accurate measurement for adults and children (Wajciechowski et al., 1991; Macfarlane, Fogarty, & Hopkins, 1989; Durant et al., 1991; Treiber et al., 1989; Coleman et al., 1997; Freedson, 1991; Freedson, 1989; Janz, 1994; Janz et al., 1992).

The long-life lithium batteries used in heart monitor receivers will typically last a year or more. Batteries in the chest straps should last three to four years with average use. All the sensors — ear lobe, finger, and chest transmitters — will deteriorate over time and will need to be replaced. Other sources of errors include damage to wires, low batteries, cross-talk between two heart monitors, and electrical/magnetic interference from television, computers, microwaves, and high-voltage power lines.

If you find you are getting erratic readings, follow these steps to diagnose the problem:

1. Check the hardware to make sure you are using the equipment properly. A proper fit consists of the monitor worn snugly around the chest with no gaps or bulges felt when the finger is run along the lower side of the monitor.
2. Try tightening the belt. Friction from even the slightest movement can cause erratic readings.
3. Check the environment. Airplanes, cars, some exercise equipment, and electromagnetic waves from computers, power poles, home security systems, and electric fences can cause interference.
4. Check interference from other heart monitors in the vicinity. The new "coded transmission" available in the high-end Polar heart monitors helps to eliminate the cross-talk from other users of heart rate monitors in close proximity.
5. Wet the electrodes using a spray bottle. Adequate moisture must be present to establish and maintain proper body contact for good readings.

I recommend either the bottom or the top of the heart monitor line (Reebok, Phase, or CardioSport). I find that the models in between don't seem to meet the needs of most physical educators. Optional features often included in these models include: time of day, stopwatch, wake-up alarm, zone alarm, count-down timer, count-up timer, backlight, calendar, water resistance, and calorie estimate counter. The heart rate monitors at the bottom of the line accurately display the student's heart rate and are relatively inexpensive. A few optional features that you may wish to consider include: ceiling and floor settings, time in zones, average heart rate, within zone heart rate, peak heart rate, time above zone, time below zone, lap with heart rate, total exercise time, cumulative exercise time, and manual

Heartalker (New Life Technologies)

This is an ECG-type heart monitor with a strap that goes around the chest. However, instead of a digital readout on a watch unit, a wire goes from the strap to a pair of earphones and the heart rate is heard at regular intervals in the earphones. The unit also announces the elapsed time since the start of the exercise. Volume and heart rate announcement intervals are adjustable. This particular heart monitor is not susceptible to interference from other equipment or other heart monitors. It comes in several models, with the more expensive model capable of calculating most used target zones (fat burning, stronger heart), providing motivational feedback, and summarizing the workout (total workout time, total time in target zone, and average heart rate).

recall. I don't recommend the Polar heart monitors, because the battery in the transmitter is not replaceable, which means you must purchase another transmitter when the battery dies.

The top-of-the-line models can store heart rate data and rapidly transfer data from the heart monitor to a personal computer. Most contemporary monitors use a telemetry or infrared downloading unit to allow the heart rate data to be transferred to a personal computer. The software analyzes the data and can print tables, line graphs, plot graphs, or bar charts. The information can then be printed out and stored.

Ideally, every student wears a heart monitor during physical education class. However, many of us are not able to purchase 20 to 60 heart monitors per teacher—at least not in one year. The next best alternative is to have students share these devices so that they wear one at least once a month. For example, assume a physical education department with four teachers, an average class size of 40, and eight heart monitors. Each teacher would have access to the monitors for one week each month. During that time, eight students per day in each class, or 40 students per week, wear the device. It is a good idea to purchase two chest straps for each heart monitor to allow cleaning time between each wearing.

The procedure for using these devices during the instructional period usually follows this sequence:

1. Students are handed a chest strap (with transmitter) before they change. Some departments have students purchase their own chest straps. Chest straps are washed or disinfected between uses.
2. Distribute a watch to each student and record the number on the watch (permanent marker and nail polish are good for marking receivers).
3. Instruct students to begin recording data.
4. At the end of the period, collect watches and straps or instruct the students to transfer the data to the personal computer on their way into the locker room and then return watches and straps to the physical education office. For heart rate monitors that don't interface with the computer - students can review a summary of their heart rate on the heart rate monitor and write it down in their journal.

Heart Monitors in Sports Medicine Class

At Bell Gardens High School, heart monitors are used during the rehabilitation unit of my sports medicine class. My students become trainers after a semester of learning how to recognize, care for, and treat specific injuries. Groups of four students are assigned to one student in the adapted physical education class. The trainers get to know their physically challenged client's case, and they focus on rehabilitation. A heart monitor is used to assess the client's current cardiorespiratory condition. Students learn how to operate, set, clear and upload the heart monitor data. Clients perform a variety of activities while wearing the heart monitor. The printouts are analyzed by the trainers and discussed with the clients. As trainers, their projects are to design appropriate conditioning programs for their clients.

Carolyn Thompson, 1994 National Secondary Teacher of the Year

ɔnitors are most commonly used to help students
ɛir heart rate during aerobic activity to ensure that
within their target heart rate zone. However, there are
ther uses. For example, students might:

1. Compare heart rates during two activities (e.g., football and jump rope), and write an essay stating which activity is more aerobic and why.

2. Analyze their recovery heart rates (how long it takes to return the heart rate to normal after a workout) in order to determine their fitness level.

3. Compare the heart rates of 10 adults, five of whom exercise and five of whom don't. Calculate over a one-year period how many more times the non-exercisers' hearts beat.

4. Analyze their own heart rate printout for the mile run. Look for trends or slopes for evidence of fatigue, number of minutes in the zone, and recovery heart rate. Printout and analysis can then be placed in either a regular portfolio or an electronic portfolio.

5. Participate in an aerobic circuit while maintaining the same heart rate, and write an essay describing the difference between pieces of exercise equipment.

6. Wear a heart rate monitor for 24 hours and then analyze the printout.

7. Monitor a parent's heart rate for 24 hours and then analyze the printout.

8. Attempt to stay in their heart rate zone without looking at the heart rate receiver watch.

9. Participate in interval training. Run 100 yards and wait for heart rate to drop 40 beats, then run another 100 yards. Repeat the process five times. Compare the number of seconds it took for the heart rate to drop 40 beats.

Caring for Heart Monitor

Don't **stretch** the electrode strips of the belt, especially when storing.

Keep the elastic chest belt clean by rinsing in cold water with a mild soap solution or spraying with a disinfectant. Hang the straps to dry.

Lubricate transmitter snaps with silicon lubricant spray to prevent corrosion from moisture and sweat.

Keep all the components of your monitor clean and wipe off any extra moisture. Never store monitor in a closed, nonventilated container such as a plastic bag or damp workout bag where moisture and humid air can be trapped. Always store the unit in a warm, dry location.

10. Complete a fitness assessment circuit that includes the following stations: blood pressure, curl ups, body composition measurement, spirometer, timed walk for distance wearing pedometer, back saver sit and reach, peak flow meter, jump rope while wearing heart monitor, heart monitor interface for downloading of data, and push ups. Write an essay describing the current fitness level based on results at each of these stations.

Heart rate printouts from students can benefit physical educators and the physical education program. They provide a visual demonstration of the fact that physical education is a part of the "high-tech" educational system of the 21st century. In addition, they document the structure of the physical education class time for students, teachers, parents, administrators, and school board members. Additional calculations (e.g., average resting heart rate, mean, median, range) can be performed and different graphs (e.g., bar, circle, line) can be generated.

Comprehensive Systems

Several of the devices mentioned in the previous sections overlap. For example, there are pedometers that also are pulse meters, heart rate monitors with internal stopwatch features, and electronic blood pressure devices that also record pulse rate. There also are some very comprehensive systems on the market that include a variety of assessment tools, software programs, and exercise options. HealthFirst and MicroFit are two popular manufacturers.

HealthFirst's TriFit is a modular program, so buyers can purchase one or more pieces. It has the ability to solicit, store, and analyze medical history, height, weight, body mass index, skinfold, impedance, resting blood pressure, heart rate, blood chemistries (total cholesterol, HDL cholesterol, total cholesterol/HDL ratio, LDL, triglycerides, glucose), girth measurements, and hip-to-waist ratio. It also can test online biceps strength, hand grip, field tests (pushup, curl up, modified sit and reach, shoulder

Comprehensive Systems

TriFit 620: polar heart rate transmitter, 620 unit, integrated Skyndex skinfold calipers, strength handle and strap, allen wrench, heart rate receiver and eight foot cable, skinfold calibration dowel, platform/scale, sit and reach unit, assessment software, and assorted cables. Optional items: Monark 828 E Bicycle Ergometer, trackmaster treadmill, Lange interactive skinfold calipers, blood pressure unit.

TriFit 600: polar heart rate transmitter, strength handle and strap, on-line Skyndex calipers with calibration dowel, multimedia monitor, keyboard/mouse, printer, TriFit unit, platform/scale, assessment software, and assorted cables. Optional items include: Monark 828 E Bicycle Ergometer, trackmaster treadmill, Lange skinfold calipers, blood pressure unit, and network ready.

MicroFit: medical-grade scale, exercise heart rate monitoring system, Monark 828 E bike, robo bike attachment, blood pressure, skinfold caliper, and flexometer.

and trunk rotation, one-mile walk, Cooper run/walk, step test), online modified sit and reach, online bike ergometer, and online treadmill. Optional software includes health risk appraisal module, group report module, meal planner, template builder, network version, and nutritional analysis. The software analyzes the data and the results are displayed in a graph format.

Once the assessment is complete, the software can develop a custom program based upon the student's needs, personal objectives, and level of experience. The program consists of templates for body composition and caloric intake goals, cardiovascular fitness, and weight training programs. All programs and exercise calendars can be modified to meet specific goals, and they are based on guidelines from the American College of Sports Medicine. The optional meal planner develops nutritionally sound menus that target composition and caloric goals along with personal preferences. All plans follow the guidelines of the American Dietetic and Diabetic Associations. Built-in meal plan templates include vegetarian, youths under 18, weight loss, and weight training. The program includes an Internet option and a Health First Encyclopedia for researching various topics related to fitness and nutrition.

The TriFit program includes group and statistical report options. This software prints aggregate and statistical results of fitness and health risk appraisal results for any given group. You can compare the aggregate results between two groups or track the progress of a particular group over time. You also can analyze how groups of individuals answered health risk appraisal questions.

The MicroFit System (MicroFit) is more assessment oriented; it includes reports for overall wellness, fitness, exercise planning, and nutritional analysis. Specific measurements include body weight, body fat, heart rate, blood pressure, flexibility, strength, cardiovascular endurance, and an area for 10 additional test items. It allows the user to conduct a wellness profile (lifestyle behavior analysis) and design a custom exercise program. The system includes software for health risk factors, personalized reports, tracking and measuring success over time, and developing individual exercise and nutrition programs. Optional modules include historical fitness data graphs and reports. When considering a comprehensive system, it is important to know which features you will actually use, calculate the cost of purchasing these devices separately, and then compare this cost to the cost of a comprehensive system. You may find that purchasing separate devices is more cost effective.

Summary

The number of fitness center/labs in school settings is increasing. This increase, coupled with the increased interest in teaching students basic motor learning, biomechanics, and exercise physiology concepts—as evidenced by the *National Standards for Physical Education* (NASPE, 2004) and the publication of *Concepts and Principles of Physical Education* (Mohnsen, 2003)—necessitates new teaching and learning methods. Exercise equipment, heart monitors, electronic blood pressure devices, spirometers, pedometers, and body composition analyzers are but a few of the devices that can help students learn these important concepts and principles and develop and maintain a physically active lifestyle.

Reflection Questions

1. Do you believe that the benefits of the technology devices listed in this chapter justify their cost? Why or why not?

2. Do you think it would be more cost effective to purchase one of the comprehensive fitness systems or the individual pieces that you need for your program? Provide support for your answer.

Projects

1. Review the various devices that can supplement a physical fitness unit. Choose the one device that you would most like to have for your program. Write a one-page proposal for your principal, describing why you need this item.

2. Select one type of fitness equipment (e.g., rower, treadmill) that you would like to have for your program. Make a list of the features you would look for when purchasing this item. Go to the Internet, find specific models that meet your criteria, and make a selection. Write a one-page description for why you choose this model.

Chapter 5

Selecting a Computer and Basic Peripherals

Sara Jones has decided to buy her own computer for both personal and professional use. She has attended several conferences and has learned that computers can be used effectively to teach students motor skills, cognitive concepts, and social skills. In addition, she knows that a computer can help a physical education teacher be more productive. Now she must decide which computer and peripherals to purchase.

Walking into a computer store can be an overwhelming experience. The choices seem unlimited and the peripherals forever growing in number. Identifying your needs, goals, and personal preferences ahead of time will help you make more informed decisions. As you read through this chapter, you should answer the following questions for yourself:

- What am I going to do with a computer?
- How much speed do I need?
- How much RAM do I need?
- What kind of storage do I need?
- How much storage do I need?
- What kind of printer do I need?
- What size monitor do I need?

There are four components in a computer system: processor, memory, input device(s), and output device(s). A keyboard and a mouse are both input devices, but an input device also can be a storage device or a modem. A file is the information to be processed, and the application is the set of instructions the computer follows when processing the data in the file. For example, a list of your students is data in a file, and the application contains the directions for the computer to alphabetize the list. When the file and application are brought into the memory of the computer, the processor manipulates the data according to the application's instructions. The processed data are then sent out of the computer via one or more output devices. Output devices include monitors, printers, and—again—storage units and modems.

Casing and Operating System

There are three sizes of computers that will be of interest to physical educators: desktop, notebook (two to 10 pounds), and handheld. In the ideal world, we would have one of each for the various tasks we perform, but most of us are limited to one or two. If I had to choose between a desktop and a notebook for a first computer, I would select a notebook. It provides me with mobility. I can access and manipulate information regardless of where I am. In addition, notebook computers are very powerful and can meet the needs of most physical educators.

Desktop

The term desktop (see Figure 5.1) is used here to refer to a stationary computer used at a desk or work station. It may be tall, narrow, and designed to sit upright on the floor (often referred to as a tower); it may be the more traditional configuration that sits on a desk, often with the monitor on top; or it may be an all-in-one monitor and case. The advantages of the desktop computer are the number and variety of ports, the lower cost,

Figure 5.1 Desktop computers

and the amenities — such as a large monitor. The numerous ports (see Figure 5.2) provide access points for the peripherals. For example, the ethernet port connects to networks, the video port to external monitors and projection systems, and the sound port to external speakers. Historically, serial and parallel ports connected to modems, printers, external storage devices, and scanners. Today, most external devices connect through Universal Serial Bus (USB) and IEEE1394 (FireWire) ports. These ports are faster and also can connect to keyboards, mouse devices, joysticks, game controllers, and video camcorders.

Once you have decided on a desktop computer, the next decision involves choosing the operating system. The operating system is the very crucial portion of the system software that enables communications between the application and the hardware. The two primary choices are Macintosh and Windows. When making this decision, consider the following:

• Which type of platform is more predominant at your school site? It helps to stay consistent with other users at your school.
• Are the applications you want to use Macintosh, Windows, or both? There must be a match between the applications and hardware. It is actually better to select your applications first and then match the hardware.

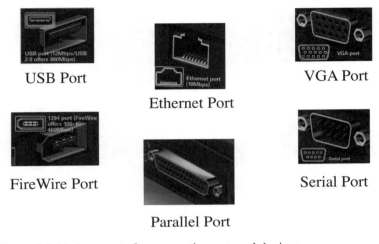

USB Port

Ethernet Port

VGA Port

FireWire Port

Parallel Port

Serial Port

Figure 5.2 Various ports for connection external devices

• Do you have a personal preference? Users tend to be more comfortable with the type of computer on which they learned.

Remember, applications purchased for one platform generally will not run on another. It is possible, however, to buy additional hardware and/or software (known as emulators) that will allow one operating system to read software designed for a second operating system. For example, *Virtual PC* for Macintosh (Microsoft) will allow you to run Windows-based software on a Macintosh computer. However, these solutions tend to be slower than the original system.

Notebooks

Notebook computers (see Figure 5.3) are light-weight mobile alternatives to desktop computers. Although the number and variety of ports may be limited and the screen may be smaller, these computers are ideal for physical educators on the go. In addition, most notebook computers can be attached to a larger monitor when in the office.

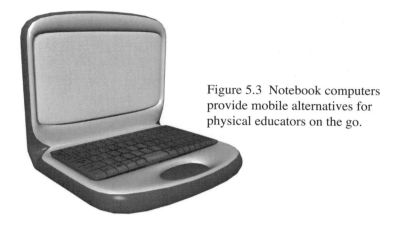

Figure 5.3 Notebook computers provide mobile alternatives for physical educators on the go.

When selecting a notebook computer you also must consider the type of operating system you desire. There are several Macintosh-based notebooks (PowerBooks, ibooks), and numerous PC-based notebooks that run the Windows operating system. The variables for choosing a specific notebook computer are similar to choosing a desktop computer.

In addition to the ports listed for the desktop computer, notebook computers typically have an additional expansion slot known as the PC card (formerly PCMCIA) slot. This slot can hold a wide variety of credit card-like devices. The most common are modems, Ethernet adapters, additional storage, and video input devices. Some notebook computers, most notably the Sony line, also come with expansion slots for memory sticks and other types of memory cards (see memory section).

Handhelds

Handheld computers (see Figure 5.4) weigh less than a pound, are battery operated, and fit in one hand. A stylus is typically used for input, but mini-keyboards also are available. The stylus allows for tapping on various buttons on the screen, tapping on a small keyboard image, or actually writing on the screen. Many

Figure 5.4 Handheld computer

come with slots for memory cards, which allows for external storage. The handheld computer can be kept in a shirt pocket or a protective case/fanny pack, and is convenient for on-the-field use. Some of the software for handheld computers—such as the Fitness Report for POS/Pocket PC (Bonnie's Fitware Inc.)—requires that you interface (connect) with either a desktop or notebook computer, while other programs—such as Teacher Observation Program (Bonnie's Fitware Inc.)—allow you to be totally self-contained. The connection between the handheld and desktop or notebook is typically serial, USB, or wireless. You can even print by connecting the handheld computer directly to a printer.

The two most popular operating systems for the handheld computer are the Palm Operating System and the Windows Mobile Software for Pocket PC. Currently, there are more applications for the Palm OS. The most important variable when selecting a handheld computer is choosing one with a transflective display. These displays provide a sharper and more brilliant image, and are far more readable in outdoor lighting. It is a good idea to put a screen overlay on the display to protect the screen from scratches.

Processor

The computer processing unit (CPU) performs the data processing functions directed by the application, and it controls the transfer of instructions and data within the computer system. Processors differ in the speed at which they operate. Computers with quicker processors typically operate at a faster clock rate, which is measured in megahertz (MHz) and gigahertz (GHz) or number of cycles (instructions) per second, than do their slower counterparts. Computers with faster processors also typically are more expensive. However, be aware that CPU rating alone isn't the only measure of a computer's speed. Other factors include the size of the computer's cache as well as the design of the motherboard on which the CPU is installed.

Most computers offer two caches—a tiny one on the CPU and a second, larger cache on the logic board. This secondary or L2 (Level 2) cache is the one to inquire about. It should be 512 K or larger, and it should be fast. The idea behind cache is that once an instruction is completed, it takes less time to recall that instruction than to perform it from scratch since the computer continually stores completed instructions for reuse.

The best way to determine which machine meets your needs is to perform a typical task on a variety of computers that operate at different speeds. The least expensive machine that meets your needs—the one that can run the software you want to use at a speed you are comfortable with—is the machine to purchase. However, your needs will change as you become more proficient with a computer, so you should plan for room to grow—both in terms of the computer's speed and the other variables identified in the following sections. I have never known anyone to be disappointed buying a more sophisticated machine when cost was not a factor.

Memory

There are two types of computer memory: read-only memory (ROM) and random-access memory (RAM). The information in ROM is placed there by the manufacturer, and it is permanent. It contains, among other things, information the computer needs to start up.

RAM, on the other hand, is where programs and data are stored temporarily when the computer is in use. When the power is turned off, the information in this area is erased. Each program requires a certain amount of RAM in order to load and run. The amount of memory that an application needs is shown on its packaging. You will probably want to load more than one program at a time, so you can move quickly from program to program. Therefore, your computer will need to have enough RAM to collectively hold all the programs you want available for use at one time. You can purchase and install additional RAM as you need additional memory; however, it is more expensive than simply purchasing it with your new computer. Larger, more complicated programs are constantly being developed that will require more and more memory.

Current operating systems support virtual memory and thus allow the allocation of additional (much slower) RAM on available hard drive space. By using extra space on the computer's hard drive, virtual memory tricks the computer into thinking there's more RAM available than there really is. The disadvantages, however, are that programs will run more slowly than with real RAM, and virtual memory uses hard drive space that would normally be available for storing data and application software. In addition, some programs won't work with virtual memory.

As you start to shop for a computer, you will notice that in addition to listing the speed of the computer, advertisers also list two numbers separated by a slash—512MB/80.0 GB. These two numbers refer to the amount of RAM and the size of the hard drive. To better understand the differences between RAM and the hard drive, consider the analogy of a desk and a file cabinet. The size of the desk is similar to the amount of RAM. The size of the file cabinet is similar to the size of the hard drive. When working in an office, your desk can only hold so many files at a time. This also is true in terms of the computer, where you only open so many files on the hard drive at one time.

Input

There are a number of options for communicating with the computer. These include keyboards, mice, joysticks, scanners, microphones, switches, touch screens, storage, and modems. Digital cameras and digital camcorders also are considered a form of input. They were addressed in Chapter 3. As mentioned previously, these devices are connected to the computer through a variety of ports, including wireless options.

Keyboard

Using a keyboard is much like using a typewriter, but with more options. Currently, the keyboard is the most common data input device. The computer recognizes the key that is pressed and displays that key's associated symbol on the monitor (unless the key has a special function). Variables to consider when selecting a keyboard include size, placement of F-keys (function keys) and the numerical keypad, whether the keyboard is angled or adjustable, and whether it requires a light or a heavy touch. Personal preference will guide your selection; however, an adjustable keyboard can alleviate wrist injuries. Finally, if you are going to purchase your keyboard from a third-party vendor, make sure it is compatible with your computer.

Alternative keyboards are available for use by those with physical disabilities. They also may be used by students who are too young to use a standard keyboard or who have developmental disabilities. Alternative keyboards are either condensed (mini) or expanded. The condensed keyboard is designed to help those with limited fields of motion but who possess fine motor skill. The keys are positioned closer together than on a standard keyboard so it requires less strength to depress each key. Examples include the Tash Mini Keyboard (Infogrip) and the Bat Personal Keyboard (Infogrip).

The expanded keyboard is a large, touch-sensitive table that can be programmed to accept overlays. An overlay might be a plastic sheet with an enlarged alphabet or a set of pictures. Overlays can be purchased or made by the user. There also are overlays that are designed to work with specific software applications. Examples include Key Largo (Don Johnston), Discover Board (Don Johnston), and IntelliKeys Keyboard and Overlay Maker (IntelliTools).

Mouse

Virtually all applications for the Macintosh and Windows operating systems require a mouse. The mouse is rolled across a flat surface or, with a trackball type, the ball is rolled around in its socket. The action of the mouse causes a pointer (cursor) on the screen to move. The computer monitors the location of the cursor and the status (clicked or not, right or left button) of the mouse. The mouse is used for pointing, selecting, and highlighting spots on the screen. Its more specific functions are determined by the application. You also can get a biometric fingertip identifer feature on a mouse which protects your computer from access by others, since it requires your finger print in order to operate.

Wireless options are especially popular when giving presentations. The teacher is free to move around the room and is not forced to stand by the computer. The wireless mouse sends a signal through the air—using either radio waves or infrared technology—to a small receiving unit that relays the signal via a cord that plugs into the back of the computer. A radio-controlled cordless mouse usually costs more than an infrared cordless mouse, which must be within a direct line of sight to operate. If your infrared cordless mouse begins to malfunction you have probably put something in front of its receiving unit.

Joystick

Joysticks are typically used in conjunction with computer games, including educational games. The joystick controls the cursor or some other screen motion with the back-and-forth, left-and-right, and up-and-down movement of its handle. There are usually one or more buttons that initiate certain types of screen action. Look for more educational games involving sports to enter the market.

Scanners

The scanner (see Figure 5.5) works like a copy machine, except that the image (graphic or text) is copied into your computer and stored as digital data. When looking for a scanner, consider the resolution (the fineness of the image). The lower the resolution, the more grainy the image. Resolutions of 1200x1200 dots per

Figure 5.5 A flatbed scanner transfers an entire page of information into a computer.

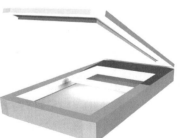

Scanner Tips:
- Warm up scanner for at least five minutes prior to use.
- Clean platen frequently.
- Scan at the size to be used.
- Scan at 72 dpi for web use.
- Scan at 300 dpi for text conversion.
- Scan at 600 dpi for graphics.
- Scan at 600 or 1200 dpi for line art.

inch (dpi) or higher with 48-bit recognition are recommended. The bit recognition refers to the scanner's ability to capture brightness and extra colors.

Scanners come in three basic types: flatbed, sheet-fed, and handheld. The flatbed is the most popular and produces the sharpest image. A sheet-fed scanner, which resembles a printer, remains stationary while the paper is rolled across it. This means that sheet-fed models can be smaller, but the images generally are not as sharp as those of flatbeds since the paper is moving. Handheld scanners are even smaller and are best used when scanning text instead of graphics.

The scanning process is controlled by the application that comes with the scanner. The image to be scanned is placed on the bed of the scanner, and you click on a button in the application —typically labeled "Preview"—to begin the process. Once the preview scan has been completed, you will be prompted to designate a location in which to save the image. You also will choose the format in which you wish to save the image. That decision should be based on how you plan to use the image. For posting on the Internet, choose "gif" for graphics, and "jpeg" for photos; for inclusion in authoring and presentation programs, "tiff" is a good choice. You now click on a button in the software program—typically labeled "Scan"—to complete the process.

Speech Input

The use of the spoken language to enter commands and text into the computer is known as speech input. Originally used exclusively by individuals with physical, visual, or other disabilities, speech recognition systems now are available for the general public. *NaturallySpeaking* for Windows (Dragon Systems), *PowerSecretary* for the Macintosh (Dragon Systems), and *ViaVoice* for Windows and Macintosh (IBM) are examples of application solutions that incorporate the latest advances in speech recognition. Speech input provides for more rapid data input and provides the non-typist with an easy interface method. It is a good idea to use an external microphone when using speech input so the computer can more clearly interpret the sound of your voice.

Switches

Switches can be used by individuals who are unable to use other types of input devices. An activated switch, used with special software, signals the student's choice or selection. A scanning array of options is displayed on the monitor and a cursor moves through a series of alternatives. The user activates the switch when the option he or she wants is highlighted.

Touch Screens

A touch screen is a device that is attached to a computer monitor or an external display system (e.g., Smart Board). The computer monitors the location of the touch on the screen and responds to it in a manner similar to a mouse movement. Touch screens are very popular in kiosks (stand-alone computers found at museums, shopping centers, and government buildings). They are useful in physical education when demonstrating software on a large external screen to a group of students.

Storage

The primary storage device used by virtually all computer users is the internal hard drive. This is the location where files are initially written for easy access, updating, and storage. Secondary devices are used for archiving files, transferring data, and making back up copies (see Table 5.1). Backing up critical data is one of the most important administrative tasks associated with using a computer. Backing up means making a duplicate copy of important data and applications. Then, if anything should happen to the original, you will have a copy.

Icons

Graphic interfaces (like the Macintosh and Windows operating systems) allow you to interact and control the computer by pointing at small pictures on the screen with your cursor (an object on the screen, usually in the shape of an arrow, that you control with the mouse) and clicking on them. These small pictures are called icons, and they represent computer hardware and software, so that you do not have to memorize commands. There are icons representing storage, folders, data files, and applications, to name a few.

Today, there are a plethora of options for secondary devices, including floppy disks (albeit rarely used today), external hard drives, CDs, digital versatile discs (DVDs), memory cards, and USB memory devices.

Hard Drive. The hard drive is a device that uses a magnetic medium to store large amounts of data. Hard drives are reliable, because they are closed systems that do not allow dirt to enter and harm the read/write mechanism (the mechanism that allows you to read, add, or delete information). Hard drives come in various sizes (measured in gigabytes) and speeds. Be aware that the data on hard drives are never permanent. All hard drives will crash (fail) eventually due to disk failure, static electricity, or other ambient factors, which is why it is important to back up data.

When saving information, especially on larger capacity storage devices, it is important to think about how to organize your files. Remember, computer storage can be compared to a file cabinet containing many folders. You may want to consider organizing your data files by class period or by the type of activity (e.g., volleyball, badminton) you are teaching, for example.

Table 5.1

Which Storage Is Best for Me?

Task   Priority   Option

Transport files   Capacity   Secure Digital Card Device
                   Price   Secure Digital Card Device
                   Speed   USB Flash Memory Card

Back-up   Capacity   External Hard Drive
                   Price   DVD-RW
                   Speed   External Hard Drive

Storing images   Capacity   DVD-RW
and audio files   Price   CD-RW
                   Speed   DVD-RW

Sharing data   Capacity   CD-RW or DVD-RW
                   Price   CD-RW
                   Speed   DVD-RW

Expand system   Capacity   External Hard Drive
storage   Price   External Hard Drive
                   Speed   External Hard Drive

Figure 5.6 Memory devices

137

CDs. Another storage device is the optical disc, which stores and retrieves data using laser technology. Optical discs can hold hundreds of megabytes of data. Applications are typically sold on compact disc-read only memory (CD-ROM). Other types of compact discs include: compact disc-recordable (CD-R) and compact-disc rewritable (CD-RW). CD-R discs let the user record information on the compact disc; however, once recorded it can not be erased. CD-RW discs let the user record over and over again on the compact disc.

DVDs. DVDs look like standard CDs, but have a storage capacity in the gigabytes. The most common formats are DVD+RW, DVD-RW, DVD+R, and DVD-R. Like the CD, the RW stands for rewritable and can be recorded over and over again, while the R format can only be recorded on once. Check the information that comes with your DVD player or recorder to determine if you should use the "+" or "-" versions. If you are purchasing a new drive, the DVD+RW seems to be a more compatible and useful format. Also, look at the size of the internal buffer—larger buffers reduce the chance of errors when writing to the disc. There is some evidence to suggest that for long-term storage, the CD-R, DVD-R, and DVD+R are better than their rewritable counterparts.

Memory Cards. A memory card is a small-size storage device that maintains its data without any external source of power. It comes in several forms--including CompactFlash, MemoryStick, SecureDigital (SD), SmartMedia, and xD--and is very popular as a storage media for digital cameras. These devices also can be used in a number of different technology devices, including desktop and notebooks computers, handheld computers, and printers. You will need a card reader in order to access the data on these memory cards. Most card readers have a USB connection, while a few have a firewire connection. There are even a few computers that come with the card reader built in; for example, the Sony notebooks typically come with the MemoryStick port.

USB Memory Devices. USB memory devices come in a variety of shapes (for example, the size of a car key and attaches to a key ring) and connect directly to the USB port. This makes it a convenient and fast method for backing up and transporting data. The USB Flash Memory works with both Macintosh and Windows, so it is an ideal method for quickly transferring files from Macintosh to Windows.

Modem

A modem is another important component of any computer system. There are internal, external, and PC-card modems. Although more and more people are connecting to networks through Ethernet ports and wirelessly, it is still important to have a modem for those occasions when dial-up is your only option for connection to the Internet. More information about modems is provided in Chapters 9 and 10.

Output

Output refers to the information the processor generates and communicates to the user. In addition to storage devices and modems (which are input and output), monitors, speakers, and printers are considered output devices.

Monitor

Size is the most obvious characteristic of a monitor. The measurement of a monitor is taken diagonally from one corner of the screen to the other. Actual monitor area is roughly proportional to the square of the diagonal length, so a 20-inch monitor is more than four times as large as a nine-inch monitor. Most manufacturers cheat on their monitor sizes by measuring from one corner of the screen (or even the case) to the other, rather than from one edge of the visible display to the other. Then they round up to the nearest inch with the result that most

14-inch monitors are closer to 12 1/2 inches when measured truthfully. The larger the monitor, the more expensive it is, and typically the easier it is on your eyes.

The second major choice is between a flat panel liquid crystal display (LCD) or cathode-ray tube (CRT) monitor. CRTs are designed like television sets. Inside a vacuum tube, a gun emits electrons, which react with the phosphorous of the screen to create the image. This electron gun makes numerous passes across the screen, from top to bottom, to create the image you see on your television or computer monitor. An LCD monitor, on the other hand, consists of a fixed number of semi-transparent crystals that are able to pass light that's emitted from rear-mounted fluorescent tubes. Rather than reacting to electrons, the liquid crystals are either turned on or off to create the image. Flat panel LCDs also are smaller and lighter, and great for reading text on the screen. In addition, they tend to last longer and produce less heat. The CRTs, however, are better for viewing graphics, especially color images, since they provide better color accuracy and contrast.

Resolution is measured in number of pixels or dots that can be displayed both horizontally and vertically. The more pixels, the finer the detail. Resolution defines how much information can be squeezed onto the screen. However, everything will appear smaller at the larger resolution, since the monitor must fit more pixels into the same space. The clearest resolution for a monitor is whatever comes closest to fitting 72 pixels (or dots) into each inch.

The number of colors and pixels that are seen on the screen actually has little or nothing to do with the monitor. A typical monitor is just a big dumb tube that does what the computer tells it to do. The part of the computer that's in charge of pixels and colors is the video board. The primary measurement of a video board is the amount of VRAM that it provides. More VRAM means more color at higher resolutions. A 2MB board provides 16 million colors up to 800x600 pixels, a 4MB board provides

16 million colors at resolutions up to 1152x864 pixels, and an 8MB board provides 16 million colors at resolutions as high as 1600x1200.

Dot pitch defines how well you can see the image on the screen. Most monitors have dot pitches of .39mm, .28mm, or .25mm. Refresh rate also affects how clear the picture appears—72Hz is the standard refresh rate for Macintosh monitors. That means the screen is repainted 72 times a second, more than twice as fast as your television screen. However, several PC monitors have refresh rates of 60Hz or even less. This begins to approach the level that contributes to eyestrain. Worse yet, many of these monitors are interlaced, which means that only half of the screen is redrawn on each pass. Interlaced monitors have a visible flicker effect, and should be avoided at all costs. Look for a monitor that's noninterlaced, with a dot pitch no greater than 0.28mm.

An alternative to a monitor is a projection system. Projection systems connect to desktop, notebook, or handheld computers and can project screen images as large as a wall. Video output cards convert the digital signal from the computer to an analog video signal, so the projection system can display the image. Many projection systems actually have the built-in capability to convert digital video to analog video. When selecting a projector, pay close addition to the number of ANSI lumens. One thousand to 2,000 ANSI lumens is good for larger groups, while 3,000 to 4,000 is required for gymnasiums. Projection systems are great for software demonstrations, electronic presentations, and video demonstrations for the entire class.

Speakers

The sound coming out of your computer can beep and squawk through its own speakers, but if you want to listen to other sounds you will want to get a set of stereo speakers—one for each side of the monitor. The speakers must be self-powered

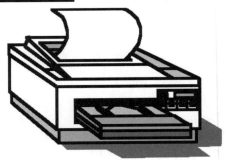

Figure 5.7   Laser printers provide higher quality text and graphics.

and they must be shielded; the magnets inside normal stereo speakers are enough to distort the image on your monitor and destroy the data on a disc.

Some students may have difficulty seeing standard, text-based software. For those students, it may be necessary to use speech synthesis, which converts written text into speech. *OutSpoken* (ALVA Access Group) offers software solutions for both the Macintosh and Windows platforms.

Printers

A printer creates a paper copy of the information you develop on your computer. Printers are typically connected to computers through a USB interface, Ethernet interface, parallel interface, or a serial interface; the interface determines how information is transmitted from the processor to the printer. Be sure to choose a printer with an interface that is compatible with your computer. If the interface is not compatible you can buy a converter, but that will add to your expense. Remember to turn the printer off when you're not printing, since printers can use up to 1,000 watts of electricity per hour. Today, educators typically choose between ink jet and laser printers.

Ink Jet. An ink jet printer is like a dot matrix printer—it prints characters in the form of tiny dots clustered together. However, a dot matrix prints either nine or 24 dots per character, whereas an ink jet sprays hundreds of dots per inch. An ink cartridge replaces an ink ribbon, and there is virtually no sound because there is no impact of metal against paper. The quality of the printing isn't quite laser-crisp, and the printed image can smear if it gets damp. Therefore, special coated paper is recommended, and it is more expensive than the paper used with laser printers.

Because it is relatively inexpensive, educators typically choose an ink jet printer for their first color printer. Colors are usually better from CMYK models (the color cartridge includes black) than from CMY models that blend cyan (C), magenta (M), and yellow (Y) inks to make black (K). The CMY models also require cartridge switching from plain text (black ink) to color printing and back. Most of the newer ink jet printers are now utilizing six and even seven or eight inks to create more refined color gradations and reproductions. The resolution for ink jet printing is typically 600 dots per inch (dpi)—higher resolution typically means better image quality. The droplet size is typically two- to five-picoliter droplets—the smaller the droplet the sharper the image. The primary disadvantage of ink jet printers is their speed (only five to 17 pages per minute). Ink jet printers do offer the best cost in terms of excellent print quality for color photos.

Laser Printers. Laser printers (see Figure 5.7) create photocopy-quality documents. The images are electronically created on a light-sensitive drum, usually with a scanning laser. Powdered toner sticks to areas where light has touched the drum and is then transferred to a sheet of paper that is briefly heated to permanently fuse the toner. Laser printers can print any text, in any style, at any size, and at any angle—and everything looks terrific. PostScript laser printers also can print phenomenal-looking graphics. They're quick (10 to 50 pages per minute), quiet, and hassle-free; most can print envelopes, mailing labels, and paper up to legal size. The more expensive the laser printer, the better its quality and the larger its memory. The resolution for laser printers is typically between 600 dpi and 1200 dpi. Laser printers are the best choice for fast, cheap, top-quality text, but the lack of color in most models means you'll need an inkjet for photos.

Power Supply

It is important to protect your investment in a computer. So, invest in an Uninterruptible Power Supply (UPS) and surge protector. The UPS provides power to the computer when the main electrical system fails. It detects the power failure and switches to battery power within a fraction of a second. This allows you to finish tasks and safely shut down. The surge protector provides protection to the computer from a fluctuation in power that can damage your equipment. Many uninterruptible power supplies have built-in surge protection. When selecting a surge protector, be sure to choose one that has a Joule Rating of at least 1000, and check that it includes telephone connections in order to protect your modem from power fluctuations as well.

Acquiring Your Computer

In many schools and districts, the type of computer you use is governed by what the school or district already owns. This is true whether you are going to an office or a lab or are purchasing the machine for your department. Some districts adopt a certain type of operating system for all schools, or a particular type of computer by grade level—for example, elementary schools use Macintosh, intermediate schools use Windows, and high schools use Windows Professional. Even if a school doesn't have a policy, departments should stay consistent with the rest of the school when possible.

Computers can be acquired through general funds, grants (e.g., from Apple Computers, Carol M. White PEP Grant, federal funds, state funds, federal block grants, and private foundations), technology funds, and other financial avenues. Physical education departments should begin by acquiring one computer for each office. Ideally, each physical education teacher should be equipped with his or her own computer and have access to a presentation workstation. At minimum, each teacher's system should include a computer, monitor, input devices (keyboard and mouse), storage devices (hard drive, CD-ROM), modem, and printer. Presentation stations should include a projection system. Once each teacher is equipped, you can begin to secure computers for student use. When purchasing, compare special educational prices (e.g., Apple school discount), computer advertisements, and mail order catalogs. When you purchase by mail order you can save hundreds of dollars by avoiding sales tax, and you tend to get a pretty good price. A good source for mail order is CDW.

Getting Started

You ordered the equipment, and it has arrived—in a variety of boxes. Now the only question is, "How does it all go together?" Fortunately, the ports (sockets where cables connect) on the rear of most computers are marked with icons that symbolize the type of equipment that should be attached to them. For example, there is an icon of a monitor where the monitor plugs in, and one of a telephone where the telephone cord plugs in.

Once you have hooked the computer up to the peripherals, it's time to turn it on. The computer itself can perform only a few functions written into its hardware (ROM). So, each time it is turned on, it needs "system software"—a set of instructions that tell the processor how to create type styles, set up the first screen on the monitor, and communicate with the input devices and output devices. System software (e.g., Macintosh operating system, Windows operating system) should already be on the hard drive when you purchase the computer.

Different operating systems use different methods for starting programs and naming files, and they offer various levels of sophistication with graphic interfaces. Be sure to complete all tutorials that accompany your computer so you can take full advantage of its operating system. Finally, put all documentation and software in one place where you can find it when you may need it. Attach tags to all the connecting power lines, printer cables, phone connection, etc., so that when, and if, you need to bring your system in for repair it will be easy to put it all back together.

Summary

Many decisions related to the purchase of a computer and peripherals are individual ones. However, it is important to purchase the best computer you can afford. That will allow you to stay up-to-date as long as possible before having to trade in your computer for a better one to meet your ever-increasing needs. Use the guidelines and recommendations from this chapter to guide your decisions. Also, refer to the many computer magazines on the market (see Appendix C) and the various companies' Internet sites for specific recommendations.

Reflection Questions

1. Describe your ideal computer. On what did you base your decision?
2. Which of the peripherals (input/output devices) would you purchase? What would you intend to accomplish with each device?

Projects

1. Make a list of all the software you would like to open at one time, determine the RAM requirements of each program, and then calculated your total RAM needs.
2. Create a list of all the features you need in your next computer. Then, thumb through a computer catalog (i.e., CDW) and list all the computers that meet your criteria. Next, go on the Internet and find reviews of these computers. Finally choose a computer and explain your decision.

Chapter 6

Physical Education Productivity Software

Bill Kwong comes in from his third period class and sits down at his computer, ready to take full advantage of his conference period. He types in his lesson plans for the next two classes, makes several locker changes, enters grades from last night's homework assignment, and prints out the students' current grades. Then, he begins to prepare the monthly newsletter he sends out to keep parents informed about the activities that are taking place in physical education.

It takes time to maintain your grades and locker system, and it takes time to do the other tasks that you must attend to each day—time that you could be using to develop new lessons and to work with students. This chapter looks at applications—specifically, applications designed to help you handle your paperwork more efficiently and professionally.

Acquiring Software

There are three basic types of applications: commercial, shareware, and public domain. Commercial applications are created and distributed by the company that holds the copyright. The company sells the application directly or through other commercial outlets such as stores, mail order houses, or online businesses. These programs are copyrighted, so it is illegal to duplicate them and give them away.

Public domain applications, on the other hand, are usually developed by someone who develops computer programs as a hobby or by someone who has received a grant. Then, either by choice or as a requirement of the grant, the programmer donates the application to the public. This means the application may legally be copied and shared with others, since the applications are not subject to any copyright restrictions. However, even though the application may not be sold, there is often a charge for the media (e.g., CD, DVD) itself, the labor involved in copying the application, and the cost for shipping and handling.

Shareware falls somewhere between commercial and public domain applications. Shareware is usually developed by part-time programmers who distribute the application freely, using a combination of copyright law and the honor system. You are requested to send a fee to the creator if you decide to keep the application. This fee usually entitles you to a copy of the manual or additional directions, and newer versions cost-free or at a reduced price. A couple of good shareware programs you should have are Aladdin *StuffIt Expander for Macintosh*, Aladdin *StuffIt Expander for Windows*, and Adobe *Acrobat Reader*.

One variation of shareware is postcardware. Programmers ask that you send them a postcard in lieu of payment, so they can track who is using their application. Another variation is donationware—instead of sending money to the application maker, you're asked to make a donation to a charity.

The other terms that you may hear are vaporware, demoware, and trialware. Vaporware is an application that has been endlessly talked about and promoted, but never seems to become a reality. Demoware is a commercial application you can test with some of its features disabled. This allows you to get a feel for the application, but you must pay to take full advantage of the application. Trialware is typically a full version of a commercial application that is set to run for a limited period of time. This allows you to try out the application, but you must pay in order for the application to continue working. Trialware is preferable to demoware, since you can evaluate the entire program and not just selected aspects.

There are not as many commercial applications for physical education as there are for other subject areas. In the late 1980s, the American Alliance for Health, Physical Education, Recreation, and Dance (AAHPERD) published the *Directory of Computer Software with Application to Sport Science, Health, and Dance* (Baumgartner & Cicciarella, 1987). It listed 208 programs, including shareware and public domain programs written by 75 programmers. Chapters 6, 7, and 8 of this book provide information on current applications for physical education, and you can find shareware and public domain programs on the Internet (see Chapters 9 and 10).

Purchasing/Installation

When purchasing applications, you must know how much random access memory (RAM) you have in your computer, and you must know the type and size of your hard drive. You also need to make sure that you secure the following:

- Macintosh applications for Macintosh computers, and Windows applications for Windows-based computers. Many programs now come as bi-platform applications, which means they will work with both Macintosh and Windows operating systems.
- Applications that requires less RAM than your computer has available.
- Applications that are compatible with your system software. Some of the newer applications will not run on an older operating system (e.g., Windows 95), and some older versions of software (designed for Macintosh System 9, for example) will not work with the newer operating system (Macintosh System X). The system requirements are noted on the packaging or marketing materials.

The majority of applications now come on a CD that contains an installation program. The user simply inserts the CD in the drive, double clicks on the Installer icon, and the software provides all necessary directions for installation. If an install program is not included, be sure to read the installation directions provided by the publisher, so as to prevent unnecessary complications.

Purchasing Options for Schools

Publishers frequently offer discounts in the form of lab packs, licenses, discounts, and/or bundles. Lab packs are good for schools interested in buying multiple copies of an application for use in a single computer lab or classroom. A lab pack generally consists of several (5-10) copies of the application and a single set of documentation. It costs considerably less for the entire lab pack than it would cost to purchase an equivalent number of individual applications.

Another purchasing option is a site or district license. This is a cost-effective way to acquire applications that are to be used widely throughout a school or district. In granting a site or district license, a publisher generally gives the licensee the right to make an unlimited number of copies of the application for use within a specific site or district. Some companies charge a standard rate for a certain type of site or district license; others base the price on the number of potential users at the site or in the district. Before purchasing software, be sure to check with your school and district, since they may already have a license.

The distribution of software via a network also is a form of duplication, because the application is available on more than one computer at a time. Therefore, most networkable versions of programs come with a network license that indicates how the software can be used on the network. Some licenses allow for unlimited use of the application on a single local area network (LAN). Others define the number of network users (or computers) that can have access to the application at any one time. Such limits are enforced by the network management system, which alerts users who attempt to access certain applications when all available copies are in use. Pricing varies, but it tends to be more cost effective than purchasing an equivalent number of individual copies.

In addition to lab packs and licenses, most companies offer other discounts to organizations that make large purchases. Some companies deduct a percentage of the cost for each order above a certain size; others offer "district memberships" that provide price breaks for participants who order a number of products during a longer period of time. Some larger entities — occasionally including entire states — have been able to negotiate special price breaks from software companies by placing especially large orders, or even by helping with the development of new products. Although individual schools and districts do not have the same buying power as a state, a number have found ways of saving money by joining together to place bulk orders. Most companies are receptive to proposals for affordable ways of making large purchases.

Many companies also offer special discount pricing for bundles of applications that include several related titles or a number of applications in a series. Increasingly, we are seeing partnerships between different companies (often including both hardware and application providers) to deliver cost-effective bundles that address specific needs (e.g., web browsing, web site development, middle school education).

Versions

Most applications are identified by a version number, and it may include one or two decimal places. These numbers refer to the version of the application. The greater the numeric difference between one version and the next, the more significant the changes in the application. The differences between version

4.0 and 5.0 are tremendous, whereas the difference between 4.01 and 4.02 may only represent the elimination of an error or bug, for example.

Using Software in Physical Education

Applications to assist physical educators can be grouped into three major categories:

- Integrated packages (word processing, data base, spreadsheet, and presentation).
- General teacher productivity tools.
- Physical education productivity tools.

The first two categories are used by all teachers; the last one is used exclusively by physical education teachers.

Remember, applications contain directions that tell computers how to perform and data files hold the information you input. Data files can be saved with special symbols embedded in the text that denote the format provided by the software, or they can be saved as ASCII, or "plain text" files, that eliminate the software-specific symbols and save the information as text only. These "plain text" files are easily transferred from one type of operating system to another and one application to another. For example, if you want to input the names of students into a spreadsheet or grading program and your school or district has a list of names in another program, ask them to export the data in ASCII or plain text so you can import the names into the desired program.

Integrated Packages

Word processing, data base, spreadsheet, and presentation applications are sold either as individual applications or as one integrated package (sometimes referred to as a suite). Some integrated packages tend to be less sophisticated, but they also are considerably less expensive and easier to use. Therefore, integrated packages are recommended as your first purchase; often they even come with the computer. You can purchase more sophisticated packages or individual applications as you develop a need for them. Most of the integrated packages are very similar, so the specific package that you buy (e.g., *AppleWorks*, Microsoft *Works*, Microsoft *Office*) should be based on cost and what others are using at your school. There are even integrated packages for handheld computers. A light version of Microsoft *Office* comes with the PocketPC operating system. On the Palm operating system side, you can purchase *QuickOffice* (www.cesinc.com) or *Documents to Go* (dataviz.com).

Word processing allows the computer to replace the typewriter. Anything that you used to do on a typewriter can now be done on a computer. Similarly, data base applications replace Rolodexes and information files. You can use data base applications to enter the information (e.g., telephone number, birth date, address) about a person that used to be placed on a Rolodex card, sort it in any number of ways, and print it out in a variety of formats. Spreadsheets, in turn, replace ledgers and inventory sheets. Spreadsheets place data in rows and columns, so that calculations can be performed. As soon as a new entry is made, the spreadsheet updates itself and recalculates any parts affected by the change. Many integrated programs also include presentation software, graphics, desktop publishing, drawing, and painting features. Let's look now at how each of these works in physical education.

Word processing. Curriculum guides, lesson plans, homework assignments, rule sheets, agendas, contracts, evaluations, worksheets, task cards, letters to parents, minutes, and policies are commonly placed in word processing files (see Figure 6.1). Such information can be updated quickly when it is time to make revisions. No longer do you have to retype entire documents to make a few minor changes. You can now keep your rule sheets up-to-date and change lesson plans at the last minute. Many

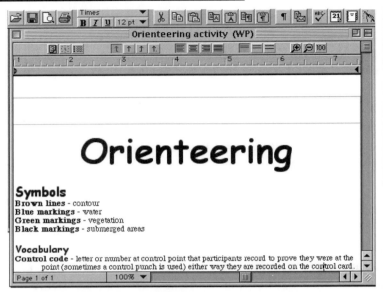

Figure 6.1 Word processing files allow you to create and update documents quickly.

word processing programs also come with templates (e.g., predesigned letters, newsletters, certificates, etc.) that make your job even easier.

Word processing applications allow the user to set margins, spacing, justification, tabs, headers, footers, and character spacing for the entire document or to change the specifications for every word, line, or paragraph. You determine font size and style (e.g., underline, bold, italic), according to preference and what is available on your computer. If, after entering information, you decide that the last paragraph should be the first, you simply select the paragraph, choose "Cut" to place the information on the clipboard (a temporary holding location), reposition the cursor at the location where you want to move the paragraph, and choose "Paste" to complete the move.

Most word processing applications come with spell checkers and grammar tools. Some applications also come with a draw or paint feature (see section on Drawing and Painting Applications

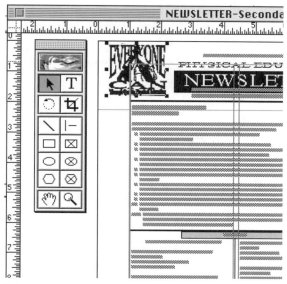

Figure 6.2 Spice up your newsletters with graphics, columns, and multiple type styles and fonts by using desktop publishing programs.

Design Rules

- Consistent typeface, type size, and spacing specifications for text, headlines, subheads, and captions.
- Uniform paragraph indents and spaces between columns and around photographs.
- Repeating graphic elements such as vertical lines, columns, or borders on each page.
- Balance spaces between text, artwork, and white space.
- Text boxes should be indented on both sides.
- Use lines, drop caps, dingbats, boxes, bullets, and reverses.
- Avoid underlining, widows, and orphans.
- Use serif fonts (those with curves — such as this) for text body and sans serif (those without curves—such as this) for headlines.
- Wrap text around drop caps.
- Use visual cueing in the form of frames, boxes, bullets, arrows, shading, bold face, and italics.
- Use captions for pictures, diagrams, and headings.
- Create and use graphics carefully.
- Avoid single words and lines at the top and bottom of pages.

in this chapter) that allows you to insert and manipulate lines, polygons, and pictures. High-end features include automatic indexing, a table of contents generator, and a thesaurus. You also can get programs, such as *Power Translator* (Globalink), that translate your word processing document into a second language. There are three basic rules to remember when using word processing programs: don't press the return key at the end of each line, put only one space after each period, and don't use the "L" key to make the number 1.

Desktop publishing programs are essentially advanced word processing programs that allow for the more complex integration of text with graphic images. Popular programs include *QuarkXPress* (Quark, Inc.) and *InDesign* (Adobe). They can create columns, generate tables, create indexes, automatically number pages, flow text automatically from one page to the next, and assemble separate documents quickly. You can import graphics from applications that provide a variety of clip art images, or you can develop your own graphics using drawing or painting applications.

High-quality, royalty-free clip art images covering a wide variety of subjects are now available. One exceptional program for physical educators is *Super Anatomy Collection* (LifeArt). It contains anatomical images of the human circulatory, skeletal, muscular, digestive, endocrine, reproductive, nervous, and urinary systems. Photographs also can be imported into desktop publishing programs. You can use this application to produce weekly or monthly newsletters (see Figure 6.2), event brochures, task cards, overheads, flyers, certificates, and material for bulletin boards. The primary advantage of desktop publishing is that it provides separate page layout views, which makes it easier to move text and graphics around the document.

Data base software. Data base software is used to organize information such as event schedules, locker assignments, student records, facility schedules, equipment checkout forms,

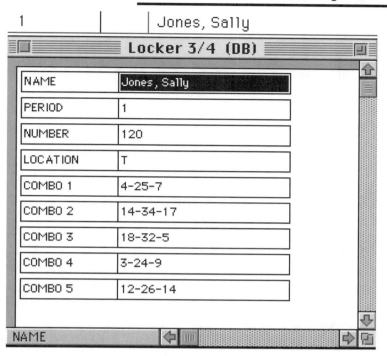

Figure 6.3 A data base view of one record with all of its fields.

eligibility lists, accident reports, and anything else that would normally be maintained on file cards or in folders. Popular databases include *Filemaker Pro* (www.filemaker.com) and *Microsoft Access* (www.msn.com) along with *FileMaker Mobile* (www.filemaker.com), *Think DB* (www.thinkingbytes.com) and *HanDBase* (www.ddhsoftware.com) for the Palm Operating System. The key benefits of a data base include: reducing data redundancy, saving time locating and updating information, and allowing for comparisons of information across files. Data bases also allow for the creation of a wide variety of reports. A relational data base is like a simple data base, but it can access data from several different data bases at one time. This is possible as long as the data bases are all related by one piece of identical information—such as a student name or number.

NAME	PERIOD	NUMBER	LOCATION	COMBO 1	COMBO 2	COMBO 3	COMBO 4	COMBO 5
Jones, Sally	1	120	T	4-25-7	14-34-17	18-32-5	3-24-9	12-26-14
	2	121	M	8-35-9	9-14-4	15-31-11	12-15-11	18-25-34
	3	122	B	13-27-15	2-19-1	8-29-14	15-31-11	9-30-2
	4	123	T	19-34-7	17-28-9	11-32-8	8-29-14	15-31-11
	5	124	M	5-26-11	11-32-8	3-12-2	11-28-8	4-30-7
	6	125	B	14-28-16	16-38-19	11-39-14	11-39-12	6-26-11
	1	126	T	16-36-19	13-24-8	22-39-26	15-29-17	16-36-1
	2	127	M	11-39-12	7-16-14	10-39-11	20-34-24	25-7-14
	3	128	B	15-29-17	5-26-11	12-26-14	8-31-18	34-17-11
	4	129	T	5-31-11	2-36-9	3-24-9	13-20-9	9-14-8
	5	130	M	9-30-2	9-30-2	18-32-21	19-21-11	12-38-11

Figure 6.4 A data base in list form shows records and fields.

A data base consists of fields (spaces in which you insert information) and records (complete sets of fields). The consistency of fields across all records is what allows data bases to quickly arrange (sort) records by one or more fields. The record selection feature permits you to specify which records are viewed at one time. For example, in a grade 9-12 data base, you may opt to view only those records for grade 10 students. Many inexpensive data bases also have the ability to do some minor calculations. A data base can be viewed in different layouts (see Figures 6.3 and 6.4), and can be printed using a number of different report formats.

Data base software is especially effective in managing locker systems. The data base in Figures 6.3 and 6.4 is based on a system where the lock is built into the locker with five different combination settings that can be changed in sequence. Nine fields are labeled Locker Number, Combination 1, Combination 2, Combination 3, Combination 4, Combination 5, Student Name, Physical Education Period, and Location of Locker (top, middle, or bottom). The locker number, location, and five combinations are keyed in advance, and the locker numbers and current combinations are printed out on labels before the students arrive at school. Student names and periods are entered as the students are assigned their lockers and combinations.

Data bases also can be used to develop and monitor the scope and sequence of curriculum. When curriculum records are kept on a data base, you can access the curriculum information that you need from your own computer. Because the information is stored electronically, schools and districts can share information more easily. On the monitoring side, you can keep track of each student's mastery of standards and more efficiently determine future learning needs.

Students also can use data bases for learning activities. When provided with a data base of information, they can be asked to search for the name of the youngest person, the name of the person with the highest blood pressure, or the name of the person with the lowest blood pressure. They also can be asked to perform filtering activities where they search for the names of individuals with blood pressure over 160 or under 110.

Mail merge. The mail merge option, available with many word processing and integrated programs, adds a new dimension to letter writing. Using this feature, you can write one letter and personalize it for any number of recipients (see Figures 6.5a-6.5c). The individualized information is entered in fields either in a data base or a second word processing document. Each record contains the individualized information for one letter. The letter is typed in a word processing program that uses special symbols to tell the computer where to insert the individualized information. By selecting the Print Merge command, you automatically print out a separate letter for each record in the data base.

Spreadsheets. Budgets, inventories, grades, and attendance records are examples of information that can be monitored using a spreadsheet program. Spreadsheets also are used to log running mileage, plan progressive resistance training programs, design interval workouts, and with any other application where the organization of numbers is useful. You can play "what if," using the spreadsheet to determine the implications of certain changes. For example, with respect to budget, what if the

File Edit Form Data Report Window
1
Josie Garcia
Rolodex5 (DB)
STUDENT
PARENT
ADDRESS
CITY
TARDIES
Josie Garcia
Juan Garcia
1883 Washington Blvd
Los Angeles, CA 90042
8

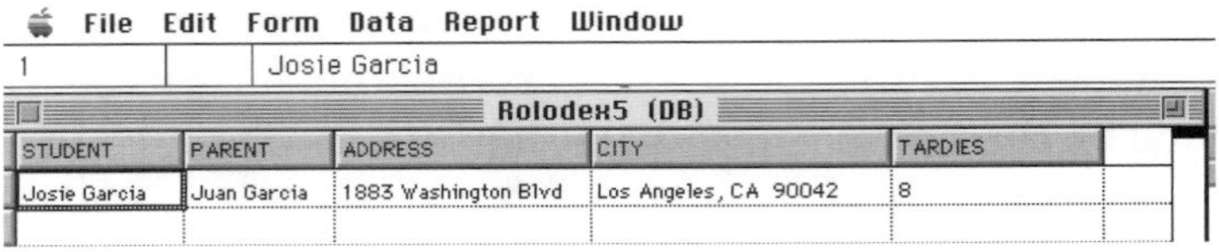

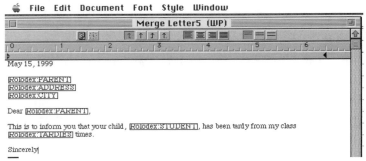

Figure 6.5a Enter selected information on each student into a single file.

File Edit Document Font Style Window
Merge Letter5 (WP)
May 15, 1999
Rolodex:PARENT
Rolodex:ADDRESS
Rolodex:CITY
Dear Rolodex:PARENT,
This is to inform you that your child, Rolodex:STUDENT, has been tardy from my class
Rolodex:TARDIES times.
Sincerely

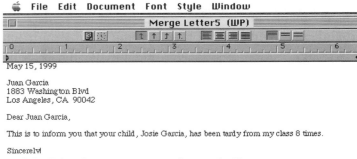

Figure 6.5b Set up your form letter by merging the field titles.

File Edit Document Font Style Window
Merge Letter5 (WP)
May 15, 1999
Juan Garcia
1883 Washington Blvd
Los Angeles, CA 90042
Dear Juan Garcia,
This is to inform you that your child, Josie Garcia, has been tardy from my class 8 times.
Sincerely

Figure 6.5c Print the merge to save time and effort.

supply account allocation increased, or what if teachers' salaries increased? How would these changes affect the entire physical education budget?

Users often are unsure when to use a spreadsheet and when to use a data base. In fact, as each of these applications matures, the lines do become blurred and sometimes one application can replace the other. However, if the fields in a data base contain mostly numbers, then a spreadsheet will probably work better. If a spreadsheet contains more labels and text that requires sorting, a data base probably will be your best choice.

Electronic spreadsheets appear as grids with rows and columns. Each intersection is called a "cell" and is referred to by its column letter and row number. You can type words, numbers, or formulas into each cell. The formulas can include math operators (+, -, *, /) and special operators called "functions" (e.g., sum, lookup, average). In Cells F2 and F3 in Figure 6.6a, both formulas add the numbers on the respective lines in Columns B, C, D, and E. In cell F3, the ":" symbol refers to "through" (in a few spreadsheet programs this symbol is ".."), thus adding numbers in Columns B through E. Other popular functions include "average" (which determines the mean for the cells specified), and "count" (which determines the number of cells that contain numbers or letters). Functions always are preceded by either "=" or "@", depending on the software package.

Spreadsheets make especially effective electronic roll books. To create an attendance record, list student names in the first column and insert dates as column headings. Type either the number "1" or a letter in the cell (the intersection of student's name and the date) to record an absence. If you use the number 1, the "sum" command will give you the total number of absences. If you use a letter, the "count" command will give you the total number of absences.

Grades also can be manipulated easily using spreadsheet software. Again, list student names in the first column, with assignments and tests as column headings. The last column is the total column, where "sum" totals the points. The spreadsheet in Figure 6.6a shows the formulas, and the spreadsheet in Figure 6.6b shows the results of the calculations. If you have a more complicated grading system, subtotals (based on the type of grade) can be calculated and different grades can be weighted using multiply (*) operator or the "average" function.

Figure 6.7 shows a more sophisticated grading file that uses the "lookup" function to calculate grades based on scores from norm-referenced tests. Set up your grading file as explained

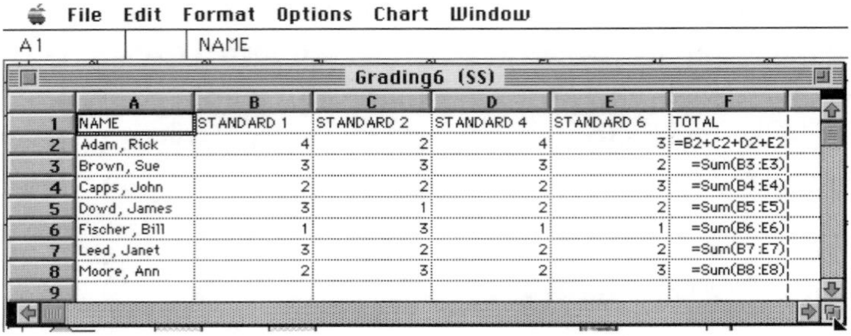

Using Technology in Physical Education

Figure 6.6a A grading file developed using a spreadsheet program, showing students' names and their scores on four assignments or tests. The formula =sum(B3:E3) tells the spreadsheet to add together the scores in Cells B3, C3, D3, and E3 and put the result in F3.

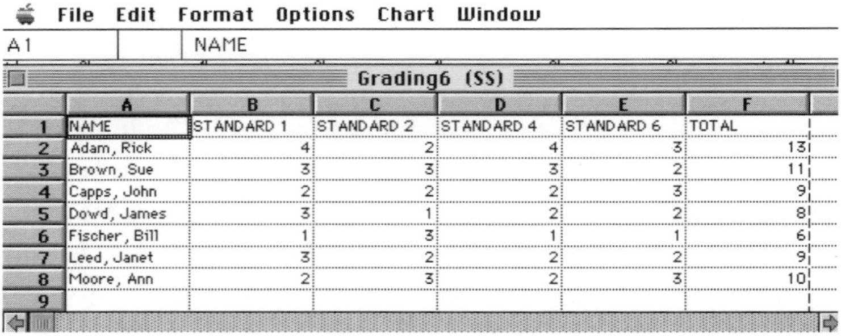

Figure 6.6b Results of these calculations.

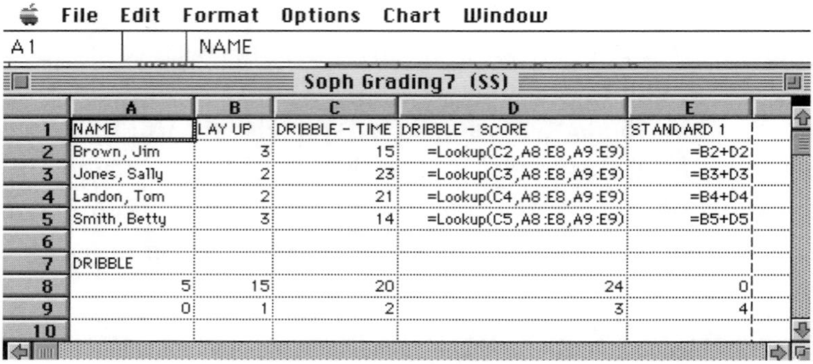

Figure 6.7 A more sophisticated grading file developed using a spreadsheet. The formula =Lookup(C2, A8:E8, A9:E9) tells the spreadsheet to look in Row 8 (A8:E8) for the number that is less than or equal to the number in Cell C2 and then return the number in the same column in Row 9 (A9:E9).

previously and establish a norm-referenced table somewhere in the spreadsheet. For example, set up a two-row table in Rows 8 and 9, listing the grades (0, 1, 2, 3, 4 represent F, D, C, B, A) in Row 9 and the corresponding times (in seconds) for a basketball dribble test in Row 8 (see Figure 6.7, Rows 8-9). Then, in the dribble score column (D), use "lookup" to tell the spreadsheet to look in Row 8 for the number that is less than or equal to the student's dribble time (found in column C) and return the grade found in the same column in Row 9.

Inventories (see Figure 6.8) are another way to use spreadsheets in physical education. Label the first column "Equipment," and list storage rooms as other column headings. In the first cell of each row, enter the name of a type of equipment, and in the following cells of that row enter the amount of equipment in each storage room. Enter "Total" as the heading for the last column, and use "sum" in each row to add together the amount of each type of equipment in the storage rooms.

A more sophisticated inventory file for equipment (see Figures 6.9a and 6.9b) will tell you when and what you need to reorder. To the inventory file I just described, add a "Number To Order" section. For example, in Rows 11 through 16 under column A, list the equipment that you need to reorder. In Rows 11 through

 File   Edit   Format   Options   Chart   Window

A1

Inventory 8 (SS)

	A	B	C	D	E	F
1		Storage	Room 1	Room 2	Room 3	Total
2	Basketballs	20	12	0	12	=Sum(B2:E2)
3	Bowling Balls	10	0	15	0	=Sum(B3:E3)
4	Footballs	6	0	0	15	=Sum(B4:E4)
5	Gloves	4	0	40	0	=Sum(B5:E5)
6	Softballs	19	0	30	0	=Sum(B6:E6)
7	Volleyballs	8	10	0	10	=Sum(B7:E7)
8						
9						

Figure 6.8 Inventory developed using a spreadsheet. The formula =Sum(B2: E2) tells the spreadsheet to add together the numbers in Cells B2, C2, D2, and E2.

16 under Column B, use the "if" function to calculate how many pieces of equipment should be reordered. With basketballs, for example, you may want to always have 30 in storage; the "if" function will compare the number in storage to 30 and determine the difference. If it is less than 30, the spreadsheet calculates and returns the difference (i.e., number to be ordered); otherwise it returns zero.

Many businesses use spreadsheets to maintain budgets, and physical education departments can do so as well. When developing a computerized budget system (see Figure 6.10), you must first determine what is to be monitored, how it is to

	A	B	C	D	E	F
1		Storage	Room 1	Room 2	Room 3	Total
2	Basketballs	20	12	0	12	=Sum(B2:E2)
3	Bowling Balls	10	0	15	0	=Sum(B3:E3)
4	Footballs	6	0	0	15	=Sum(B4:E4)
5	Gloves	4	0	40	0	=Sum(B5:E5)
6	Softballs	19	0	30	0	=Sum(B6:E6)
7	Volleyballs	8	10	0	10	=Sum(B7:E7)
8						
9						
10		Number to Order				
11	Basketballs	=If(F2<30,30-F2,0)				
12	Bowling Balls	=If(F3<12,12-F3,0)				
13	Footballs	=If(F4<30,30-F4,0)				
14	Gloves	=If(F5<50,50-F5,0)				
15	Softballs	=If(F6<60,60-F6,0)				
16	Volleyballs	=If(F7<40,40-F7,0)				

Figure 6.9a. The addition of the formula =If(F2<30,30-F2,0) tells the spreadsheet to compare the number in Cell F2 to 30 (F2<30) and, if the number in F2 is less than 30, return the difference between 30 and the number in F2 (30-F2). Otherwise, return 0.

	A	B	C	D	E	F
1		Storage	Room 1	Room 2	Room 3	Total
2	Basketballs	20	12	0	12	44
3	Bowling Balls	10	0	15	0	25
4	Footballs	6	0	0	15	21
5	Gloves	4	0	40	0	44
6	Softballs	19	0	30	0	49
7	Volleyballs	8	10	0	10	28
8						
9						
10		Number to Order				
11	Basketballs	0				
12	Bowling Balls	0				
13	Footballs	9				
14	Gloves	6				
15	Softballs	11				
16	Volleyballs	12				

Figure 6.9b Results of these calculations.

D19

	A	B	C	D
			Budget (SS)	
1	EQUIPMENT			1000
2	5/15/99	Gymnastics Mats	500	
3				
4				
5				
6	TOTAL SPENT			=Sum(C2:C5)
7	BALANCE – EQUIPMENT			=D1–D6
8				
9	SUPPLIES			500
10		Basketballs	84	
11		Stop Watches	96	
12				
13				
14				
15	TOTAL SPENT			=Sum(C10:C14)
16	BALANCE – SUPPLIES			=D9–D15
17				

Figure 6.10   This typical physical education budget, produced using a spreadsheet, shows beginning balances, expenses, and remaining balances for equipment and supplies.

be accomplished, and how results are to be used. For example, suppose a department chairperson is allocated $1,000 for equipment and $500 for supplies. Each amount is listed as income, and each requisition is listed as an expenditure. By maintaining a total of the expenditures and calculating the difference between the original allocation and the total expenditures, the department chairperson can immediately ascertain the amount still available to spend in each budget category. Since most spreadsheets have graphing capabilities (see Figures 6.11, 6.12, and 6.13), he or she can depict the type of expenditures in graph form.

Presentation software. PowerPoint (Microsoft) has basically dominated the market for presentation applications; however, Apple has recently release a presentation software entitled *Keynote* which it hopes will compete. Presentation software (see Figure 6.14) allows for the easy creation of slide shows. The user makes an outline of the presentation. The outline is converted by the software into a slide show. The user then can add pictures (e.g., jpeg), sounds, and videos. There are even programs, such as Pocket SlideShow (CNETX), Presenter to Go

Figure 6.11 Spreadsheets also allow you to create informative graphics that can add perspective to facts and figures. This is an example of a pie graph.

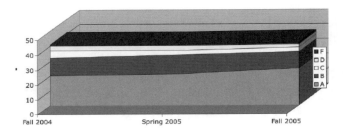

Figure 6.12 This is an example of a stacked graph.

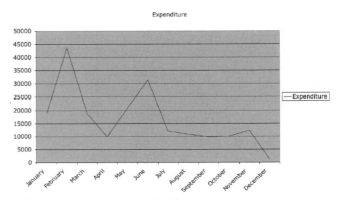

Figure 6.13 This is an example of a line graph.

(Margi) and Pocket Slides (Conduits Technologies) that allow you to take your presentation files with you and show them from your handheld computer.

PowerPoint is used by physical educators to create presentations that can be shown during a lecture or used by students who were absent to catch up. They also can be used during back-to-school nights and other presentations for community groups. Some educators also use *PowerPoint* to create graphics and task cards, although there are other programs specifically designed for these tasks. Good presentations contain no more than six lines per screen and six words per line. The text should be flush left and unjustified except for headings, and none of the words should be in all CAPS. In addition, the pictures should be meaningful and scanned at 72 dpi.

Drawing and painting applications. There are numerous drawing and painting applications, including Adobe *PhotoShop* (paint), Adobe *Illustrator* (draw), Macromedia *Freehand* (draw), and *Sketchy* (paint for Palm operating system). Paint programs allow you to use a variety of tools (pencil, paint brush, paint can, eraser) to create images on the screen, pixel by pixel. Advanced painting programs allow the user to integrate all sorts of interesting effects (e.g., gradients, smudges).

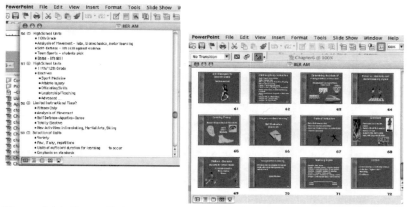

Figure 6.14 *PowerPoint* converts an outline into a slide show.

Drawing applications allow the user to create images as objects that can be edited and manipulated. These are often referred to as vector graphics, since the objects are mathematically described and resolution independent, allowing for enlargement, reduction, rotation, overlap of one object with another, and colorization with no loss of detail. Using either program, you can create diagrams of fields or even simple stick figures that depict various motor skills. When purchasing clip art, look for vector graphics.

3D image applications. 3D applications, such as *Carrara* (Eovia) and *Bryce* (Corel), extend the features of drawing and painting applications into the third dimension. These images are best used on the screen where they can be rotated for viewing all three sides. Although you can print three separate images in 3D showing each perspective, 3D images are effective for showing motor skill, strategy situations, and biomechanic concepts.

Types of Graphics

gif: Used for bitmapped pictures that are transmitted over the Internet.

jpeg: Used to create a standard for color/grayscale image compression. It is effective on continuous tone color spaces. Best used on the Internet and for monitor presentations.

png: Designed to replace the older and simpler gif format and to some extent the much more complex TIFF format.

eps: used for storing vector graphics and bitmapped artwork.

wmf - Common vector graphics file format.

.tiff - Very versatile commonly used method for storing bitmapped or picture images in various resolutions, gray levels, and colors. It was created specifically for storing grayscale images and it is the standard format for scanned images such as photos.

.pict - Oldest generic file format for Mac.

.bmp - Bitmap storage on the Windows platform.

Red Eye Correction

In *PhotoShop*, you will find this feature in the "adjust" menu. Selecting it yields the red-eye removal dialog box. This dialog box has two default settings, but you can choose from numerous settings. You can set the eye color and iris size. You can add a glint to the center of the eye and you can increase or decrease the lightness of the pupil. You can outline the pupil in a freehand or point-to-point manner. You do not just remove the red eye; you redesign the eye to look the way you want.

Using a program like *QTVR Authoring Studio* (Apple), *3D-Stitcher* (Realviz), or *Photovista* (MGI), a series of linear pictures can be stitched together in a panoramic picture (three-dimensional image). Dragging the mouse up moves you closer, dragging the mouse down moves you away, dragging the mouse to the right turns your view to the right, and dragging the mouse to the left turns your view to the left. These programs also can create 3D objects by placing an object on a rotating platform and taking several pictures, rotating the platform before each shot. These pictures are then stitched together, creating a 3D picture. Dragging the mouse rotates the object so that all sides can be viewed. Teachers can create panoramic or 3D object pictures for instruction and students can use them in their projects.

Animation applications. This category of applications, including *Flash* (Macromedia), *Poser* (CuriousLabs), and *LifeForms* (Credo Interactive), creates moving objects. Animations are much more effective than a still graphic, yet they require much less memory than digitized video. The process involves creating the first and last frames to be used in animation. The application then fills in the middle frames, adjusting for the changes that take place. This process is repeated for the entire sequence so that you end up with an animation segment for your program. Animation projects are especially effective for creating dance sequences and tumbling routines (see Chapter 8 for more information).

Audio software. Audio digitizing is the process of converting a sound from analog to digital format so that it can be manipulated, saved, and used for instruction and electronic projects. Digitizing sound requires a sound source (tape cassette, CD), a microphone attached to the computer or a line port so that a cable can connect the sound source to the computer, and software, such as *SoundEdit* (Macromedia) or *SoundJam* (Sound Step) to digitize and manipulate the sound. Sampling rates determine how often an analog audio signal is cut up to make a digital audio clip. The higher the number of samples per second (5K, 7K, 11K, or 22K), the more lifelike the digitized sound—and the more memory it will require. Whenever possible, digitize sound at 22K in order to maximize the quality. You can always reduce the sampling rate when you compress the sound for storage. A great compression format for sound is MP3. MP3 files also can be played from a handheld computer or an MP3 player, such as an iPod.

Digitizing Audio

1. Turn on audio cassette recorder or CD player.
2. Place audio cassette or CD in recorder or player.
3. Press play on the audio cassette recorder or CD player.
4. Double click on audio digitizing software
5. Use fast forward/rewind on the audio or track button on the CD player to select a segment to capture.
6. Press play on the audio cassette recorder or CD player.
7. Click record on the computer screen.
8. At the end of the segment, click stop button on the computer screen.
9. Select File-Save to save the audio clip to your disk.

Digitizing Video

1. Start with high-quality video.
2. Turn on video source.
3. Press "play" on video source.
4. Find segment to transfer.
5. Double click on video digitizing software.
6. Capture at full screen resolution.
7. Click "record" button on the computer screen.
8. At the end of the segment, click "stop" button on computer screen.
9. Select File-Save to save video clip.
10. Select File - Quit or Exit.

Video Editing. You or your students also can digitize (convert analog video to digitized video) video clips. The quality is not quite as high as with digital video (transferring digital video from a digital video camera to the computer via a firewire cable), but it will do the job. Again, these files can be used for instruction or electronic projects.

A video digitizing card (e.g., Dazzle) or USB VideoBus (Belkin) is necessary to convert the analog video into digital video. The input source for digitized video is any analog medium, such as an analog video camera, videocassette player, or broadcast television signal from an antenna, cable, or satellite. A cable connects the video source to the video card on the computer, and a second cable connects the audio port on the video source to the audio port on the computer. Software distributed with the video card controls the computer display. Most digitizing programs also allow the user to cut, copy, paste, and alter the clips. If this is an area of interest for you, then it is a good idea—and it will be cheaper—to purchase the video card when you purchase your computer. Or better yet, go the digital route and get a digital video camera and a computer with a firewire connection. Then, using software that comes with the operating system (e.g., Macintosh's *iMovie* or Windows' *MovieMaker*) you can create and edit (i.e., cut out pieces, add transitions) your clips.

Multimedia Hard Drives

- 7,500 rmp (revolutions per minute).
- Large storage capacity.
- Access time of less than 10 milliseconds.
- Sustained data transfer date of 3 MB per second.

General Teacher Productivity

General teacher productivity software can make any teacher's job, including a physical educator's easier. This section provides information on software specific to a number of tasks that many physical educators perform. If you don't want to put extra money into these programs, then consider purchasing an integrated program like *AppleWorks* or *Microsoft Works*, which come with numerous templates and assistants to help you design your own certificates, calendars, brochures, grading reports, lesson plan formats, statistics, banners, presentations, and posters using the tools already available in the program. You also will find several programs in this category on the Internet where they can be accessed or used for free (see Chapters 9 and 10). Remember, the programs suggested here are for those who currently perform these tasks. There is no intent to suggest that everyone should be performing all of these tasks.

Organizational Programs

Organizational programs, such as *Kidspiration* (Inspiration) or *Inspiration* (Inspiration), can help students and teachers organize their thinking. The software allows quick access to concept maps, webs, and other graphic organizers. The integrated outline view enables the user to quickly prioritize and rearrange ideas. Organizational programs are especially effective for brainstorming about future goals and objectives.

Banner and Poster Programs

Bulletin boards are an important element of the classroom and gymnasium environment. In the past, teachers without artistic skills were forced to either cut and paste magazine pictures or purchase commercial bulletin board displays. With a computer, anyone can easily produce professional looking bulletin boards. Several programs (including desktop publishing programs, described earlier in this chapter) can assist with this task. However, there also are specific banner and poster programs, such as *Print Shop® Pro Publisher* (Broderbund) and *PrintMaster®* (Broderbund).

Certificate Makers

AwardMaker® (Baudville) for the Macintosh and Windows environments makes creating your own certificates and awards a snap. The software contains a border library, prewritten text (or you can create your own), graphics, and award seals. It also comes with a variety of templates for various achievements. The physical educator selects the appropriate template and enters the appropriate information for each student. Or, if awards are being given to a number of students, then the built-in "mail merge" feature can speed up the process.

Calendar Programs

Calendar programs help you and your students create calendars and keep track of projects and activities. Depending on their size, you also can use these programs to keep track of lesson plans. Calendar programs to consider include single function programs such as *Now Up To Date* (PowerOn Software) or multi-task programs that also feature a calendar program, such as *Lotus Notes* (Lotus).

Puzzle Programs

Puzzle programs provide you with quick and easy ways to develop crossword puzzles, word searches, and other puzzles as learning activities. For example, *Crossword Puzzle Maker* (Crossword Weaver) is a popular, user-friendly program for making crossword puzzles of any size. The crossword puzzles can be viewed on screen or printed out. Other popular puzzle makers include *Crossword Studio* (Nordic Software) and *Wordsearch Studio* (Nordic Software). The word search program allows the user to create word puzzles in a variety of shapes and sizes. The teacher enters the words and/or definitions and the software creates the puzzles.

Testing

Your computer can help you construct written tests by storing and sorting your questions. You have the choice of using a word processing program, a data base program, or a packaged testing program that formats the test for you.

Test Designer Supreme for Windows (Super School Software) and *MicroTest* for Macintosh and Windows (Chariot) are test generating programs that give you a choice of formats, including multiple choice, matching, true/false, fill in the blank, puzzle questions (e.g., crossword puzzles), and short essay. *ExamView* (FSCreations) is a testing tool that lets you create a paper and online tests. This test generator is ideal for building tests, worksheets, and study guides (practice tests) in any subject. Using the online testing features, you can access numerous reports that help you focus on your students' learning needs.

QuizWiz (PalmTop Learning) is an easy-to-use program that lets the user create quizzes on any topic using flashcards, multiple-choice questions, or true/false questions. The quizzes are created using the Palm operating system's built-in memo pad and then imported to the program. After you have developed a battery of test items within one of these formats, the program will randomly select a desired number of questions based on topic, level of difficulty, and type of question.

Micro Test (Kendall Hunt) is a test generator for physical education that supports the *Looking Good, Feeling Good* textbook. It comes on a multi-platform CD-ROM for Windows and Macintosh. It has preformatted screens for easy entry of multiple choice, true or false, and matching questions. Tests may be created by picking questions manually from the question bank or automatically by the program. Questions can be categorized by chapter and question type as well as level of difficulty and key words.

FitSmart (Human Kinetics) is a 50-item, multiple-choice test designed to measure high school students' knowledge of basic fitness concepts. It is based on the National Youth Physical Fitness Knowledge Test. Students take the test online or from a printed form. Either way, the computer can grade the test using a weighted system. It also can convert raw scores to standard scores and provide feedback to students about the test results.

NASPE also has produced a computer-based test aligned with its *Concepts and Principles of Physical Education* book. It comes on a multi-platform CD-ROM for Windows and Macintosh. It has preformatted screens for easy entry of multiple choice questions. The test may be created by picking questions manually from the question bank or by adding your own. Questions are categorized by subdiscipline.

IEP Assistants

Individual Education Program (IEP) assistant applications can help special education teachers, including adapted physical educators, with the paperwork required by Federal Legislation. These programs provide on-screen prompts that remind users of the required components. They essentially provide a blueprint for each special student's instructional activities that is printed out on the required forms. Three popular programs for both Windows and Macintosh are *IEP Works Pro* (K-12 MicroMedia Publishing), *IEP Pro* (Chalkware Education Solutions), and *IEP Writer* (Super School Software).

IEP Works Pro helps teachers create an IEP in less than 15 minutes. With more than 1,300 goals and objectives, you can easily select those that are appropriate for your students and customize as necessary. IEP state-approved forms are available for a number of individual states.

IEP Pro provides most, if not all, the forms needed for the IEP process. But, just in case you need another form, district forms also can be designed using the text formatting and spell check functions in this program. Included in the program are 12,000 goals, objectives, and prewritten statements that can be searched using key words. These goals and objectives are then linked to the various IEP forms.

The IEP Writer is similar to *IEP Works Pro*, but it also includes special education program planning tools, inservice training materials for regular and special education teachers, and diagnostic checklists. Both programs allow data to be saved in a format that facilitates the writing of IEPs in subsequent years.

Electronic Gradebooks

Earlier in this chapter, I showed you how to set up grade files using spreadsheet programs. But you may prefer more user-friendly programs for recording grades. Grading programs prompt you for student names, test/assignment names, and grading practices. Then, you enter the grades and the program calculates the final grade for you. Grading programs also can create and print class lists and blank score sheets and produce progress reports.

There are a wide variety of grading programs on the market for teachers in all areas of the curriculum. Popular desktop grading programs that work for physical education include *Making the Grade* (Jay Klein Productions) and *Grade Machine* (Misty City Software). Popular handheld grading programs designed for physical education include *Record Book for Palm Operating System and Pocket PC* (Bonnie's Fitware) and *Companion* (Polar/Health First). Base your selection on the specific features and report formats you need. Just make sure the program you select can handle the number of students you have in each class and the total number of classes you teach.

Making the Grade (Jay Klein) accommodates multiple grading schemes, including points, letters, and symbols. Additional options include tracking attendance and behavior, weighting grades (up to 10 assignment categories), and arranging groups. The program has room for 80 students per class with 320 assignments and 250 days of attendance or behavioral data. All calculations are instantly and automatically updated on the screen. Data can be viewed in numerous formats, including a seating chart. A variety of reports can be generated in English or Spanish.

Grade Machine (Misty City Software), which is designed to look like a grade book, also accommodates multiple grading schemes defined by the teacher, including letter grades and points. Additional options include weighting grades, sorting students, using excused scores for long-term absences or late arrivals, and an automatic backup system. The program has room for 250 students, 250 assignments, 10 weighted categories, and 20 grading periods. Full-screen editing lets you scroll through students, assignments, or scores to enter and edit grades. *Grade Machine* generates progress reports for individuals, a certain category of students, or an entire class. This software program even allows you to post grades on the web.

Record Book for Palm OS/PocketPC (Bonnie's Fitware) allows for the collection of attendance, behavior, and grading information using the Palm operating system or the Pocket PC operating system. The program allows you to enter assignments, categorize assignments according to the standard assessed, weight assignments and standards, record grades, note absences and tardies along with behavior issues, and transfer the data to the computer where they are analyzed. Once analyzed, a number of different reports are available for print out.

Polar/Health First also has developed a software program entitled *Companion* that includes the monitoring of attendance, grading, fitness, and heart rate monitoring. It is sold with a PocketPC and, once licensed, the companion management software is accessed via the Internet at http://www.healthyschools.net.

Comparison Criteria for Grading Programs

- Customer support.
- Suitability for physical education.
- Documentation, tutorial, and online help.
- Cross-platform compatibility.
- Number of students per class.
- Number of assignments per class.
- Grading periods.
- Assignment categories.
- Overall grade summaries.
- Grading scales.
- Scoring options.
- Special scores.
- Easy score entry.
- Types of reports.
- Password protection.
- Importing and exporting features.

Physical Education Productivity

Physical education productivity software is specifically designed to simplify many tasks involved in teaching physical education—such as calculating the nutritional values of foods and monitoring fitness scores. Since students typically enter their own eating habits into the computer, nutritional software will be examined in Chapter 7. However, we will look at fitness monitoring software in this section.

One program, the *Physical Education Clipboard* (Bonnie's Fitware) is a multi-faceted program designed to meet all of the physical educator's miscellaneous needs. It is preformatted for the collection and maintenance of lesson plans, locker system information, video inventory, music inventory, equipment inventory, and master scheduling of physical educators.

Fitness Reports

Fitness reporting programs comprise one of the earliest uses of computers in physical education. These programs analyze raw fitness scores, print summaries, and store data for pre-/post-test comparisons. Fitness reporting programs can follow a student from kindergarten through twelfth grade, providing year-to-year comparisons. Raw scores can be analyzed quickly to provide information on student improvement. In addition, class averages for each test item allow you to ascertain if the instructional program is producing the intended learning outcomes. You can easily print a variety of reports, and you can send them home to keep parents up-to-date on their children's progress. Keep in mind, however, that entering data can be very time consuming unless you use some type of scanner or handheld computer.

Since the 1980s, a variety of software programs have been developed to monitor physical fitness data. Some of the more popular ones include *Fitnessgram* (Human Kinetics), *Fitness Report for Palm Operating System and Pocket PC* (Bonnie's

179

Fitware), and *MS Fitnesstracker* (MicroServices). Each program offers unique features. Choose the one that fits your needs, your computer, and the test items to be administered.

Fitnessgram (Human Kinetics). *Fitnessgram* focuses on health-related fitness, providing users with the option of pacer walk/ target heart rate or one-mile run for cardiorespiratory endurance; push ups, pull ups, modified pull ups, or flexed arm hang for upper body strength and endurance; curl ups for abdominal strength and endurance; trunk lifts for lower back strength and flexibility; back saver sit and reach or shoulder stretch for flexibility; and body mass index (calculated from height and weight data) or skinfold measurements (triceps and medial calf) for body composition. Data can be entered by keyboard or scanner, or it can be imported. The program outputs results onto a preprinted student report card with a graph showing which test scores were above or below the criterion level, the actual test score, an individualized exercise prescription for where the student's scores were low, a total fitness index, and a cumulative record of test results.

The program allows for one pre- and one post-test, with both scores written on the second fitnessgram. The back side of the fitness card has space for the student to record out-of-school activity levels. Reports include a class summary by student with test score. Statistics include number of students, mean score, standard deviation, highest score, lowest score, and percentage of students achieving the minimum standard for each test item.

Fitness Report for Palm OS/Pocket PC (Bonnie's Fitware). *Fitness Report for Palm OS/PocketPC* is available for Macintosh, Windows, Palm operating system, and Pocket PC. It includes several test batteries, including one that focuses on health-related fitness, providing users with the option of pacer, walk/target heart rate, or one-mile run for cardiorespiratory endurance; push ups, pull ups, modified pull ups, or flexed

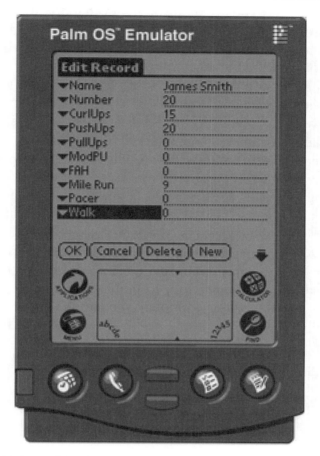

Figure 6.15 Bonnie's Fitware offers the option of collecting fitness scores while still on the field using the handheld computer.

arm hang for upper body strength and endurance; curl ups for abdominal strength and endurance; trunk lift for lower back strength and flexibility; back saver sit and reach or shoulder stretch for flexibility; and body mass index (calculated from height and weight data) or skinfold measurements (triceps and medial calves) for body composition. A President's Challenge version also is included as well as test batteries for individual states, including Missouri, California, Connecticut, and Virginia.

Input is by keyboard or through the handheld computer (Palm operating system (see Figure 6.15) or Pocket PC. The fitness pre-test printout (see Figure 6.16) shows the pre-test score, minimum standards, whether the student met the minimum standards, and the recommended improvement. It provides space for students to write their own goals for improvement. The fitness post-test printout includes the pre- and post- fitness scores, pre- and post- met or not met, and the minimum competency scores. The statistics program includes averages for each test item and the number of students meeting minimum standards on six out of six, five out of six, four out of six, three out of six, two out of six, one out of six, and zero out of six test areas. Reports that list class summary by students and scores also are available. This program does require that you have the current version of FileMaker Pro on your desktop computer.

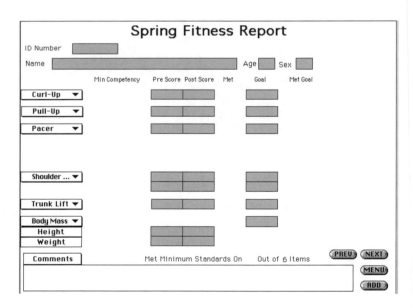

Figure 6.16 Bonnie's Fitware offers fitness reports for goal setting at the start of the school year (see above) and reports that include pre-test and post-test scores for the end of the school year.

Athletic Director and Coaching Software
Do You Also Coach?

Sports Director - Users can store and manage information about players, teams, leagues, coaches, officials, and other support personnel, including contact information, calendar, medical information, honors or awards, eligibility, and evaluations. The application manages and tracks information on facilities, equipment, and supplies. It also assists with the planning and scheduling of practices, contests, tournaments, and administrative appointments, as well as recording the results of contests and tournaments. *Sports Director* generates 36 reports, including athlete information and eligibility; uniform, supplies, and equipment inventory; game results and rankings; tournament brackets; player registration forms; and medical and parental consent forms.

Football Statistics - provides offensive, defensive, and special team statistics. Printed reports are available for single games and cumulative games for both individual and team statistics. Two-way transfer of data between handheld and Windows-based computer. Real-time offensive statistic summaries on the handheld.

Basketball Statistics - provides instant visual shot chart and statistical analysis. Generates printed reports that show team and individual shot charts and statistics for both teams. Runs on all handhelds using the Palm OS handhelds and interfaces with Windows and Macintosh-based computers.

Soccer Statistics - provides real-time screen summaries for team and individual statistics, and printed reports including shot charts. Runs on all Palm OS handhelds, 3.1 or higher, and interfaces with Windows-based computers.

Volleyball Statistics - provides real-time statistical summaries for teams and individuals. The printed report includes all statistics and attack charts. Users may choose from four levels of game tracking: Lite, Full, Pro, and No Chart.

Softball Statistics or Baseball Statistics - provides real-time statistical summaries for teams and individuals. The application runs on all handhelds using the Palm OS, 3.1 or greater, and interfaces with Windows-based computers.

*Available from Bonnie's Fitware Inc.

MS FitnessTracker (MicroServices). This Windows-based program is a data base application that electronically tracks President's Challenge fitness test scores. A wide variety of reports come with *FitnessTracker*, and by using the filtering and sorting options available for each report, you can tailor them to meet your own specific needs.

Evaluating Software

The important points to consider when selecting software are user friendliness, anticipation of user errors, error free programming, text and graphics that are easy to read, accuracy of content, and documentation. User friendly means the program is easy to use. Just as important as user friendliness is the software's ability to anticipate user errors. Programs that crash when the user makes an entry error are not as desirable as programs that let users know they have made an error and give them an opportunity to correct it.

It also is important that the program is sound—that it does what it is supposed to do. Programs with bugs, or programming errors, are very frustrating, especially to beginning users. Readability of the text and precision of the graphics also should be considerations when evaluating software. And—while this point is sometimes missed in the hype of the technology—it is important that the content in the software is accurate. You will find most documentation to be useful as long as you are willing to take the time to read it or use it when a problem occurs.

Summary

There are a number of software programs that can assist the physical educator with daily chores. These include word processing, data base, spreadsheet, grading, and fitness programs. Such programs can help you become more efficient—but only if you know how to take advantage of their many features. Why not take a course this year, or buy a book that includes a tutorial so you can take full advantage of the software you already own!

Reflection Questions

1. Considering that there are many free software programs available to educator—including web based, shareware, and public domain, why would an educator purchase a software program such as Crossword Magic?

2. How might the use of fitness reports help students to improve their daily levels of physical activity and physical fitness?

3. Which applications discussed in this chapter are you the least familiar with, and what can you do to become more familiar with them?

Projects

1. Create a spreadsheet based on your grading system.

2. Create a newsletter that describes your physical education program.

Chapter 7

Computer–Assisted Instructional Software

Students in a volleyball class are about to learn a new skill—the spike—and apply their skills to a game setting. The teacher has set up learning stations around the gymnasium. There are skill practice stations, fitness development stations, and a computer station where the spike is demonstrated. There also is a second computer station where students learn the 4-2 offense for volleyball.

I nstructional software (applications designed to provide instruction) enhances the learning process by setting up a direct interaction between student and computer. The computer allows students to proceed at a rate that is meaningful to them. It is forever patient, providing corrective feedback when needed and positive feedback when appropriate.

More than 30 research studies have found that the average learning time is reduced for 50 percent of the students who use multimedia instructional programs. Several studies also have shown 23 to 70 percent greater mastery in students who use interactive technology, as compared to students who use more traditional methods (Levin & Meister, 1986; Niemiec, Blackwell, & Walberg, 1986; Gu, 1996; Kulik, 1994). Students also show greater motivation and enjoyment when they use multimedia programs—they are actively involved and their attention is

Why Use Instructional Software in Physical Education?

- Provides students with the "why."
- Introduces students to motor skills techniques before they actually practice them.
- Provides simulation, problem-solving experiences, and practice with offensive and defensive situations that would not otherwise be available.
- Provides a logical sequence from simple to more complex concepts.
- Provides unlimited practice, review, and remediation.
- Provides feedback and reinforcement quickly and efficiently.
- Helps create a richer, more varied instructional setting.
- Meets a variety of student needs.
- Provides information, calculates answers, manages student progress, and prints out results.
- Programs are more easily updated than are other types of instructional material.
- Programs promote cooperation and collaboration among students, and good teachers can capitalize on these opportunities.

focused (Wilkinson, Pennington, & Padfield, 2000). Multimedia programs can be used for full-class presentations, small-group tutorials, and student projects. It is not unreasonable to expect that the textbooks of tomorrow will be multimedia interactive.

Before you use computer-assisted instructional software in your class, you need to do four things:

1. Identify the standard(s)/instructional objective(s) of the lesson or unit.
2. Determine the most appropriate teaching strategy, including instructional materials, for meeting the standard(s)/objectives of the lesson or unit.
3. If the instructional materials include technology, select the software that will best help students meet the objective(s).
4. Decide how best to incorporate instructional technology into the lesson.

Steps 1 and 2 are common procedures for planning any lesson. While you might consider any number of teaching strategies and instructional materials, there are several reasons for selecting instructional software. Once you decide to use software, you must select the specific application and plan your lessons. This chapter will introduce you to a variety of instructional programs, give you tips on how to evaluate them, and provide you with ideas for incorporating them into your lessons.

Instructional Software

There are several different types of instructional software on the market, including drill-and-practice programs, tutorials, analysis, reference, mind mapping, educational games, and simulations. Many have trial versions available for download from their web site. When selecting applications to review, follow the steps in the Selecting Instructional Software for Review. Then, use the assessment criteria in the Reviewing Software during the review process. To help you narrow your search, descriptions of each type of software and examples for physical education are provided in the following sections. Most programs cost between $25 and $100 per computer, although some are more expensive. All programs are available for Macintosh and Windows and can be used, at least partially, for grades four through 12, unless otherwise noted. Additional

Selecting Instructional Software for Review

1. Analyze your needs.
2. Specify your requirements (e.g., operating system, content).
3. Identify promising software.
4. Read relevant reviews.
5. Preview software.
6. Make recommendations.
7. Get post-use feedback.

examples are included at the end of this chapter and vendors are listed in Appendix A.

Drill-and-Practice Applications

Drill-and-practice applications can help students memorize facts, such as the rules of a sport. These programs provide computer-directed instruction, so the learner merely answers questions. The basic format of drill-and-practice applications are as follows: The student reads and responds to the questions presented by the application. The application then evaluates the student's response to each question, provides immediate feedback, and presents a summary performance report. Some drill-and-practice applications include graphics and video. Drill-and-practice applications have always been a very low level use of the computer, and today these applications pale in comparison to other applications. However, as a drill medium, the computer has some advantages. Just make sure the content of the application is important and is something students truly need to memorize. An example of this type of application follows.

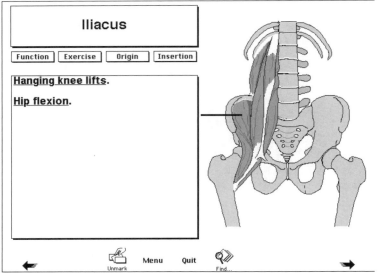

Figure 7.1 A screen from Muscle Flash (Bonnie's Fitware).

Reviewing Software

- The objectives are clear.
- The content is accurate.
- The program keeps track of how well students are doing.
- The program is easy to use.
- The program offers second chances when users respond incorrectly to questions.
- The program provides motivation.
- The program runs correctly (no bugs).
- The content moves from lower level objectives to higher level skills.
- Graphics are clear and appropriate.
- Sound is used to enhance program.
- The program makes effective and appropriate use of the computer as an instructional tool.
- The pace of the material can be controlled by the teacher or the student.
- The level of difficulty can be controlled by the teacher or the student.
- The student can easily access the program's "Help" function.
- The student is actively involved with the program.
- The program's instructional strategies are based on research findings.
- The presentation is free of any objectionable stereotyping.
- Inquiry processes are well integrated into the software package.
- The program's feedback responses are appropriate, informative, and timely.
- The program encourages two or more students to interact with one another.
- Program documentation is comprehensive, clear, and consistent with observed program behavior.
- It is available in both Macintosh and Windows formats/

Muscle Flash (Bonnie's Fitware). Muscle Flash (see Figure 7.1) is a flash card program designed to teach students the names of muscles. It displays a graphic of a single muscle and asks the student to identify it. Students receive feedback on the accuracy of their responses. There are five levels: Primary Muscle Flash,

Elementary Muscle Flash, Middle Muscle Flash, Senior Muscle Flash, and College Muscle Flash. The application also asks the muscle's location, function, and exercises for strengthening. In addition to self-testing, there also are four quizzes that can be assigned and the results recorded for the teacher.

Tutorials

Tutorial applications combine text, graphics, sounds, and videos to introduce new concepts. They also provide an opportunity for the students to interact with the application by answering questions. More sophisticated applications offer learners several options after each question is presented: enter an answer, review the topic, have the question asked differently, or select additional topics to explore. The application may even be able to evaluate the learner's performance and automatically adjust the difficulty level of future questions accordingly. Good tutorials should include one or more practice sequences.

Bowling Tutorial (Bonnie's Fitware). This application is designed to teach students how to score in bowling. It includes rules, symbols, and scoring for spares and strikes. *Bowling Tutorial* also allows student interaction through self-check questions and the scoring of a sample game.

Softball Basic Strategy Tutorial (Bonnie's Fitware). This application presents the basics of defensive softball strategy, including base coverage for infield and outfield hits. Students interact by clicking on the base where they would throw the ball in a given situation. The application provides the students with feedback and an opportunity to select another base.

Analysis Applications

Analysis applications add another level of interaction. Students input real or fictitious data directly or through probes, and the software conducts the analysis. Four types of analysis software

are used in physical education: nutritional analysis, risk assessment, exercise planning, and data collection.

Nutritional Analysis. Many nutritional analysis applications are currently available. These programs ask the user for age, weight, height, gender, and amount of physical activity, and then calculate the individual's nutritional needs. The user records the types and amounts of foods he or she eats daily, and the program creates a report that lists calories ingested, the nutrient values for all foods, and the total of all nutrients ingested. You can use these reports to determine if the student has met the recommended dietary allowances (RDA) and whether the number of calories ingested was excessive. Some programs allow the user to indicate the type and length of activity performed. The software then determines the number of calories expended for a specified amount of time and the relationship between caloric intake and caloric output.

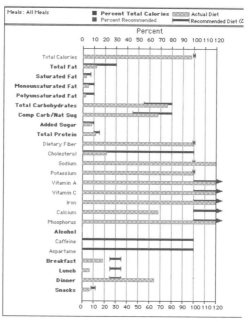

Figure 7.2 A screen from DINE Healthy (Bonnie's Fitware).

DINE Healthy (DINE Systems) exposes poor nutritional and fitness behaviors through its analysis of daily food intake and physical activity. Appropriate menus and exercises are recommended for a healthier lifestyle. The application serves as the student's personal trainer for fitness and nutrition. It is especially effective for students who desire a reduction in body fat, cholesterol level, and blood pressure.

Balance Log (HealtheTech) provides you with the opportunity to set personal nutrition and weight loss goals, track daily food consumption, and monitor progress on a handheld computer (Palm operating system). You can keep an accurate count of calories, carbohydrates, protein, fat, sodium, and fiber.

Risk assessment. Risk assessment programs ask the user to input data regarding his or her lifestyle. Questions include height, weight, gender, age, cholesterol level, blood pressure, smoking habits, alcohol usage, physical activity habits, family medical history, nutritional information, and use of seat belts. Based on the data received, the program determines the individual's life expectancy, cardiovascular disease risk, and/ or cancer risk. There are several shareware programs for risk assessment; as well as web-based software at sites such as http://www.bodybalance.com/hra/.

Exercise planning. Exercise planning applications can help a student develop an individual workout plan based on his or her current fitness level and physical activity goals. In addition to desktop/notebook versions, there also are software programs in this category that fit on a handheld or palm computer.

UltraCoach (FitCentric) is a Windows-based multi-sport athletic training program. It can provide students with a personalized workout program for cycling, running, swimming, inline skating, weight lifting, and/or aerobics, along with cross-training programs. It keeps track of all workouts, equipment, and routines, and gives feedback using graphs, charts, and reports.

For heart rate monitor users, it will produce heart zone training for warm-up, workout, and cool down based on manually entered data or data transferred from a Polar heart monitor. The program ensures that students do not overtrain, and therefore can reduce the chance of injury.

Physical Education Workout (Bonnie's Fitware) includes Cardio for Palm OS and Weights for Palm OS. Weights for Palm OS has been designed for rapid workout creation. Lifts, sets, and supersets can be created with little effort using 78 pre-defined lifts as well as user-defined lifts. Duration of rest periods between sets and lifts can be defined for each exercise. Users can maintain notes before and after each workout and export/import workouts to share with friends or clients. Weights for Palm OS replaces your handwritten workout journal with an electronic one, taking your workouts into the new millennium. Cardio for Palm OS does the same for your aerobic workout.

Management Tips

1. Teach students to respect and properly care for the equipment.
2. Have students bring their own CD-R to school to use for physical education.
3. Have the students write their name and their teacher's name on the label of the CD-R.
4. Teach students to use reasonable names to save projects.
5. Teach students to save their projects every five minutes while they are working.
6. Have students keep CD-Rs in storage boxes.
7. If your computer has enough memory or you are working from a   server, have students keep projects in folders labeled with their names.
8. Use a timer so students know how much time they can spend on   the computer.
9. Assign students to specific computers.
10. Provide task cards for each computer assignment and have computer helpers available to trouble shoot problems.

Interdisciplinary Lesson: Physical Education/ Science/Math/Computer Multimedia Project

Instructional Unit: Swimming/SCUBA.

Cognitive Concepts: Exercise physiology and biomechanics.

Facility: Swimming pool.

Supplies: SCUBA gear such as tanks and regulators, masks, snorkels, fins, boots, and gloves.

Interdisciplinary Concepts:

Physical education—application of swimming skills in the lifetime activity of SCUBA diving.

Diving physiology—effects of diving and pressure on the human body and its various systems.

Diving physics—gas laws and the connection between scientific laws and safe diving.

Navigation mathematics—navigation and orienteering. Gain insight into the geometry concepts used by everyone from divers to pilots to locate their position and direction.

Scientific laws—Boyle's law, Dalton's law, Henry's law, buoyancy.

Life science—marine life encountered by SCUBA divers.

Human physiology—effects of SCUBA diving on body temperature, senses, circulation system, respiratory system, oxygen debt in muscles, and balance or equilibrium.

Multimedia project—students work in small groups to do research, design experiments, and present their findings. Each student team prepares a project proposal for their desired topic. Completed projects are presented at the end of the term.

*Additional lesson examples are available in *Integrating Technology and Physical Education*—available from Bonnie's Fitware Inc.

Data collection. Motion measurement is the term used in biomechanics to describe the collection and analysis of two-dimensional and three-dimensional data. The data are collected using reflective markers, so that the movement is automatically recorded and analyzed by high-end computer systems. At the lower end, the performance is recorded and analyzed by the computer allowing the user to identify (usually through a mouse click) the location of joints in each frame. The data then are analyzed for factors, such as displacement, velocity, and acceleration. When recording for the purpose of quantitative analysis, be sure to:

- Record the motion at right angles to the camera.
- Physically move the camera back and use the zoom lens to frame the subject.
- Limit camera motion (including panning).
- Create a field of view two to three times larger than the subject.
- If the clip will be used for slow-motion replay then zoom in on the subject (Knudson & Morrison, 1997).

It also is very important to know the number of frames per second at which the video was recorded and the length (in inches) of a physical object in the field of view. These are the two variables that allow for the analysis of the data. The following three programs are appropriate for middle and high school students.

Dartfish Video (Dartfish) is available in a Windows-based professional model, standard model, and basic model. This software allows for a wide variety of analysis. But most significantly, it can overlay one student's performance on top of an expert's performance for comparison and it has drawing tools for illustrating proper technique. It uses StroMotion to break down performance frame-by-frame, and even has multi-play for comparison of two performances.

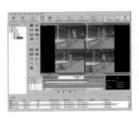

Figure 7.3   DartFish

The *Neat System* (Neat Sports) allows you to capture and analyze full motion video on any Windows-based PC. This system provides several graphic tools (line, circle, semi-circle, rectangle, parallelogram, angle, grid, pencil, back swing trace, and follow through trace) for isolating and highlighting positions on the video screen. The graphics appear over the video as it plays or advances frame by frame. The system also allows for the simultaneous playing of several video files. Users can select two-, three-, or four- window mode.

The *Peak Motus®* (Peak Performance Technologies) is another Windows-based motion analysis program. Its modular design allows users to select only those specific applications that they need. The Peak Motus Basic Video System collects video data at a maximum of 25 Phase Alternate Line (PAL) or 30 National Television Systems Committee (NTSC) pictures per second. The use of reflective markers is optional, and the system can provide two-dimensional and/or three-dimensional data as needed. The system is capable of calculating accurate and precise kinematic measurements.

Teaching Biomechanics

Biomechanics is the science of how and why movement occurs, and whether it is efficient. The Elements of Physical Education class covers the principles of gravity, stability-balance, Newton's Laws, force, types of motion, levers, projectiles, application of force and absorption of force. Students work in groups of four at learning stations as they study these principles. Each station has a task card that challenges students' motor, problem solving, and movement analysis skills. The textbook *Moving for Life* (Spindt et al, 1991) is used at one station, where the students read several paragraphs and answer two questions. At other stations, the students experiment with different motor skill techniques in order to determine the biomechanical principles involved. A computer station allows students to interact with the concepts, check their understanding with a quiz, and see the motion being studied.

–Carolyn Thompson, Bell Gardens High School

Reference Software

Reference software provides users with the opportunity to explore and retrieve information relevant to their learning. It runs the gamut from electronic encyclopedias, to medical CD-ROMs, to sport-specific software. In many of these programs, students enter search words and are presented with a number of related documents, graphs, tables, pictures, sounds, animated graphics, video clips, three-dimensional interactive tours, and/or interactive activities. Hypermedia (similar to the hyperlinks on the World Wide Web) frequently is used with reference software; it allows for interactive linking. Thus, access to reference software is nonlinear. Users can skip certain information and target the specific information they need.

Encyclopedia Britannica (Britannica). The standard edition is an interactive reference tool that features a comprehensive, visually-enhanced encyclopedia, dictionary, and world atlas - all in one resource. Using Britannica's renowned knowledge index and innovative search technology, students have a dependable tool to collect information on thousands of topics.

Other electronic encyclopedias include World Book Multimedia Encyclopedia–Deluxe Edition (World Book), which includes three-dimensional models of human anatomy and an online component for current downloads from the World Book web site, Encarta Encyclopedia (Microsoft), and Grolier Multimedia Encyclopedia (Grolier).

Elementary Physical Education Dictionary (Bonnie's Fitware). This A to Z dictionary addresses physical education terminology appropriate for grades two through six. It includes pronunciation, picture or animation, and description. It also contains quizzes to test student understanding of physical education vocabulary.

Awesome Athletes (Sports Illustrated). This Windows-based program uses a fun approach to teach students about the greatest athletes of all times. There are photos and facts about 250 athletes. Live action videos are combined with interviews. In addition, there are a number of games that test sports knowledge.

Soccer (Bonnie's Fitware). This comprehensive soccer instructional CD features: video demonstrations of drills and techniques, video discussion of strategies and tips, rules for the game, player positions and responsibilities, game tactics, and a printable playbook and reference manual.

Golf Tips (Bonnie's Fitware). This CD-ROM comes in two formats: *Golf Tips: Breaking 100*, and *Golf Tips: Breaking 90*. Both provide tips and techniques from the best golf instructors from around the world. Both are organized in four sections—5-Day Lesson, Analyze Your Trouble Areas, Build Your Own Golf Workshop, and Play the Hole—and are designed to provide a comprehensive instructional package. The *Breaking 100* application is recommended for middle school students and the *Breaking 90* application for high school students.

The 5-Day Lesson, Analyze Your Trouble Areas, and Build Your Own Workshop sections cover the same material, but in

Sample Instructional Stations for Golf

1. Video golf stroke
2. Review video of golf stroke*
3. Use Measurement in Motion to analyze golf stroke*
4. Practice putting
5. Practice driving
6. Practice golf stroke with peer feedback
7. Practice putting
8. Practice driving
9. Use *Golf Tips* software to review golf stroke
10. Practice golf stroke

* Do not start groups at stations two or three

different ways. The 5-Day Lesson covers more than 50 topics in a sequential, instructor-led form. Each day builds on the skills and techniques learned the previous day.

In Analyzing Your Trouble Areas, students can focus on a specific problem with a particular aspect of the golf game. For example, the software will organize a series of lessons around playing out of hazards.

In Building Your Own Workshop, the student designs his or her own workshop and customizes the learning. The student chooses the lessons he or she wants to pursue—such as hitting from a bunker—and clicks on related topics of interest as he or she progresses through the lesson. The CD includes 360-degree video clips, video clips (slow and normal motion), audio coaching cues, and photography sequences to assist with instruction.

Finally, Playing the Hole provides students with the opportunity to play a championship par five hole to test their knowledge of golf strategy and club selection. This virtual reality simulation of an actual hole enables the user to specify average score, choose a club, and then play the hole customized to his or her

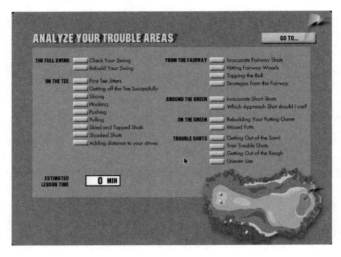

Figure 7.4 A screen from Golf Tips (Diamar).

skill level. The user receives feedback from the pros on club choices and strategies.

Olympic Gold (Discovery Channel). This Windows-based software provides a 100-year history of the summer Olympic games. It includes video, photos, and in-depth articles. Also included are individual and country-wide statistics relating to medals, times, and records.

My Amazing Human Body (DK). *My Amazing Human Body* is designed for students between the ages of six and 10. It presents information on human anatomy, health, nutrition, and much more. Students learn about their skeleton, organs, and body systems as they follow the activities of a specially created three-dimensional skeleton host. Activities include Build Me a Body, where students answer multiple-choice questions to earn bones and organs; What Am I Made Of, where kids examine, manipulate, and learn about 35 body parts; and Me and My Day, where students determine the events of the skeleton's day by selecting activities and meals. In Secret File, students record information about themselves such as favorite foods, height, and weight, as well as developmental milestones.

Ultimate 3-D Skeletal System (DK). This CD-ROM provides a medically accurate, three-dimensional digital skeleton. The software identifies every bone, shows every muscle attachment, pronounces every word, manipulates in three dimensions every bone in the human body, and shares a wealth of information pertaining to bones and the skeletal system. The three-dimensional images are derived from an x-ray scan of real bones. The detail of images is extremely fine; every small pit and crevice can be viewed. The name of each part of the skeleton is heard and viewed as the cursor is placed on it. The Amazing Facts section provides interesting information related to the bones and the Extra News section allows bones to be viewed from unusual angles. A quiz tests knowledge of the names of particular bones. Students may copy text, graphics, or an entire screen to the clipboard of their computer. An index allows access to any part of the program at any time. A teacher's guide offers supplemental activities and ideas for classroom use.

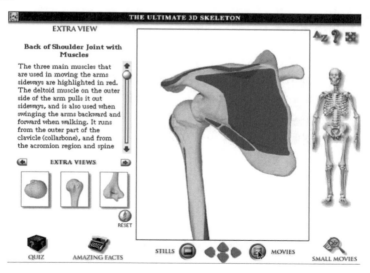

Figure 7.5 A screen from Ultimate 3-D Skeletal System (DK).

A.D.A.M. Essentials (A.D.A.M.). Designed for high school students, this CD-ROM contains a multimedia reference program on the fundamentals of human anatomy and physiology. The 12 body systems are described, along with each of their functions. There are more than 4,000 anatomical structures in approximately 100 medically accurate layers, along with 38 narrated animations on the inner workings of the body that include pronunciation of structure names. Students can participate in interactive puzzles and build different body structures. A complete teacher's guide with lessons for all body systems is included. Note: Genitalia can be covered using a fig leaf at the time of installation.

BioMechanics Made Easy (Bonnie's Fitware). This program instructs students on analysis of movement. It provides a reference section on each of the biomechanical principles (e.g., stability, projection, levers). In addition, there is a simulation section where students apply their knowledge in "real-life" situations and their performance is monitored and recorded.

Mind Mapping

Mind mapping software, including *Kidspiration* and *Inspiration* (Inspiration), *PicoMap* for Palm OS (Hi-Ce), and *Pocket PC MindMap* (JKRB Software), allows teachers and students to conceptualize and communicate ideas. The programs allows users to structure their ideas by enabling the drawing of a map with help boxes, graphics, and colors. Some of the possible project ideas for mind mapping software include:

1. Compare and contrast locomotor and nonlocomotor movements (see Figure 7.6):

2. Compare and contrast different aspects of fitness (see Figure 7.7):

3. Compare and contrast skills used in different sport (see Figure 7.8):

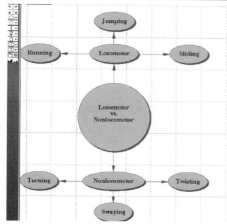

'Figure 7.6 A mind map comparing and contrasting locomotor and nonlocomotor movements.

Figure 7.7 A mind map comparing and contrasting different aspects of fitness.

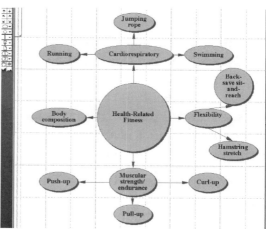

Figure 7.8 A mind map comparing and contrasting skills used in different sports.

Instructional Games

Instructional games usually contain rules for how questions will be answered or problems will be solved. A score keeping element, designed to increase student motivation, separates games from other types of computer-assisted instruction. Some educators may prefer not to encourage competition in learning; however, most of these programs can be set up so students compete against themselves or against a standard.

Football Rules Game (Bonnie's Fitware). The *Football Rules Game* uses a game-like setting to teach and/or reinforce touchdown rules. The game can be played by an individual or by two teams. The ball is kicked off by one team, and the receiving team gets the ball at the 25-yard line. The offense has four opportunities (questions) to move the ball across the next quarter line. The team can choose to answer a 5-yard, 10-yard, or 15-yard question. A correct answer moves the ball the number of yards indicated. If the team crosses the quarter line, they get a first down and four more opportunities to advance the ball. Otherwise, the other team gets possession of the ball and the chance to answer questions.

Softball Rules Game (Bonnie's Fitware). The *Softball Rules Game* is similar to the *Football Rules Game*. It uses a game-like setting to teach and/or reinforce softball rules. Students choose a single, double, or triple question. After three outs (incorrect answers), the other team gets a turn at answering the questions. Automatic outs are included with the single questions to prevent students from selecting only the easier questions.

Simulations

Simulations are the most sophisticated form of computer-assisted instruction. The computer is programmed with a definite number of rules related to an event. These are accompanied by extensive graphics to enhance the illusion of the actual situation. An event is presented, and based on

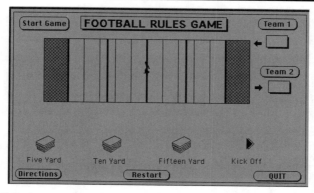

Figure 7.9 A screen from Bonnie's Fitware *Football Rules Game*. Students select 5-, 10-, or 15-yard questions to answer. If their answer is correct, the ball advances that many yards.

the user's interaction with the program, different results are obtained. Simulations are ideal for teaching problem solving and decision making, especially in situations where the real event can be dangerous or expensive. The strength of simulations is that they simplify circumstances in order to highlight special conditions and create realistic problem solving environments. A weakness is that they may be oversimplified and some details may be omitted, giving the user a false impression of reality. Simulations also may provide a false sense of accomplishment, since a high score on a simulation does not guarantee a high score in the real situation.

Sim Athlete (Bonnie's Fitware). Instructs students on how to develop their own practice plan. *SimAthlete* provides a reference section on each of the motor learning principles. It also has a simulation section where students can assume the role of a coach and develop a practice plan for an athlete. If they create an effective practice plan, their athlete performs well. If their plan is ineffective, then their athlete performs poorly. The scores for the simulation are recorded so teachers can monitor student progress.

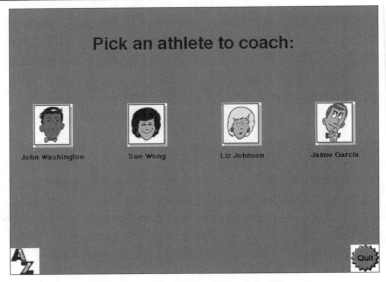

Figure 7.10   A screen from *SimAthlete* (Bonnie's Fitware).

Virtual Reality

Virtual reality is defined as "a computer-generated 3 D experience in which a user can navigate around, interact with, and be immersed in another world in real time, or at the speed of life" (Briggs 2002, p. 35). Instructional materials (diagrams, models, textbooks, videos, software, laserdiscs) have augmented physical education instruction in grades K-12, and now virtual reality is another type of instructional material holding *promise* for the future. That promise comes in the form of: 1) greater student learning related to NASPE's (2004) *Physical Education Standards*, 2) increases in student motivation for learning, and 3) fewer student accidents in the learning environment. Albeit the research is not definitive; virtual reality does appear to be an ideal training medium (Weiss & Jessel, 1998; Haggerty, 1999). And, as Normal (1993) notes after years of learning studies, motivation to learn may well be more powerful than even the cognitive variables. One need only look at the entertainment industry to see how successful it is at getting adolescents engaged in activities.

Dance Dance Revolution (available from Bonnie's Fitware). A dancing simulator based on the popular coin-operated game. Users mimic dance steps by following onscreen cues. Special workout mode provides aerobic exercise routines for players. Wide variety of contemporary dance music includes pop, disco, techno, and hip-hop. Single-player modes, as well as cooperative and competitive multiplayer modes. It includes software and interface dance pad.

NetAthlon (FitCentric). Uses multi-disciplinary technology to enable users of indoor fitness equipment to train or compete in a realistic immersive outdoor training environment and have their training data auto stored. FitCentric pioneered the concept of virtual reality athletic training in 1997 with *UltraCoach VR,* which provided users of exercise machines the ability to simulate outdoor reaction activities in a 3D real-time virtual environment. Three years of research and development have produced *NetAthlon™*, FitCentric's second generation of virtual athletic training system with many new features and improvements, including the support of multi-sport systems (e.g., cycling, running, rowing, stepping/climbing, and cross-country skiing); real-time feedback using realistic and motivating real-time visual, audio, and tactile (resistance) feedback, and real-time data display.

Using Instructional Software

Once you have selected the appropriate software for the learning objective, you must determine how best to incorporate it into the lesson. Of course, it is important that you feel comfortable using a computer for your own purposes before you try to use one for instruction with students.

Your first experience using instructional software may simply involve typing notes into a word processing or presentation document and projecting the information onto a screen through a projection system or television set. (This use of the computer can help to increase your technology comfort level, but it does not address the requirements of the fourth step listed at the start of this chapter—selecting the best method of incorporating computer-assisted instructional software into a lesson.)

You have at least four options for using instructional software. The first three require one computer (although for the third method a few more would be better); the last option requires a computer lab. For Method 1, you connect the computer to a projection system or to several 25-inch monitors. This method is used for class activities, with class members taking turns reading the tutorial part of the software. During the question-and-answer phase of the program, individual students are called on to answer questions, or, better yet, a cooperative learning strategy called "numbered heads" is used—students work in groups of four and collaborate within their groups to determine the correct answers to randomly asked questions. This is called numbered heads because each student is given a number from one to four, and the teacher calls out a number instead of a student's name. This technique should be used only when you want to cover a small piece of information with the entire class at the beginning of a lesson. It is not recommended for an entire class period.

Method 2 requires that you set up learning stations, including one computer station. A few management tips for student use of the computer will facilitate the process. Students work in cooperative learning groups of four students each, rotating from one station to the next. Each student should be assigned a role—for example, navigator (controls the movement through the software), encourager (reinforces the contributions of the other individuals in the group), expander (elaborates on answers given by other members), and summarizer (brings closure to group learning). Method 2 is used most commonly in physical education because it allows for a high percentage of time on

Biomechanics Sample Worksheet

Principle assigned:

Using *Biomechanics Made Easy*, look up your assigned principle. List the concepts and examples for each principle.

Principle stated:

      Rule   **Example**

Remember for each concept listed, you need to create one station that reinforces the concept.

You need to include the following to support your station:
• instructions for each station
• study card for each principle and concept
• worksheet for your principle and concept
• assessment sheet
• a list of other activities or exercises to support your principle

Taking Screen Pictures for Task Cards

Macintosh

Press the command key, shift key and the number 3 simultaneously
- listen for the click.
The image will save to your hard drive with the name PICTURE X.
x = number

Windows

Press the Print Screen (PrtSc) button on the top of your keyboard.
The image saves to the clipboard. Use Edit->Paste in Paint to paste
the image and save it.

task and keeps students physically active during most of the
lesson. However, the actual amount of time spent with the
computer is rather limited, so students should be directed to
either follow task cards, respond to a series of questions, or
conduct specific research. This method also can be structured
to provide additional computer opportunities for those students
who have medical excuses.

Method 3 is similar to Method 2, in that it uses one computer
station. However, in this method, the groups that are not
using the computer are preparing to do so. For example,
students prepare their tumbling routines on paper, then
use the computer to input their routines and view a visual
representation. Students then can evaluate and refine their
routines. Another example of this method is for a sport like
orienteering in which students learn, in expert groups, various
elements needed for orienteering. The computer program
simulates an actual experience. Method 3 should be used
only when students have time to prepare for what they will
be doing on the computer.

In Method 4, each student or pair of students must have
access to a computer, and each computer must be supplied
with the software, either individually or by a network. There

are three situations in which Method 4 is recommended: The first is when the objective for the lesson requires the use of the software for an extended period. The second is when students have computer lab time during the school day, separate from their other classes, and the lab teacher is open to using a variety of software (including physical education software) to teach students computer skills. Finally, the lab setting can be used when students create multimedia projects during out-of-school time or technology class. These projects might be specific to physical education or they might be interdisciplinary in nature. All uses of technology bring your students closer to meeting the technology standards for K-12 students.

Summary

Instructional software—including drill-and-practice, tutorial, analysis, reference, mind mapping, educational games, and simulation programs —is available to physical educators. And, even though we would like to see more high-quality instructional programs, there is much that we can do with the software that is available. Our students will benefit from learning health-related cognitive concepts, viewing model skill performances, interacting with sport-related experiments, and investigating up-to-date fitness information.

Make sure you are using all of the instructional resources available to you, including instructional software.

Reflection Questions

1. Why do you think there are fewer instructional programs for physical education than there are for other subject areas?
2. Which strategy will you use when incorporating instructional software in your lessons? Why did you choose this strategy?

Projects

1. Secure a trial version of one application. Design a lesson plan. Be sure to align the lesson with one or more of the National Standards.

2. Outline an application you would like to see designed. Be sure the objectives of the application align with the design. Consider submitting your outline to a software publisher for review.

Motor Skill

Backyard Baseball (available from Bonnie's Fitware) - Select teammates from a group of neighborhood personalities. Each team is augmented with kid-sized versions of pro players. Once your team is in place you can play the actual game on-screen.

Backyard Basketball (available from Bonnie's Fitware) - Kids are able to move, pass, shoot, steal, jump, and in defense situations, switch players (on offense, kids control whoever has the ball).

Backyard Football (available from Bonnie's Fitware) - Choose a field to play on, set the weather conditions, and decide what rules you want to use. Then pick your team and get ready to play. Once the basics are mastered you can learn more advanced tricks, like tapping the mouse button to throw a pass with a high arc versus holding the button down to throw in a straight line. You can lead your receivers, perform fake punts, put specific players in specific positions for every play, and do just about everything else.

Backyard Soccer (available from Bonnie's Fitware) - In addition to picking a team, players also choose a team name, playing surface, one of three levels of game difficulty, and duration. Once the team is in place you can play the actual game on-screen.

Backyard Hockey (available from Bonnie's Fitware) - Teams up with the National Hockey League to bring you kid versions of goal-scoring, fast-skating and puck-passing players. Create the lineup, customize a team, take the ice, and get ready for action.

Golf Resort Tycoon (available from Bonnie's Fitware) - Design a golf resort and maximize resources to attract more guests.

Real Pool (available from Bonnie's Fitware) - Play a real game of pool using the mouse as the cue stick.

Sailing Simulation (available from Bonnie's Fitware) - Learn how to sail using this simulation.

Virtual Pool (available from Bonnie's Fitware) - Billiards simulation.

Volleyball Complete (Bonnie's Fitware) - Provides information on volleyball for all eight subdisciplines. Includes a portfolio section where students can record their learning related to volleyball.

Biomechanics Concepts

Volleyball Complete (Bonnie's Fitware) - Provides information on volleyball for all eight subdisciplines. Includes a portfolio section where students can record their learning related to volleyball.

World of Sports Examined (available from Bonnie's Fitware) - Incredible graphics give users a close look at the body as it performs in different sporting events from around the globe. The Success in Sport section utilizes role-playing games where users are challenged to design training programs, work the muscles, and jump over hurdles as they answer questions.

Motor Learning Concepts

Volleyball Complete (Bonnie's Fitware) - Provides information on volleyball for all eight subdisciplines. Includes a portfolio section where students can record their learning related to volleyball.

World of Sports Examined (available from Bonnie's Fitware) - Incredible graphics give users a close look at the body as it performs in different sporting events from around the globe. The Success in Sport section utilizes role-playing games where users are challenged to design training programs, work the muscles, and jump over hurdles as they answer questions.

Social Skills

Choices, Choices (Tom Synder) - Kids face difficult choices every day, balancing their own values with the expectations of friends, parents, and teachers. *Choices, Choices* helps students develop the skills and awareness they need to make wise choices and to think through the consequences of their actions. K-6.

Inspire! **Team Building and Group Development** (available from Bonnie's Fitware) - This volume of *Inspire!* includes 20 activities for teaching effective group communication and team-building skills. The activities on this CD-ROM address critical thinking, leadership, collaboration, individual self esteem, competition, group dynamics, and team confidence. Includes 20 activities for helping youth learn team building and group development. Using interactive multimedia, *Inspire!* shows you how to set up, lead and process each activity. In addition to watching and hearing video, you can read and print instructions for any activity.

Physical Activity and Fitness

Fuel Nutrition Software (available from Bonnie's Fitware) - One of the most revolutionary analytical tools available to help trainers and nutritionists effectively analyze nutrition and energy needs for clients.

Health-Related Fitness (Bonnie's Fitware) - Knowledge base covering all the frequency, intensity, time, and type (FITT) concepts. Program also allows students to create their fitness portfolio.

Media Pro (ADAM) - Contains over 2000 anatomical clinical illustrations for use in presentations and on Internet pages.

Pyramid Challenge (available from Bonnie's Fitware) - Uses the food pyramid to instruct children about food choices.

Pyramid Explorer (available from Bonnie's Fitware) - This CD-ROM is full of fun and education for ages 10-100! Four game-like modules are loaded with nutrition information and interaction. Hunt for Red Tomato and other foods in a grocery store scavenger hunt, or scour a kitchen for some healthy eats in Cupboard Quest. Then discover answers to nutrition questions in Pyramid Mysteries and 3-Square. A complete teacher's guide includes activities for reinforcing the *Pyramid Explorer* concepts. Use in classrooms, libraries, computer tech labs, homes—this state-of-the-art nutrition resource should be added to every collection. Each CD-ROM includes both Mac and PC versions. Package includes: CD-ROM software with four modules, teacher guide plus reproducibles.

Ultimate Human Body (DK) - Overview of the systems of the body.

Historical Perspectives

An Olympic Journey: The Story of Women in the Olympic Games (Amateur Athletic Foundation) - Women in the Olympics.

Sports Illustrated for Kids (Creative Multimedia) - Information on the history of 50 major sports.

Chapter 8

Assessing Student Learning

Jeremy Washington works in a small K-8 school. Because he is the only physical educator, he has the same students for nine consecutive years. At the beginning of each school year, Jeremy records his students and stores the clips in individual electronic portfolios. The older students record their own clips and transfer the images to their portfolios. They also review their images through the years and write essays describing their progress. Finally, they analyze their strengths and weaknesses, and indicate how they can improve their performances.

A quality physical education program provides meaningful learning experiences for all students. Physical educators in such programs assess student learning, analyze assessment data, and use the assessment analysis to plan future learning experiences. However, because many physical educators teach hundreds of children every week, documenting their learning can be a real challenge. What they need is an efficient and effective means for recording and analyzing assessment data.

Technology can definitely help make assessment an easier task. Some aspects of computer-assisted assessment were described in Chapters 4, 6, and 7 in the sections on fitness assessment, spreadsheets, grading programs, programmed instruction, and motion analysis. This chapter focuses on more authentic assessment methods, including using technology to assess performances, create projects, and maintain portfolios.

Assessing Performances

Authentic assessment requires students to apply skills, knowledge, and attitudes to real-world situations. These authentic tasks tend to motivate students, since the value of their work goes beyond the demonstration of competence in school, and relates to their actual lives and futures. If your standards are written so that they are observable, measurable, and require evidence of students' ability to create new knowledge or apply skills in new situations, then the development of assessment tools will be a relatively easy task. The key to assessment is that there is a match between an assessment tool and each standard.

The *Rubricator* software program (New Measure) is designed to assist with this process. *Rubricator* is a template for designing performance assessments and indicators aligned with standards, and rubrics (descriptions of qualitative levels of performance on specific tasks) aligned with indicators. It also is an organizer for assessing content standards, performance tasks, performance checklists, scoring rubrics, and self-reflection questions/statements.

Rubistar (High Plains Regional Technology in Education Consortium) is another tool to help you create your own rubrics or checklists in English or Spanish from any of several templates. It contains prompts for different subjects areas and grade levels (www.4teachers.org/projectbased).

Student Projects

In Chapters 2 and 3, we considered student use of videocassette recorders and camcorders for student projects. In this chapter, we will look at student projects that involve the use of the computer. Projects require students to create products from their research. Students find projects very motivational, since projects often provide them with an opportunity to select their own topic for study, use skills associated with their primary intelligence, and demonstrate creativity. Projects also promote self-reliance and reflection, since students must assume responsibility for determining when their projects are complete and ready for display.

A number of physical educators across the country are beginning to require their students to create multimedia projects. However, their situations vary widely. Some physical educators have only one computer in their department, others have one computer per teacher, while still others have access to complete computer labs. Their instructional strategies also vary. Some teachers have students rotate through a series of learning stations, one of which involves the use of a computer. Other teachers have students create their own projects using different media (e.g., one group uses the computer, one group uses a video camera, one group uses markers and chart paper). Still others have students create multimedia projects—by themselves, in small groups, or as a class project.

Student projects, or project-based learning, allows teachers to assess student learning and provides feedback for students. Moursund (1998) has defined several key elements for project-based learning:

- Learner-centered lessons: Students should have a choice in the selection of the projects.
- Authentic content and purpose: The project should be linked to real world work.
- Challenging: The project should require students to put forth an extra effort.
- Product for presentation or performance: Once completed, the project should be presented to the teacher, other students, parents, and possibly even the community at large.
- Collaboration and cooperative learning: Whenever possible, projects should be developed in groups to facilitate collaboration and cooperation skills.

- Teacher facilitation: The teacher should assume the role of advisor, or the "guide on the side," as opposed to the "sage on the stage."
- Rooted in constructivism: The individual learner should construct his or her own knowledge by building on current knowledge. Thus, each group may require different information to complete its project, depending on the group members' current understanding and the depth of the project.
- Explicit educational goals: Students should be expected to learn specific technology skills as well as cognitive, social, and psychomotor skills related to physical education.
- Incremental and continual improvement: Students should receive ongoing encouragement to improve their projects and not to be satisfied with their first efforts.

In order to ensure that your students' projects include the key elements, consider the Project Design Steps. Each of the 12 steps are crucial in order to ensure continual learning and improvement.

The possibilities are endless when students use computers to develop their projects. They can combine text, still images, digitized sound, and digitized video clips (see Chapter 3). In addition, various software programs—from presentation software, to animation software, to authoring software—can help them bring the entire project together.

Software

There are four types of software that can be used to create student projects. They are presentation, animation, authoring, and web authoring tools. Presentation software, such as *PowerPoint* (Microsoft) or *Keynote* (Apple), provides the user with a template on which to create an electronic slide show. Students

Project Design Steps

1   The teacher sets criteria for the project and lets students know his/her expectations.
2. Students brainstorm and determine the type of project, the subject, and the audience.
3. Students write a proposal to present their ideas.
4. Students confer with the instructor regarding their proposal.
5. Students present their proposal to the entire class or another group if class size is large, and revise it based on feedback from the group.
6. Students create a script and storyboard for their project.
7. Students confer with the instructor regarding their script and storyboard.
8. Students conduct research using the Internet, CD-ROMs, and books.
9. Students complete their project.
10. Students confer with the instructor regarding their project and make revisions based on teacher feedback.
11. Students demonstrate their project to the entire class and revise it based on feedback from the group.
12. Students add their project to their personal portfolio.

can incorporate text, graphics, videos, and/or sound on each slide. In addition, they can choose the type of transition and the timing between the slides.

Animation software allows the user to combine a large number of still images in sequence to create a moving image. This is the same process used for animated cartoons. Computer programs such as *LifeForms* (available from Bonnie's Fitware) and *Poser*

Electronic Project

Students develop an electronic presentation to help other students learn the basic skills of ...

The project must include:
- An introduction page with title.
- One page for each of the five basic shots in the game of ...
- A picture demonstrating the critical elements for each skill.
- Three tips or cues for each shot.

(available from Bonnie's Fitware) are available to help you with the process as well as with the design of human figures. The process involves creating the first frame and the tenth frame (or wherever a major change occurs) to be used in the animation. The program then fills in the middle frames, adjusting for the changes that will take place. Continue the process for the rest of the sequence, and you end up with an animation segment for your program. This software can be used for an array of projects ranging from illustrating a motor skill technique, to illustrating a movement technique, to creating dance performances, to creating tumbling routines.

Authoring software, such as *HyperStudio* (Knowledge Adventure) and *Director* (Macromedia), let you bring together in one package text, still images, animation, sound, analog video, and digital video. While presentation and animation software allow for a linear presentation, authoring software uses buttons or "hot spots" that let the user create a variety of pathways (known as hypermedia) to move through the program. Buttons are most commonly used to link one screen to another, but they can provide for other actions as well. The action is determined by the designer, and might include playing sounds, displaying images, asking questions, playing video clips, checking for correct answers, displaying animations, or performing calculations—almost anything that you can imagine.

Project-based learning involves creating a product for presentation to others. What better way to share one's product than by posting it on the World Wide Web! This can be accomplished in several ways. Some of the programs mentioned above—including *PowerPoint*, *HyperStudio*, and *Director*—create files that can be posted on the web using a "plugin." The second method is to use a web authoring program, such as Adobe *GoLive* or Macromedia *Dreamweaver*, to create web pages (see the web section in Chapter 10). If your school does not have its own server for posting work, you can use one of several existing web

Fair Use Guidelines for Educational Multimedia

Educational uses include:
- Student multi-media creations.
- Faculty-produced curriculum materials.
- Distance learning—provided that only their students access it.
- Demonstrating multi-media creations at professional symposia.

- **Motion Media** - up to 10 percent or three minutes, whichever is less.
- **Text** - up to 10 percent or 1,000 words whichever is less.
- **Poems** - up to 250 words. Three-poem limit per poet; five-poem limit per anthology.
- **Music** - Ten percent or 30 seconds, whichever is less.
- **Photos/Images** - up to five works from one author; up to 10 percent or 15 works, whichever is less, from a collection.
- **Data base information** - up to 10 percent or 2,500 fields or cell entries, whichever is less.

All other uses are protected by U.S. copyright law. Software, music, and graphic arts publishers are serious about enforcing copyright laws and will prosecute offenders.

Web Design Guidelines for Students

1. Start small.
2. Add material gradually.
3. Create one main folder for your entire site.
4. Create a separate folder inside the main folder for each major category of information.
5. Create one folder named "images" inside your main folder.
6. Keep each level to 5 to 10 items.
7. Develop a plan for maintenance and updates.
8. Put contact information (name, address, telephone, and fax numbers) on each page.
9. Include an e-mail link on each page.
10. Add new content weekly.
11. Check all links weekly.
12. Use a consistent look and feel.
13. Put navigation on each page.
14. Use no more than three images per page.
15. Put no more than two screens of information on each page.
16. If you must use more than two screens of information, provide a menu at the top of the page.
17. Design for 72 dpi, 256 colors, RGB, and 640x480.
18. Load time for a page should not exceed 30 seconds.
19. Test all pages on two browsers—Netscape/Explorer—and on two platforms—Macintosh/Windows.
20. Linked text should not exceed 20 percent of a passage.

sites where student work can be posted for free (see Web Design Resources). Be sure to check your school's policy regarding the posting of student work.

Whichever software program is chosen, it is imperative that a storyboard be designed first. The storyboard is a paper display of what the project will look like once it is finished. I have found it most helpful to give students a stack of 3x5 or 5x8 cards. They use one card per anticipated screen. Each card illustrates the general layout of the screen, including sketched illustrations and written text. When creating a web site, write the name of the particular file on the card. Instruct students to be as detailed as possible at this stage.

Developing Projects in Physical Education

Project-based learning can be used as an end-of-the-year activity, with students researching and presenting information on a unique sport. Other methods for creating projects related to physical education, include:

- Interdisciplinary projects where physical education is the content, language arts is the process, and technology is the means.
- Homework assignments where students work on their projects during out-of-school time and use computers in the media center or computer lab during after-school hours.

Students need not limit their projects to sports. They might focus on one of the following topic areas:

- Tumbling routines
- Stretching techniques
- New games
- Dance routines
- Sports nutrition
- Sports medicine
- Rules of the game
- Weight training
- Healthy hearts
- Motor learning concepts
- Motor skills
- Biomechanic concepts
- Historical perspectives
- Sport strategy

Web Design Resources

Clip Art
clipart.com   http://www.clipart.com
Icon Bazaar   http://www.iconbazaar.com

Audio Clips
Sound Central   http://www.soundcentral.com

Video Clips
Video Collection   http://www.videocollection.com

Animation Clips
Animation Factory   http://www.animfactory.com

Posting
GeoCities   http://www.geocities.com/
Teacher Web   http://www.teacherweb.com/

Electronic Portfolios

A student's portfolio is similar to an artist's portfolio, and can contain a wide range of materials (e.g., plans, projects, scores) that indicate progress toward the identified grade level standards. Too often, when physical educators first begin to use portfolios, they have their students create collection portfolios that include everything they have done throughout the year. However, the goal of portfolios is actually for each student to develop a performance portfolio—a purposeful collection of work that demonstrates that student's efforts, new learnings, emerging insights, progress, and achievement over time. Some of the work will be from earlier in the year and some from later in the year. Most of the work should be selected by the student; however, some teachers like to designate certain required items. Typically six to 10 pieces of work are selected for each student's portfolio. Most portfolios also include an end-of-the-year reflective essay, in which the student comments on his or her progress during the year.

At the end-of-the-year, the portfolio provides the teacher and student with concrete information for discussion of his or her progress and the setting of goals for the next year. During the end-of-the-year conference, the teacher should ask students to

Multimedia Projects in Physical Education

At the end of each school year, I conduct an eight-week Technology in Physical Education instructional unit for my eighth grade students. During this unit, the students select one sport that is unfamiliar to them to research. They use *HyperStudio* to create multimedia projects that demonstrate their learning, and they practice the skills related to the sport. This instructional activity assesses student progress toward National Standard 1 as the students work on their motor skills for the new sport, and National Standard 2 as they apply motor learning and biomechanical principles.

-Carol Chesnutt,
1997 NASPE Southern District Middle School Teacher of the Year

explain the connection between the grade level standards and the pieces of work they selected to demonstrate their learning. This process will help students understand how learning occurs. Students also may be asked to share their work with their parents during end-of-the-year parent conferences. In many schools, the teacher takes a secondary role during these conferences, while students explain their own progress to their parents. This is also an opportunity for students to reflect on their work and celebrate their learning (Mohnsen, 2003b).

Electronic portfolios are an extension of the paper portfolio. Students can store text, graphics, video clips, and audio clips along with complete multimedia projects. The electronic version provides both students and teachers with a means of tracking and accessing large amounts of data from a variety of formats in a short period of time. For example, video is ideal for documenting growth in physical education, but it can be cumbersome to store videotapes and time consuming to access a particular clip, unless the images are digitized and stored in an electronic portfolio. Once digitized, students can view pre- and post-clips and write an essay describing the differences and how they illustrate personal growth. Other items commonly placed in an electronic portfolio include motor skill rubrics, fitness scores, biomechanical analysis of skills, social rubrics, and personalized motor and movement learning plans.

Physical education classes across the United States range from 20 to 80 or more students per class. Physical educators who wish to use electronic portfolios often are faced with time constraints and limited access to computers. For individualized portfolios to be successful, a physical educator must have access to at least one computer for every eight students, or access to a computer lab. In the former case, students form eight groups and rotate through a circuit. The circuit's computer station contains a computer for each student. Physical education teachers with access to a computer lab send their students to the lab on a rotating basis. In the lab, students enter data into their personal portfolios. At the end of the year, the electronic portfolio provides the teacher and student with concrete information to use in discussing progress and setting goals for the following year.

Portfolio Applications

Students can use one of three methods to create electronic portfolios. They can use authoring software, discussed earlier in this chapter. This method requires that students create not only the work that goes into the portfolio, but also the structure for collecting that work. They can use one of several generic electronic portfolios on the market that are used by a number of subject-area teachers — *GradyProfile* (Aurbach & Associates) or The *Portfolio Assessment Kit* (Super School Software). All of these programs are capable of capturing illustrations and writing samples, evaluations and observations, student reflections, self-assessments, and parent observations. The third method involves using portfolio templates specifically designed for physical education. Currently, three such templates are on the market, and there are plans for additional sport-specific versions.

Health Related Fitness Tutorial/Portfolio (Bonnie's Fitware). The *Health Related Fitness Tutorial/Portfolio* is a two-part program (see Figures 8.1 and 8.2). The first part is a tutorial on health related fitness that incorporates hypermedia so students can locate specific areas of interest. It includes cognitive concepts related to principles of fitness, safe versus dangerous exercises, training protocols, taking one's pulse, and warm-up/cool-down procedures, along with a variety of exercises for each fitness area. The second part is an electronic portfolio where students enter fitness scores, select exercises, calculate caloric input/output, produce drawings or video clips, write journal entries, and design fitness plans. The program is set up to record fitness scores for pull ups, push ups, modified pull ups, flexed arm hang, curl ups, back saver sit and reach, shoulder stretch, trunk lift, mile run, pacer, body mass index, and skinfolds.

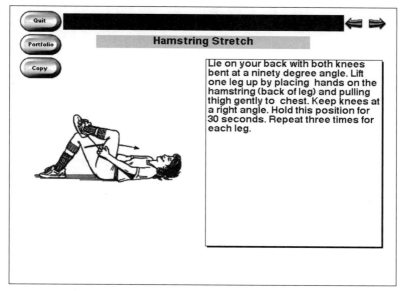

Figure 8.1 A screen from *Health-Related Fitness Tutorial/Portfolio - Tutorial Stack* (Bonnie's Fitware).

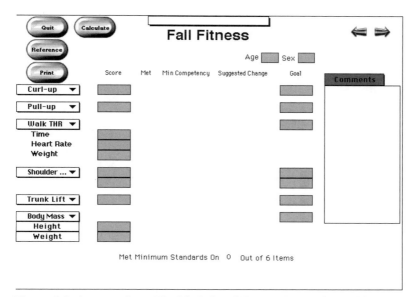

Figure 8.2 A screen from *Health-Related Fitness Tutorial/Portfolio - Portfolio Stack* (Bonnie's Fitware).

Skills

Figure 8.3 A screen from *Volleyball Complete* (Bonnie's Fitware).

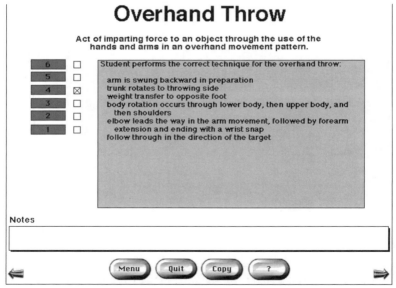

Figure 8.4 A screen from *Physical Education Portfolio* (Bonnie's Fitware).

Volleyball Complete (Bonnie's Fitware). This portfolio (see Figure 8.3) relates each of the eight subdisciplines of physical education (exercise physiology, motor learning, biomechanics, psychology, motor development, aesthetics, sociology, and historical perspectives) to the teaching of volleyball. This is a two-part application, similar to the *Health Related Fitness Tutorial/Portfolio*. One part is a tutorial, and the second part is a portfolio. Using the tutorial part, teachers and students can access and interact with information on volleyball skills, techniques, strategies, training, and teamwork. Then, using the portfolio part, students enter journal writings, interactive activities, rubrics for volleyball skills, and video clips. This two-part sport concept will continue to expand, with additional titles added each year (softball and bowling are already on the drawing board).

Physical Education Portfolio (Bonnie's Fitware). This portfolio (see Figure 8.4) is formatted around the eight subdisciplines of physical education. Students can enter fitness scores, journal entries, and video clips. It also contains rubrics for basic movement (run, hop, skip, etc.) and motor (throw, catch, kick, etc.) skills. Students simply select their level of competency.

Using Portfolios in Physical Education

Electronic portfolios are relatively new. Typically, each student is given (or purchases) a CD-R (or uses a CD-RW, DVD, or folder on a server or the Internet) that contains his or her portfolio. Then, in either a computer lab setting or as part of a circuit, students use a computer to enter information into their portfolios. Some physical educators require that their students work on their portfolios during time outside physical education—during school breaks, after school in the media center, or at home if they have access to a computer. When time and access to computers is limited, teachers often will create task cards to ensure that students use their computer time efficiently.

Summary

The educational community as a whole continues to move toward more authentic types of assessment, and it is imperative that physical educators do the same. Technology can facilitate the monitoring, documentation, and storage of assessment items. In this chapter we examined the role of technology in multimedia projects and electronic portfolios that allow students to demonstrate and improve their learning in the content area of physical education. In the next chapter, we will look at how technology can improve the quality of teaching.

Reflection Questions

1. What do you consider the benefits of multimedia projects and electronic portfolios to be for your students?

2. What are some items you might have students include in an electronic portfolio to demonstrate their understanding and performance related to the standards?

Projects

1. Practice digitizing audio and video clips. Share the results with others.

2. Design an instructional unit that culminates with students creating their own multi-media projects.

Chapter 9

Using Telecommunication Applications in Physical Education

Ann Chu sits down at her computer between classes and calls up the messages left for her on her handheld computer while she was teaching the previous hour. One message is from the district office, reminding her of an upcoming curriculum meeting. Another is from the main office at her school, requesting this quarter's grades. Ann brings her grade report up on the screen, recalculates it to include this week's grades, and sends the grades to the main office. Ann then composes an e-mail message requesting information on a good video clip to introduce a unit on Frisbee and sends it to the NASPE listserv. She is confident that one of the many physical educators on the list will respond within a few hours.

Telecommunication refers to any type of data transfer between two points. Sending messages to others in your school system, requesting a calendar listing of conferences and workshops from an association, and collaborating with colleagues hundreds of miles away on new instructional strategies are examples of how you can use telecommunications to improve your effectiveness and save time. This chapter introduces you to telecommunication hardware and software, describes various telecommunication applications, and provides you with ideas on how to use this technology.

Computer Connections

A network consists of individually controlled computers that are in communication with one another. The network can connect two individuals in a physical education office, or it can link a group of offices in a school. Most local area networks (LANs) use one powerful computer as a host and link many less powerful computers to it. The host machine stores network versions of software programs, and through it other computers on the network can legally access the software. Networks also allow computers to share hardware devices such as a laser printers, color printers, and scanners, and to exchange messages between computers.

School networks are typically connected by an ethernet cable; however, some schools are connecting computers wirelessly. They use the 802.11 standards, since they are specifically designed for running wide and local area networks and connecting users to the Internet. From the user's perspective, you simply open your browser and access web pages.

Those of you not on a wireless system or cabled to a network will need some type of modem (the name is an abbreviation for modulator/demodulator). "Modulate" means to change data into electronic pulses, and "demodulate" means to change pulses back into data. There are different modems, including dial-up, cable, and DSL, and they come in external, internal, and PC card sizes. See the Major Connections Options box for a comparison of the various connection options.

You will need to connect the telephone or cable wire from the wall to the line port on the modem in order to use your modem. The software that controls the modem typically comes with the modem or when you register with an Internet Service Provider (ISP--see the section on the Internet). When you send information from a file on your computer to another computer, you are uploading. When you receive information from another computer and store it on your disk, you are downloading.

Major Connection Options

	Speed (sec.)	Cost	Note
Dial Up	56KB	$50 modem $19.95/mo	Slow access speed
Cable Modem	500 KB-10MB	$150 modem $30-50/mo	Not available in all areas
DSL	256KB-7MB	$200 modem $30-70/mo	Not available in all areas Uses regular phone lines
Satellite	400 KB	$200 for dish $29.95/mo	

Networks allow schools and districts to submit data and allow different institutions and departments to access the information as needed. For example, fitness scores can be submitted electronically to the district office, which in turn will compile reports and submit them to the state department of education. Later, anyone on the education network can access those scores. This type of information is especially important when writing grants.

Internet

The Internet is a collection of smaller networks that provide a connection between computers located around the world. Each local network is connected to one or more other networks, usually via high-speed digital phone lines. There are hundreds of thousands of networks, including commercial, academic, and government networks. The Internet also is referred to as the Information Super Highway or the World Wide Web (www), although the web is actually a subset of the Internet.

Along with setting up your connection, you must select an ISP in order to connect to the Internet, unless your school or district provides one for you. When selecting an ISP, talk to a technology expert in your area about local service providers. At a minimum, the provider should assign you an e-mail address, connect you to the Internet, allow you unlimited access to the web, feature a helpline, and provide local access numbers. If you have difficulty selecting a service provider, I recommend Earthlink.

Telecommunication Applications

Once you are connected to the Internet, you will have access to a number of different telecommunication applications. These include electronic mail (e-mail), fax services, listservs, newsgroups, web discussion groups, chat sessions, chat conferencing, audio conferencing, and video conferencing. Each one of these applications can provide physical educators with a new way to reach out and communicate with colleagues. An additional telecommunication application, searching for information on the World Wide Web, is addressed in Chapter 10.

Electronic Mail

Having an Internet account is somewhat like having a post office box. Your friends and colleagues can send mail to your post office box. Then, when you have time, you go to the post office, open your post office box, and retrieve your mail. The process is the same for accessing electronic mail. However, instead of a physical post office box, you have a mail box with your ISP. Your friends and colleagues send electronic mail to your electronic mailbox located on the computer of your Internet Service Provider, and when you have time, you access (e.g., connect with) the ISP and retrieve your mail (see Figures 9.1).

In an electronic mail system, all users have a private mailbox address and a password to use when accessing that mailbox. Once you have an e-mail address, you can send and receive mail just like you do with snail mail (the Internet users' name for traditional mail service). If you would like to try sending a message, feel free to send me one at: bmohnsen@ pesoftware.com ("bmohnsen" is my mailbox number, and "pesoftware.com" is the network on which I have my mailbox). The main difference between e-mail and snail mail is that your message is delivered immediately and, if the receiver is available and wishes to do so, immediately answered.

You compose an e-mail message on your computer and send it to your ISP's computer. That computer processes it and sends it to the address you designate. All electronic mail applications provide you with a template for sending mail. The process is similar to snail mail. You type in one or more addresses, write your message, and send the message (by clicking on the "Send" button). The recipient retrieves the message, opens it, reads it, and—if he or she wishes—sends a reply. The recipient also may forward the message to other individuals. All e-mail applications have something that resembles an in box, where incoming mail is stored until it can be read; an out box, where e-mail messages that have been sent are stored; and a trash can, where deleted messages are stored until you empty the trash. You can even attach files to an e-mail message—just make sure that the receiver has an application that can open your file. For example, if you send a Word file, then the recipient needs Word in order to open the file.

E-mail is especially helpful when you are trying to connect with colleagues to share information or get answers to questions. For example, in one school system, a college supervisor, master teacher, and student teacher were all linked by electronic mail. The student teacher wrote her lesson plans and submitted

E-mail Etiquette Rules

Write subject lines that describe the main theme of your message and then stick to that theme.
Be careful with sarcasm and humor.
Don't use all capital letters - it means you are shouting.
Don't send a mass-mailing advertisement.

Figure 9.1 Netscape mail

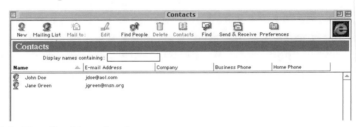

Figure 9.2 E-mail address book

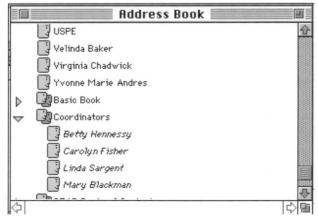

Figure 9.3 E-mail address book

E-mail Abbreviations and Emoticons

IMHO	in my humble opinion
BTW	by the way
FYI	for your information
:-)	basic smiley or happy face
;-)	wink
:-(	frown

them simultaneously to the supervisor and the master teacher. The supervisor and master teacher read the lessons and sent suggestions back to the student teacher at their convenience, prior to the time of the lesson.

Just like with telephone numbers and addresses, it easier to set up an address book for electronic mail addresses than to remember them. Most e-mail applications (Outlook, AOL, Netscape) have the capacity to store electronic mail addresses. The address book (see figure 9.2) typically accepts both the name of the individual and his or her address, so that when you are ready to send a message you simply click on the person's name and an electronic mail template (addressed to the recipient) is created. Most address books also allow you to group individuals so that you can send a message to a selected group. Figure 9.3 shows a group listing.

Fax Services

Fax services (e.g., efax.com) let you send and receive faxes for free. They provide you with an unique fax number that you can give to people who want to send you faxes. These faxes are then routed to your e-mail account. Most of these services require that you download some "free" software before you can use their service. Most also will provide you with an 800 fax number for a monthly fee.

Listservs

A listserv is an extension of e-mail that works much like a mailing list. You send one message to the listserv distribution address and a copy of the message goes to everyone on the list. If you would like to join a physical education listserv, then follow the directions below for joining NASPE-L (National Association for Sport and Physical Education):

1. Send an e-mail to the listserv address:
   join-naspe-talk@lyris.sportime.com
2. Leave the subject line blank
3. You will receive a message regarding your acceptance to the list
4. You may now send a message to the list at naspe-talk@lyris.sportime.com

If you would like to remove yourself from the listserv, then follow the directions below for unsubscribing to NASPE:

1. Send an e-mail to the listserv address:
   leave-naspe-talk@lyris.sportime.com
2. Leave the subject line blank
3. You will receive a message regarding your removal from the list

Once you have joined a listserv, there are a number of commands you can use to request additional information. Refer to Common Listserv Commands box for these special commands.

Listservs are a great source of support for isolated physical educators. They provide you with the opportunity to connect with other physical educators. You can ask questions (e.g.,

Finding People on the Net

Yahoo Search - http://people.yahoo.com//
Who Where? - http://www.whowhere.lycos.com/
Switchboard - http://www.switchboard.com/

Common Listserv Commands

Lists: get a description of all lists
Subscribe Listserv: subscribe to a list
Unsubscribe Listserv: unsubscribe to a list
Review Listserv: review a list
Index Listserv: order a list of listserv files
Get Listserv: order a file from listserv
Set Listserv nomail: suspends mailing of materials from the list
Set Listserv mail: resumes mailing of materials to your account
Set Listserv digest: all mail is collected on the server and sent out daily in the form of a single message
Set Liserv nodigest: removes the digest option

Note: Listserv refers to the name of the listserv

what is a good video for teaching juggling, which instructional strategies are best for students with Attention Deficit Disorder). Listservs also can be set up locally for your students, so that discussions can occur between your students and between you and your students. With permission from your administration, you can set up your own listserv at http://egroups.yahoo.com/ or perhaps your district or school has an application that can facilitate this for you.

Newsgroups

Internet discussion groups, known as newsgroups, serve as forums on almost any topic imaginable. They are essentially bulletin boards where people can read and post messages about topics of their choice. When you post a message to a newsgroup, everyone who visits that newsgroup can read your comments and respond if they wish. Newsgroups are accessed by using a "newsreader" software program or the built-in version included in Netscape Navigator and Internet Explorer. The messages are organized by topic, allowing the viewer to designate an entire conversational strand as already read if it is not relevant. A listing of all newsgroups can be found at http://groups.google.com/.

Web Discussion Groups

Web-based discussion groups provide an alternative to newsgroups. Individuals interested in a particular topic are given a URL (universal resource locator) address (see Chapter 10 for how to access a site) where they can read messages that have been left and leave messages of their own. Web discussion groups can be useful in many circumstances, although they currently lack many of the amenities provided by newsgroups. Most such groups do not provide an easy way to mark, hide, or delete previously read postings, or to mark an entire topic thread as read with a single keystroke. Web discussion groups can be used as online bulletin boards where you leave messages for your students and, they in turn, leave messages for you. You can create your own web discussion board at http://www2.eboard.com/.

Chat Sessions

This form of telecommunication is known as instant messaging, because it offers real-time conversation with another person in text form by way of a pop-up box on your computer screen. Most instant messaging programs let you set up a list of people with whom you'd like to converse, and when those people go online and are ready to accept messages, the software will notify you. The most popular example is AOL's Instant Messenger (http://www.aol.com), which is available to non-AOL members as well as AOL members. You can use instant messaging much like you use regular e-mail, except that the communication will be faster, since it is in realtime.

Chat Conferencing

Internet Relay Chat (IRC) is like an international CB system or conference call on your computer. You might think of it as a virtual area where people gather to use their computers and modems to "chat" in real time. The server is a central place where you join in discussions with other users who are connected to the same chat server.

In order to participate in chat conferencing, you must first obtain an IRC program called a client. Two of the most popular are mIRC (Windows) and MacIRC (Macintosh). After installing the client, you can log onto a server where you can find the IRC's individual channels. Pick a "handle" (online name) and choose a public channel (topic) to connect to, ask to join a private one, or create a channel of your own. A "#" symbol in a channel name means the channel is available worldwide. An "&" symbol in a channel name means the channel is available only on the IRC server to which the user is connected.

Selecting a channel from the thousands that exist can be the most difficult part of IRC. You have a range of topics from which to choose—including everything from sports groups, to computers, to education. Once you join a channel, you can communicate with the other people there by simply typing what you want to say.

A browser-based IRC is now available through web sites such as Talk City. Using Netscape Navigator or Internet Explorer you can access and communicate in various chat rooms (channels). Simply follow the directions:

1. Type in URL: http://www.talkcity.com/.
2. Click on "Chat."

3. Choose a chat room.

4. Complete the log in.

5. Type a message and click on send.

Again, this type of communication allows for instant conversation with several people on a topic of interest. Physical educators can use this form of communication to share questions, concerns, and updates related to teaching physical education or prepare for National Board Certification (see Chapter 11).

Audio Conferencing

An audio conferencing uses telephone conference equipment, Internet telephony (a combination of Internet and telephone using software such as net2phone), or the Internet to link geographically dispersed people for audio communication. When connecting via the Internet, users enter the IP address (computer number) of the computer they are trying to reach. Individuals who are connected via a network typically have a static or unchanging IP address. However, if you use a dial-up connection you will usually be given a dynamic IP address. This means that each time you connect, your computer will be assigned a temporary address for the duration of your call.

This technology is great for communicating with guest speakers, content experts, and colleagues across the United States and around the world. Several teachers and/or students at each site can communicate simultaneously, allowing for "real-time" interaction between participants. Students can interview athletes, medical doctors, nutritionists, professors, and other experts as part of a research project or report.

Desktop Video Conferencing

Desktop video conferencing uses the Internet to take advantage of text, audio, and video transmissions in real time. Full-motion video, which provides 30 new frames per second (fps), requires a very fast baud rate. Since many users are unable to connect at these speeds, compressed video (CODEC) analyzes each new frame and transmits only the pixels that have changed. Because audio quality is far more important than video quality, users will forgive diminished video quality if your content is substantive.

Placing an audio/video call via the Internet is similar to placing an audio call—simply enter the IP address of the person you're calling. The receiver needs to be connected and have compatible conferencing software (e.g., NetMeeting, iChat AV) running. Good practices to follow when using audio/video conferencing include reducing movement, speaking clearly, waiting for others to stop talking before speaking, wearing solid colored clothing (avoid bright red, yellow, or orange), and muting the microphone when not speaking.

Desktop video conferencing provides the same opportunities as instant messaging, chats, and audio conferencing—with the added bonus of being able to see the other individuals. This makes the conversation seem even more like a real, in-person conversation. However, if your Internet connection is slow it is better to bypass the video conferencing and stick with instant messaging, chats, or audio conferencing.

Browser-based video conferencing is now available through web sites such as cam frog (www.camfrog.com). Using Netscape Navigator or Internet Explorer you can access and communicate in various chat rooms (channels). Simply follow the directions and make sure you have a camera connected to your computer.

Telecommunication Projects

There are many worthwhile learning activities on the Internet that physical educators and their students can join. These include keypals, guest speakers, question-and-answer forums, information searches, data base creation, electronic publishing, electronic fieldtrips, pooled data analysis, parallel problem solving, sequential problem solving, telepresence problem solving, simulations, and social action projects (many of these are covered in Chapter 10), since they involve using the World Wide Web. Students also can compete in virtual track meets and make connections with Olympic athletes.

Key Pals for Students

Many of us had pen pals when we were students. Today, our students can have key pals. Key pals are students who connect with one another via electronic mail. They share ideas, concerns, physical education/activity experiences, information, written assignments, and research. And, they learn to accept individuals from other communities and cultures. If the key pal idea is of interest to you, go to the Physical Education Keypal Internet site (http://www.pesoftware.com/pepals.html) to find pals for yourself, your students, or both.

TeleOlympics

TeleOlympics (http://www.ofcn.org) allows students from across the United States and abroad to compete in a number of different track events. Teachers post students' times on the Internet so comparisons can be made and winners determined. The students share information, via e-mail, about their schools, communities, interests, hobbies, and cultural differences. Students can access the Mapquest (http://www.mapquest.com) web site to locate one anothers' schools.

Connections with Famous People

Electronic mail also can provide access to an array of individuals with knowledge and expertise who are of interest to physical educators and their students. Olympic athletes, professional athletes, biomechanists, exercise physiologists, motor learning specialists, outstanding physical education teachers and leaders, and others are available to any one of us via electronic mail.

E-mail from an Olympic Athlete

In the next two weeks we will begin the difficult process of selection. Today there are about 20 athletes training here for the Olympics. Our coach has to pick the top eight for the premier boat, then four for the next boat, and two for the last boat. Selection is often the hardest part of the year because it is the time when people's dreams are realized or their failures are faced. Everyone wants to be in the top boat, but there are only eight seats available. And after the four and the two-man boats are chosen there are some guys who won't get to go to the Olympics at all. You can imagine how hard it would be to train all these years and not make the team. The other hard part about selection is that we are all friends. We have established strong emotional ties over the years and it will be tough to see friends feel such disappointment.

Bonnie's Fitware, Inc. sponsors the Olympic Athlete Project. During the 1995-1996 school year, an Olympic rower was identified who was willing to share his trip to the Olympics with students. Steven Segaloff was a potential Olympic coxswain when he began communicating with students across the United States. He sent e-mail messages (see Box) every other week that dealt with his sport, his training program, the selection process, his relationship with the other rowers (teammates), and his feelings about training and participating in the Olympics.

Summary

Many physical educators feel isolated from their colleagues. They miss the interaction and sharing of instructional ideas, class management techniques, assessment tools, and resources. Telecommunications can help fill this void by providing them with the opportunity to communicate with other physical educators via e-mail, listservs, newsgroups, web discussion groups, chat sessions, and audio/video communications.

Reflection Questions

1. Which of the telecommunication tools would best fit your communication style? Why?
2. Which of the telecommunication tools would work best for your students? Why?

Projects

1. Join a listserv. Sit back for a while and observe the conversations, then jump in with your own comments or questions. Write a one-page summary description of your experience.
2. Arrange a time to meet a friend or colleague at the TalkCity web site to participate in a chat session. Write a one-page summary description of your experience.

Chapter 10

Accessing the World Wide Web

Carolyn Brown wonders whether there are any data to support her concern that students need daily physical education instruction. So, during her conference period, she boots up her browser application and begins to visit sites she feels may have relevant information, including the Centers for Disease Control and the Institute for Aerobic Research. Although she finds some information, Carolyn still thinks she needs additional information for the school board presentation she is planning. So, she visits the AltaVista search site and enters the following words: + "daily physical education" +benefits. Immediately, 1,000 hits are listed. Carolyn's next decision is whether to search all 1,000 sites or to refine her search. With only 30 minutes left in her conference period, she decides to refine her search. She clicks on "Refine," and by the end of her conference period has more than enough information to present to her Board of Education.

W hen the Internet was introduced in the late 1960s, the goal was to develop a global network of computers. Today, the Internet has met that goal. You can access journals, books, research papers, clip art, and news reports plus a variety of information on topics ranging from computers, to education, to sports. The World Wide Web (www), a subset of the Internet, provides access to information through a graphical user interface. Specifically, the World Wide Web allows you to look at information stored on computers around the world by typing in an address or pointing the mouse at a link (typically text in a different color and underlined) and clicking. Different links access different pieces of information on different computers.

Web Browsers

A web browser is an application designed to facilitate viewing information on the World Wide Web. Browser applications support hypertext markup language (html), which allows you to see text, graphics, and pictures. Browsers also allow you to bookmark your favorite pages and save or print pages for viewing off-line. Plug-ins can be added to make these programs even more powerful. The two most popular web browsers are Netscape Navigator (http://www.netscape.com) and Microsoft Internet Explorer (http://www.microsoft.com/). Both can be downloaded for free.

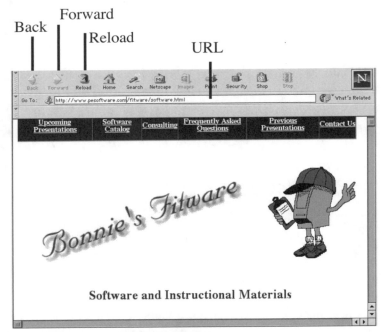

Figure 10.1   Anatomy of a web page

Browser Commands

Open/Location Field - Where you can enter an address. Type in the URL and you instantly bring the information from that site to your computer screen.

Back - Clicking the Back button allows you to retrace your steps and return to sites you've already visited.

Forward - Reverses the action of "Back."

Reload/Refresh - Reloads the page currently on display. This may be necessary if the page loads incorrectly or the content of the page changes frequently.

Stop - Stops the loading of the current page.

Print - Prints all the pages on the current screen without any prompts.

Home - Brings the web page you have designated as your opening location back to the screen.

Plug-ins

In order to access some audio/video clips on the Internet, you will need special plug-ins. Plug-ins (and their cousins, helper applications) expand upon your browser's basic functions. With plug-ins, you'll be able to hear live radio broadcasts, watch videos of sport skills, and explore 3D universes without leaving your browser. Plug-ins are small utilities that give your browser the ability to display a wider variety of documents, images, and other online files.

The current sophistication of Netscape Navigator and Internet Explorer include code that can handle most of the files you are likely to encounter on the Internet. Additionally, both browsers include Apple's QuickTime plug in, which can play nearly any multimedia file you are likely to encounter. However, older browsers may require the installation of one or more plug-ins.

Most plug-ins are free and are downloaded from the sites that use them. Web sites that use special plug-ins will actually check your system and alert you to the need for a plug-in. Adding plug-ins is one of the easiest procedures on the Internet—your browser does most of the work. When you load a page that requires a plug-in that you have not installed, Netscape notifies you and lets you see a list of suggested plug-ins. If you use Microsoft Internet Explorer and ActiveX, the browser automatically downloads and installs the necessary plug-in. However, rather than waiting to install plug-ins when you need them, you may want to gather and install several at once.

The plug-ins listed in Browser Plug-ins box are the most important for your continual enjoyment of the Internet. When you download a plug-in, pay attention to where it is saved on your hard drive. After you download a plug-in, you may need to quit your browser and locate the downloaded file in order to install it. You typically will be asked to register your name, workplace, address, e-mail, and other identifying information when you download the plug-in. You also will be asked to read the terms of agreement for use and agree to those terms before the installation can be completed. Once the installation is complete, your new plug-in will be active.

Helper Applications

Helper applications run or display files that are not integrated into web pages and do not display inside the browser's window. Three popular helper applications are Adobe *Acrobat Reader*, Aladdin *StuffIt Expander*, and *WinZip* (WinZip).

Securing Helper Applications/Plug-ins

1. Go to the appropriate web site.
2. Register your name and address (not required at all sites).
3. Select the appropriate plug-in or helper application for your computer platform and language.
4. Click on the "Download" button, then read the installation instructions.
5. Click on the geographically appropriate download link to download the plug-in or helper application.
6. Wait for it to load (time depends on your modem and connection speed).
7. Follow the installation instructions.

Browser Plug-ins

Quicktime VR: http ://www.apple.com/quicktime/
Flash: http://www.macromedia.com
ShockWave: http://www.macromedia.com
RealPlayer: http://www.real.com/
PowerPoint: http://www.msn.com/
Cortona (VRML): http://www.parallelgraphics.com/products/cortona/

Helper Applications

Acrobat Reader: http://www.adobe.com
StuffIt Expander: http://www.aladdinsys.com
WinZip: http://www.winzip.com

Portable Document Format (PDF) is a file format that enables the user to retain the typographical format (fonts, line breaks, graphics) of a document. Using Adobe *Acrobat Reader,* you can open, view, browse, search, and print PDF files on any of the major desktop computing platforms. You can tell that a file is in PDF format by the file name extension—.pdf. When properly configured on a computer, the browser launches *Acrobat Reader* whenever a PDF file is encountered. This is the easiest way to ensure that the document you receive resembles the original document.

StuffIt Expander and *WinZip* are applications that assist with the transfer of files from the Internet to the user's computer. Many times, files are encoded and/or compressed prior to transfer (see the File Transfer section in this chapter). The encoding helps to retain the document's original format, and compression makes the file smaller so that it can transfer more quickly.

StuffIt Expander decompresses files that have been compressed (or "stuffed") using the *StuffIt* program, and *WinZip* can do the same for files compressed using *Zip*. You also will find self-extracting archive files on the Internet. A self-extracting file (.sea) is an executable program, which when loaded, automatically translates and decompresses itself.

Locating a Web Page

Everywhere you look today, you see long strings of text that look something like this: http://www.pesoftware.com/

These strings are referred to as universal resource locators (URLs). They begin with a protocol, like "http://" (HyperText Transfer Protocol) or "ftp" (File Transfer Protocol) followed by a variety of letters, numbers, and punctuation marks. URLs are to the World Wide Web what telephone numbers are to the phone system. They allow you to connect with the location you desire. Typically, the first section after "http://" contains www, indicating that the site is on the World Wide Web. However, you may also encounter www2, which is a separate group on the Internet for educational resources. The next section is the name of the server or computer (pesoftware) that houses the information. The computer's name often ends with a period, followed by a three-letter combination such as edu, com, gov, or org. Each suffix refers to a particular type of organization. For example:

> com = commercial
> edu = education
> gov = government
> org = organization

More recently, we have begun to see suffixes that refer to the physical location of the computer. For example, "ca.us" refers to a site from California, USA, and "gov.ab.ca" to a government organization in Alberta, Canada. The most common errors when typing in a URL include omitting one of the parts, using the

Changing Font Size

Internet Explorer - Go to the View menu, point to Text Size, and then choose a larger or smaller font for the text on that page.

Netscape -Go to Edit, then Preferences, then the Category scroll list. Choose Fonts under Appearance, then choose a different size or type of font.

wrong domain designator (edu, or com, or org), punctuation errors (e.g., "~") or omissions, misspellings, using either upper or lower case when the other is called for, and using a space instead of an underscore.

All browsers have an "Open" button where you can enter an address (URL). By typing in the URL (http://store.pesoftware.com), you can instantly bring the information from that site to your computer screen. This is often referred to as the home page. It is the first in a series of linked documents. You can think of the home page as the main menu or the table of contents in a book. In order to move from the home page to linked pages, you simply click on the hyperlink (special text embedded with a URL, often a different color and underlined) that brings the new document to your screen. By clicking the Back button you can retrace your steps and return to sites you've already visited. You also can go directly to these pages if you know the URL. For example, in the URL , http:/www.pesoftware.com/ fitware/software.html, "software.html" is the name of the document or page, and it is located in a folder entitled "fitware" that is located on the computer named "www.pesoftware.com." When typing in the URL, you can omit the http://.

The difficulty in going directly to sites such as these lies in remembering the long series of letters, numbers, and punctuation marks that make up the URL. Luckily, all browsers contain a "bookmark" or "favorites" feature that allows you to mark a page you may wish to revisit. Your bookmarks or favorites will become extremely important to you, so be sure to back up the files. The Saving Bookmark/Favorite Files box provides directions. You also can save or back up your bookmarks online at sites such as http://www.hotlink.com/.

A bookmark is a valuable tool that can save you time by taking you to a previously explored web page without having to go through multiple menus or hyperlinks. However, be aware that there are some situations (i.e., visiting a link from within a site with frames) in which you cannot bookmark a site.

Suggested Physical Education Web Sites

Aerobic Steps: http://www.turnstep.com/

Ancient Olympics: http://www.upenn.edu/museum/Olympics/olympicintro.html

Ancient Olympics: http://www.perseus.tufts.edu/Olympics/index.html

BAM: http://www.bam.gov

Bike Safety Lessons: http://www.creativeclassroom.org/subaru/lesson-plans.html

Busy Body Fitness Equipment: http://www.busybody.com/

Children's Fitness: http://www.oitgrvl.k12.sc.us/beachcomber/lessons/norrislesson.htm

Circus Skills: http://www.juggling.org/

Cooperative Games: http://www.coopsports.com/

Exploratorium: http://www.exploratoriu.edu/sports/index.html

Fitness Jumpsite - http://primusweb.com/fitnesspartner/

Folk Dances: http://www.folkdance.com/

Franklin Institute Museum: http://sln.fi.edu/

Freddie the Frog Exercises: http://www.justsaywow.com/freddie.htm

Global Fitness: http://www.global-fitness.com

Golf: http://www.teachkidsgolf.com

Kids Health and Fitness: http://www.kidshealthandfitness.com.au/

Kids' Running: http://www.kidsrunning.com/

Kidscience: http://kidscience.miningco.com/kids/kidscience/msub36.htm

Line Dance Fun: http://www.linedancefun.com/

Mountain Biking: http://xenon.stanford.edu/~rsf/mtn-bike.html

Museum of Science: http://www.mos.org/home.html

Olympic Movement: http://www.olympic.org/

Olympic Studies Centre: http://blues.uab.es/olympic.studies/

Online Sports Videos: http://www.sportsid.com/sid2000/default.htm

Orienteering: http://www.learn-orienteering.org/

PBS: http://www.pbs.org/teachersource/health.htm

PE Links: http://www.pelinks4u.org/

Rules - http://www.rulescentral.com

Science and Olympics: http://whyfiles.org/019olympic/index.html

ShapeUp America: http://www.shapeup.org/

Skate in School: http://www.rollerblade.com/

Sports Figures: http://sportsfigures.espn.com/sportsfigures/index.jsp

Sports Illustrated for Kids: http://www.sikids.com

Sports Medicine: http://www.physsportsmed.com/

Suggested Online Teacher Resources

A to Z: http://www.atozteacherstuff.com/
AAHPERD: http://www.aahperd.org
Ask ERIC: http://ericir.syr.edu/
Assessment Tools: http://www.rubrics.com/
Brainium: http://www.brainium.com/
Brain Pop: http://www.brainpop.com
Certificate Creator: http://www.CertificateCreator.com/
Dictionary: http://dictionary.reference.com/
Educate Now: http://www.educatenow.com/
Education World: http://www.educationworld.com/
Encyclopedias: http://responsiblekids.net/encyclopedias.htm
Exemplary Teacher Videos: http://www.intime.uni.edu/
Fact Monster: http://www.factmonster.com/
4Teachers: http://www.4teachers.org/
Free Worksheets: http://www.freeworksheets.com/
FunBrain: http://www.funbrain.com
Gateway to Ed Materials: http://thegateway.org/
Grants: http://www.schoolgrants.com/
Handhelds: http://www97.intel.com/education/index.asp
ISTE: http://www.iste.org/
Language Translators: http://www.freetranslation.com/
Lesson Plans: http://schools.eastnet.ecu.edu/pitt/ayden/physed8.htm
Microsoft Lesson Connection: http://www.k12.msn.com/
National Board Professional Teacher Standards: http://www.nbpts.org
PBS: http://www.pbs.org/teachersource/
PE Central: http://www.pecentral.org/
PE Links for You: http://www.pelinks4u.org/
PE Software: http://www.pesoftware.com/
PE Zone: http://reach.ucf.edu/%7Epezone/home.html
Promote Physical Activity: http://www.VERBnow.com
Quiz Creator: http://eleaston.com/quizzes.html
Research It: http://www.itools.com
Sport Quest: http://www.sportquest.com/
Sports Science: http://www.sportsci.org/
Teacher Web: http://www.teacherweb.com/
Teach Nology: http://www.teach-nology.com
Tools: http://school.discovery.com/teachingtools/teachingtools.html
U.S. Department of Education: http://www.ed.gov/index.jhtml
Virtual Tours: http://www.virtualfreesites.com/tours.html

Suggested Health Education Web Sites

*ADAM, Inc. - http://www.adam.com/

American Heart Association - http://www.americanheart.org/

Anatomy for Kindergarten - http://www.tdh.state.tx.us/kids/lessonplans/kanatomy.htm

Anatomy & Physiology - http://biology.about.com/cs/anatomyphysiology/

Bio-Med Net - http://biomednet.com/hmsbeagle/

Bluecares: Body Atlas - http://www.bluecares.com/guide.atlas.html

Calorie Counter - http://www.caloriescount.com/

Centers for Disease Control: http://www.cdc.gov/

Children's Wellness: http://www.accentpub.com/kidspage.html

Combined Health Information Database - http://chid.nih.gov/

Conflict Management- http://www.knowconflict.com/

CPR - http://depts.washington.edu/learncpr/

Dairy Council -http://www.dairycouncilofca.org/

Dealing with Pressure - http://www.goodcharacter.com/

Dental Health: http://www.colgatebsbf.com/

Discovery Health - http://www.discoveryhealth.com/

Dole 5 A Day - http://www.dole5aday.com/

Eat Right - http://www.eatright.com/

Everett Koop - http://www.drkoop.com

Fast Food Facts - http://www.olen.com/food/

Fighting Disease - http://www.un.org/Pubs/CyberSchoolBus/special/health

First Aid - http://www.bbc.co.uk/health/first_aid_action/

Food and Nutrition Information - http://www.nalusda.gov/fnic/

Food Finder - http://www.olen.com/food/

Food Pyramid - http://www.ganesa.com/food/index.html

Free Software - http://www.ualberta.ca/healthinfo

Gander Academy's Human Body Systems - http://www.stemnet.nf.ca/CITE/body.htm

Good Character - http://goodcharacter.com

Growing Healthy Online Training - http://www.nche.org/

Health Careers - http://www.telehealthnc.com/hce.html

Health Center of Excellence - http://healthbehavior.com/

Health Education - http://www.health.org/

*Health Help - http://www.hhni.com/

Health Information Library - http://www.ynhh.com/online/health_lib_frset.html

Suggested Health Education Web Sites

Health Resources - http://dewey.chs.chico.k12.ca.us/heal.html
Health Teacher - http://www.healthteacher.com/
Healthfinder - http://www.healthfinder.gov/
Human Body Adventure - http://vilenski.org/science/humanbody/
    hb_intro.html
Human Body Experiments - http://www.galaxy.net/~k12/body/
Human Health - http://www.epa.gov/students/health.htm
Infection, Detection, Protection - http://www.amnh.org/explore/
    infection
Injury Prevention - http://www.cpsc.gov/kids/kidsafety/index.html
***InteliHealth** - http://www.intelihealth.com
Kids Health - http://kidshealth.org/
MayoHealth - http://mayoclinic.com/
Medicine Through Time - http://www.bbc.co.uk/eduation/medicine
Medscape - http://www.cbs.medscape.com/
My Gross and Cool Body - http://school.discovery.com/lessonplans/
    codeblue/gutreaction.html
NOVA: Cut to the Heart - http://www.pbs.org/wgbh/nova/heart
Nutrition Exploration - http://www.nutritionexplorations.com/
Nutrition Information - http://www.kidfood.org/
Online Interactive Nutrition - http://www.usda.gov/cnpp
Operation Clean Hands - http://www.education-world.com/a_curr/
    curr016.shtml
Public Health Links (comprehensive) - http://www.tmfnet.org/pss/phlinks.htm
Quackery Site - http://www.quackwatch.com/
Real Scoop on Tobacco - http://www.itdc.sbcss.k12.ca.us/curriculum/
    tobacco.html
Riverdeep: http://www.riverdeep.net
Stay Safe: http://www.accentpub.com/kidspage.html
The Bad Bug Book - http://wm.cfsan.fda.gov/~mow/intro.html
The Heart: http://www.fi.edu/biosci/heart.html
***Veritas** - http://www.veritasmedicine.com/
Virtual Hospital - http://www.vh.org/
Virtual Pediatrician - http://www.mdchoice.com/
Visible Human Project - http://www.uchsc.edu/sm/chs
***WebMD** - http://www.webmd.com/

*URAC - American Accreditation HealthCare Commission
    Recommendation

Saving and Printing

As you visit various sites, you will no doubt run across information you either want to save or want to print. The browser allows you to do both easily. For example, using Netscape Navigator, go to the web page that is of interest to you. Select "File" from the menu bar, and then select "Save" to save the information from the web page to your hard drive. Or, select "File" from the menu bar, and then select "Print" to generate a hard copy of the information. Be careful when printing web sites with frames. You must first click the mouse on the information you wish to print, and then select "File-Print."

However, when you print the information from the site you might get pages you do not need. To avoid this, go to Print Preview and determine how many pages you need. Now specify in the print dialog box which pages you want to print. If your browser does not have Print Preview, arbitrarily set a fixed number of pages in the print dialog box.

You also can save images/audio from the web onto your computer. Again, using Netscape Navigator, perform the steps in one of the following methods to save an image:

Method 1:
1. Macintosh: Click and hold the mouse over the image. Windows: Right click and hold the mouse over the image.
2. When the pop-up menu appears, choose "Save this image as."
3. Type in a name for the image.
4. Select the location on your hard drive where you would like the image to be saved.

Method 2:
1. On Macintosh: Click and hold the mouse over the image. Using Windows: Right click and hold the mouse over the image.
2. Choose the command, "Copy this image."
3. Using Macintosh: Go to the apple, drag down to scrapbook, and select Edit-Paste. Using Windows: The image will automatically be placed on the clipboard.

Searching the Web

No doubt you have heard the term "surfing the net." It is much like window shopping—it means roaming around online until you find something of interest. This is actually the least efficient method of searching for information. In fact, it is only beneficial once you find a page that has numerous links to related information. Search engines, on the other hand, make it possible to find the information you need quickly.

There are several kinds of search tools (see Search Tool box), including search engines, directories, and meta search tools. A meta search tool lets you build a single search and then apply it to multiple search sites simultaneously. However, these searches take much longer than a single search, and they are not as focused as a single search engine.

Directories are organized collections of links to web resources, somewhat like a book's table of contents. Links are usually added by human operators who solicit Internet users to submit links and actively search for new links to add themselves. You look for keywords in subdirectory headings titles and descriptions of links to web sites.

Search engines consist of data bases containing the full or partial text of sites. Their data bases are built by automated tools called bots, crawlers, or spiders, that roam the web exploring links and collecting the entire content or abstracts of the content found at different web sites. When you use search engines, you search their entire data base.

The same query will get different results from each of these tools. There is no charge to use search tools, because they are supported by advertisers who post banners on the search result pages. There are dozens of search tools; two particularly popular ones are Yahoo (web directory) and AltaVista (search engine). You access the search tool by typing in its Internet address.

Once at the web site, you will see a rectangular area where you can type in a topic (e.g., volleyball, Medieval games). You then click on the word "Search," and the software shows you a list of locations where related information is stored. When you click on one of those locations, the information from that site appears on your screen. Search engines list the best matches first—those pages that have the highest number of matching keywords or phrases on them.

No matter which tool you use, a focused search will produce more exact results. You will need to be as specific as possible in order to conduct a successful search. It is not unusual to type in something general like "sports" and end up with more than one million sites. Therefore, it is better to perform many narrow searches that result in fewer matches than to make your search too broad and spend valuable time looking at information that does not interest you. A narrow search is performed by using limiting words such as AND (+) or PHRASE. If you enter the words—teaching adolescents volleyball—separated by spaces, some search engines will perform an OR search and return all the pages that have the word "teaching" and all of the pages that have the word "adolescents" and all the pages that have the word "volleyball." This isn't exactly what you wanted.

Some engines require you to specify a search phrase, put your phrase in quotes, put the word AND between your search words, or use a plus sign in front of each word (see the directions on the search engine web site for specifics). In these scenarios the user types in:

    "teaching adolescents volleyball"—phase search
    teaching AND adolescents AND volleyball—AND search
    +teaching +adolescents +volleyball—+ search

Search engines do have their limitations, including out-of-date sites. The information associated with the link may have been moved or eliminated. In addition, not all search engines are created equal. You are usually better off with search engines that support phrase searches.

Search Tools

Directories

http://www.yahoo.com

http://www.dmoz.org/

Meta Search Tools

http://www.search.com

http://www.monstercrdawler.com

http://www.metacrawler.com

Search

http://www.altavista.com/

http://www.google.com

http://www.excite.com

http://www.go.com/

http://www.aj.com/

Niche Searches

Academic Journals - jstor.org - archival collection of full-image, full-run academic journals

Ask ELibrary - ask.elibrary.com - searchable archive of books, articles, newspapers, transcripts, pictures, and maps

Cite Seer - citseer.nj.nec.com/cs - cited research papers

Education Domain - searchedu.com - search the edu domain

Find Articles - findarticles.com - indexing published articles from more than 300 sources

Government Stats - access.gpo.gov/su_docs/multidb.html - government stats, publications, and history

Kids Search Engine - www.yahooligans.com - one of the best kid-oriented search sites

Map Quest - www.mapquest.com - location finder

Medicine Journals - highwie.stanford.edu - 12 million fully indexed articles

National Library of Medicine - www.ncbi.nlm.nih.gov/entrez/query.fcgi - 12 million citations

Speeches - speechbot.research.compaq.com - indexes over 16,000 hours of broadcasts

Technology Books - safari.oreilly.com - electronic versions of technology books

File Transfer

File transfer protocol (FTP) is a procedure for defining how files are transferred from one computer to another. You can use FTP by going to a site (ftp://) on the World Wide Web and letting your browser handle the details, or you can use an FTP client (software) to access FTP sites. The most popular FTP clients are

Saving Bookmark/Favorite Files

In Navigator, open your Netscape folder (it's probably in your Program Files\Netscape\Navigator subfolder or System\Preferences\ Netscape) and locate the bookmark.htm file. Copy it to another storage device.

In Internet Explorer, go to Windows\Favorites subfolder and locate the Favorites file. Copy it to another storage device.

FETCH (Fetch Softworks) for the Macintosh and WS-FTP Pro (Ipswitch) for Windows. With FTP, you can send and receive files as long as you have permission from the site.

Files can contain text, executable programs, graphics, or compressed data. Archive files are single files that contain many files in compressed form, making it faster and easier to transfer them by modem. Most files available by FTP have been compressed and encoded to allow them to more easily pass through different computers (see section on plug ins).

Web Activities

Web technology can bring resources into the classroom to facilitate active, problem-based, collaborative learning and can provide information that otherwise would be unavailable or prohibitively expensive. Teachers no longer need to rely exclusively on the resources available within their districts. When you are searching the web it is important to find high-quality sites that contain accurate information. Sites sponsored by professional organizations and journals are excellent places to begin your search. There also are portals (subscription-based or free) that provide gateways to the best information on the web. You can follow the hyperlinks noted on these sites, since they usually have been reviewed prior to inclusion.

Physical educators can find a great deal of information on the web to help in developing curriculum, planning lessons, and producing instructional materials (see boxes on Suggested Web Sites). The web also can be an extremely valuable instructional resource for students. They can use the Internet to engage in treasure hunts, complete WebQuests, conduct research, participate in electronic field trips, solve problems, complete tutorials, and perform simulations.

Treasure hunts. In treasure hunts, students are given questions about a specific topic along with specific web sites where they can find the answers. Well-written questions can extend understanding beyond isolated facts and guide students to deeper thinker. Culminating with a "big idea" question allows students to synthesize what they have learned and apply it to real-life settings.

Treasure Hunt– Multicultural Games Germantown Academy

Sites:

http://www.germantownacademy.org/Academics/MS/6th/MCGAMES/
   Gamelink.htm

http://www.germantownacademy.org/Academics/MS/6th/MCGAMES/
   Directory.htm

http://www.germantownacademy.org/Academics/MS/6th/MCGAMES/
   Template.htm

Questions:

1. List countries where the game originated and where it is currently played.
2. Describe how your game is played. State the object of the game. Describe rules/boundaries. List equipment.
3. Recommend the type of athlete who would enjoy playing this game. What skills does the game demand? What are your impressions of this game? Did you enjoy playing it? Would you recommend it?

WebQuests. WebQuests were created by Bernie Dodge, as a means to purposefully search the World Wide Web through cooperative learning, the process of inquiry, and problem-based learning. In WebQuests (http://webquest.sdsu.edu), students are given an authentic problem to solve along with web resources on the topic. Students typically work in collaborative groups or teams. Each student explores the linked sites related to a specific role on the team. Students then teach what they have learned to the other team members. Finally, higher-level questions guide students toward more challenging thinking and a deeper understanding of the topic being explored. A well-written Quest demands that students go beyond fact finding. It asks them to analyze a variety of resources and use their creativity and critical-thinking skills to derive solutions to a problem.

WebQuests have six parts:
1. An *introduction* that sets the stage and provides some background information.
2. A *task* that is doable and interesting.
3. A *set* of information sources needed to complete the task.
4. A *description* of the process the learners should go through in accomplishing the task.
5. *Guidelines* on how to organize the required information.
6. A *conclusion* that brings closure to the Quest, including reminding the learners what they have learned.

WebQuest developers have created a template to help educators create their own webquests. It can be found at: http://webquest.sdsu.edu/LessonTemplate.html. Examples of WebQuests are shown in the boxes, along with URLs for additional examples.

Research projects. Students can use the Internet to research areas of interest. For example, they can investigate proper exercises, new motor skill techniques, the history of a sport or dance, or investigate the validity of a diet or exercise claim. However, it is

Personal Trainer WebQuest

http://www.itdc.sbcss.k12.ca.us/curriculum/
personaltrainer.html

Choose one of the people below and develop a menu and exercise program to improve their overall health. You must:
Find the appropriate goal weight for the person.
Develop a weekly exercise program.
Develop a one-week menu.
Provide helpful survival tips.
Give your client specific recommendations.

Sample Client:
Michelle is a 17-year-old high school junior. She stands 5' 6" tall and weighs 135 pounds. Michelle is involved in Key Club and sings in the school choir. Michelle spends her evening hours talking on the phone, watching TV, and/or hanging out with her friends. Michelle's family isn't big on family meals, so Michelle is responsible for preparing most of her own meals. Michelle doesn't eat breakfast, eats fast food a lot, and is on a first-name basis with the fine folks at Taco Bell. Michelle feels her body may still be growing but is concerned with the fact that some of her clothes are getting tight. She would like to drop a few pounds.

Jump Rope WebQuest

http://lincoln.midcoast.com/~wps/pewriting/
introduction.htm

This WebQuest is an opportunity for children to explore the topic of jumping rope while at the same time allowing them to make strong connections within the curriculum areas of English and language arts, health, physical education, and technology. Your children will act as jump rope enthusiasts. Their job will be to research the benefits of jumping rope, finding specific information concerning the numerous benefits. Students will need to complete reading and exploring activities. A note-taking sheet containing eight reasons why jumping rope can be beneficial will be completed. This information will be helpful to the children as they create a pamphlet that will persuade others to participate in the sport of jumping rope. As a culmination, there will be an oral presentation to classmates. All facts included in the pamphlet need to be supported by the information that they have researched in this lesson.

Sample WebQuests

Health Education

Addiction WebQuest: http://technoteacher.com/WebQuests/ADDICTION/index.htm

Food WebQuest: http://www.manteno.k12.il.us/drussert/WebQuests/PaulaHall/Foods%20of%20the%20US.html

Honey Bees WebQuest: http://www.manteno.k12.il.us/webquest/elementary/Science/HoneyBees/Honey%20Bee%20Webquest/Honeybee%20Webquest.htm

I am Joe's Heart WebQuest: http://www.ufrsd.net/staffwww/stefanl/Webquest/joe/heart.htm

Substance Abuse WebQuest: http://www.technoteacher.com/Health/schedule2.htm

Physical Education

Ancient Olympics WebQuest: http://www.sinc.sunysb.edu/Class/est57280/kmeehan/webquest.htm

Basketball WebQuest: http://www.plainfield.k12.in.us/hschool/webq/webq116/

Fitness WebQuest: http://www.manteno.k12.il.us/lweedon/webquest.htm

Olympic WebQuest: http://web54.sd54.k12.il.us/vrkit/supplements/sixth/olympics/student.htm

Olympic WebQuest II: http://www.kent.wednet.edu/staff/dlapp/Olympics/olympic_webquest.html

Volleyball WebQuest: http://www.csulb.edu/~emyrw/Modules/Module1kpe257/Connect.html

important that you prepare your students to use this research tool. Online encyclopedias are an excellent place to start, but other sites also contain excellent information. Students must learn to double check all references and to examine author credentials (see What Makes a Good Web Site box). It also is important that your students learn how to properly cite references (see Web Citations box) from the Internet.

Electronic field trips. An electronic field trip can be a valuable Internet experience. The high cost of field trips and the sheer size of the earth may make it impossible for students to physically explore the world outside their school district. However, students can explore the world through virtual field trips. Your students can explore the materials from past trips or join a trip in progress. There are opportunities to share ideas with the travelers as well as with other students following the trip. Many virtual field trips provide daily updates with photographs, movies, sound clips, and journal entries.

Turner Educational Services has been one of the leaders in the area of electronic field trips. They have sponsored field trips to the Indianapolis 500 and to baseball training camps. During their "Calculations on a Curve Ball: The Many Figures of Baseball" field trip, students learned to use mathematical equations to

Web Citations

Basic Citation:
Author's Last Name, First Name. [author's Internet address, if available]. "Title of Work" or "title line of message." In "Title of Complete Work" or title of list/site if appropriate. [Internet address]. Date accessed.

Listserv Citation:
Sender's Name. [Sender's e-mail]. "Title of e-mail." In "Name of listserv." [listserv address]. Date accessed.

E-mail Citation:
Sender's Name. [Sender's e-mail]. "Title of e-mail." Private e-mail message to name of receiver, [e-mail address of receiver]. Date accessed.

Newspaper Online Citation:
Author. "Title." Newspaper name. Date: paging or indicator of length. [Type of medium]. Available: web site/path/file or supplier or database name. [access date].

Magazine Online Citation:
Author. "Article Title." Magazine name. Date: paging or indicator or length. [Type of medium]. Available: web site/path/file. [access date].

calculate the percentages of runs, hits, and errors of their favorite players. Using the sciences of physiology, physics, chemistry, and meteorology, students learned to improve motor skills related to the game of baseball. Through history and literature they explored the relationship between baseball and American culture. And, they applied economic principles to the business of baseball as they "became" the team owner and created a budget for a winning season.

Throughout the journey, the students met players, coaches, trainers, announcers, statisticians, and others related to the baseball environment. Information was sent via live interactive telecasts and received either by satellite or cable. There were live Internet chats and discussion groups as well as toll-free phone numbers to call with questions. Data disks and web sites provided primary and secondary resources. Turner Educational Services continues to produce new electronic field trips during each school year. Online services such as America Online and CompuServe also sponsor free electronic field trips.

Problem-based learning (PBL). PBL is learning organized around the investigation and resolution of an authentic, ill-structured problem. PBL includes three main characteristics (Torp & Sage, 1998):
- It engages students as stakeholders in a problem situation.
- It organizes curriculum around this holistic problem, enabling students to learn in relevant and connected ways.
- It creates a learning environment in which teachers coach student thinking and guide student inquiry, facilitating deeper levels of understanding.

The difference between project-based learning and problem-based learning, is that the problems are messier in PBL. The teacher designs a problem that fits the current standards. Then, students collaborate with other students to solve the problem using a number of different resources to investigate and recommend a solution. The teacher's role includes: building the teaching/

What Makes a Good Web Resource?

Accurate	Author credentials	Free
Current	Fast load	Short pages
Reliable	Good information	Readability
Graphics	Links to other sites	Purpose
References	Reviewed	Searchable
Style	Updated	Well organized

learning template, coaching students on critical learning events, and providing embedded assessment of student learning.

The critical components of PBL include:
-Prepare the learners
-Introduce the problem
-Identify what the learners need to know
-Define the problem
-Gather and share information
-Generate possible solutions
-Determine the "best" solution
-Present solutions
-Debrief the activity

Web tutorials. Web tutorials are designed to teach a particular concept. Good tutorials address a specific objective and provide new information, including lots of examples. The tutorial should include an introduction, options for help, and opportunities for students to practice. Feedback also should be provided. An example of an outstanding tutorial is the Science of Cycling (http://www.exploratorium.edu/cycling/), which combines information on science and physical activity.

Virtual simulations. Virtual simulations help students apply their skills to "real life" situations by providing an environment in which they can manipulate variables, examine relationships, and make decisions. Simulations can help to prepare students for a field trip or a real experiment. While some simulations have a particular mission to accomplish, others are intended to help students explore a particular

273

Other Web Activities

Database Creation - Collecting and organizing information into databases that project participants and others study and analyze.

Electronic Appearance - Interpersonal exchanges that host special guests who communicate with students either in real time or asynchronously.

Electronic Publishing - Collect and organize information into electronic periodicals (e-zines), report repositories, and online galleries.

Global Classrooms - Group-to-group exchanges - two or more classrooms in different locations study a common topic together during an agreed-upon time period.

Impersonations - One participant in an online group communicates as a character.

Information Exchanges - Sharing information that is collected locally.

Information Searches - Online problem solving. Students are given clues and must use either online or more traditional resources to answer questions. Sometimes referred to as scavenger hunts or treasure hunts.

Parallel Problem Solving - Students discuss each other's problem-solving processes. A problem is presented to and explored by students in several locations before they come together online to compare, contrast, and discuss their separate problem-solving methods.

Peer Feedback Activities - Participants offer constructive responses to others' ideas.

Pooled Data Analysis - Learners pool similar data from different locations and then analyze the patterns that emerge from combined samples.

Question-and-Answer Activities - Online activity with a subject matter expert.

Sequential Creations - Collaboration on a common product that occurs sequentially rather than simultaneously.

Social Action Projects - Students learn about and take action to solve authentic global challenges.

Telementoring - Internet-connected specialists from universities, businesses, or schools serve as electronic mentors to students who want to explore specific study topics.

Telepresent Problem Solving - Real-time brainstorming and problem-solving using text chat and/or videoconferencing.

Web Lessons

Health Education

Body Quest: http://library.thinkquest.org/10348/

Cloning: http://powayusd.sdcoe.k12.ca.us/ewe2/

Dissection: http://george.lbl.gov/ITG.hm.pg.docs/dissect/
dissect.html

Elementary Substance Abuse Lessons/Activities: http://
www.teachervision.com/lesson-plans/lesson-5186.html

Environmental Awareness: http://www.gsn.org/cf/categories/
cat7.html

Health and Fitness Research Lessons (8 lessons K-12): http://
www.learningspace.org/instruct/lplan/library/hfit.html

KidLink Health Activities: http://www.kidlink.org/english/general/
c/curric11.html

Label Me Activities: http://www.EnchantedLearning.com/subjects/
anatomy/titlepage.shtml

Life Expectancy: http://moneycentral.msn.com/investor/calcs/n_
expect/main.asp

MedMan: http://library.thinkquest.org/2824

Middle School Alcohol Addiction Lesson Plans: http://
www.thirteen.org/edonline/lessons/alcohol/alcoholov.html

Time of Your Life: http://orr.mec.edu/~cbasile/web_quest.htm

Truth in Advertising: http://education.indiana.edu/cas/tt/v3i3/
advertising.html

Physical Education

History of Physical Education: http://schools.eastnet.ecu.edu/pitt/
ayden/hist/hist.html

KidLink Physical Education Activities: http://www.kidlink.org/
english/general/c/curric10.html

Olympic Dream: http://www.wc4.org/Moucha-Ruble2.htm

Physical Education Lesson Plans: http://schools.eastnet.ecu.edu/
pitt/ayden/physed8.htm

Physical Education Lesson Plans: http://www.nysatl.nysed.gov/
PhysEd/index.htmlPhysically Fit: http://www.widgeon.com/
22chfitness.html

situation or environment. In most cases, simulations should be used as a culminating activity after students have basic skills in the concepts being addressed either on the web site or in other classroom activities. The classic virtual simulation is the Virtual Frog Dissection Kit at http://www-itg.lbl.gov/ITG.hm.pg.docs/dissect/info.html.

Some physical educators have actually combined the formats of virtual simulations and virtual field trips by having their students design community activities. An educator in Iowa had her students design a virtual canoe field trip. They were given x amount of fake money with which to buy equipment and arrange for transportation and lodging. They used MapQuest to plan their travels, online shopping to make purchases, and research tools to locate the "skill-appropriate" river/lake and to hone their canoeing skills.

Working Offline

If you do not have access to the Internet at your teaching location, you can still provide your students with Internet learning opportunities. Programs such as *Web Buddy* allow teachers to collect pages and even entire sites from the web for viewing offline. Many professional speakers use these programs so they can demonstrate the Internet without having to wait for the transfer of information or worry about a disconnection. Physical educators can do the same by downloading the web pages and placing them on a local server or computer. Students can access the information as if they were actually on the World Wide Web.

Developing Web Pages

If you would like to add to the Internet information on physical education and sports you can set up your own web page. Web authoring programs such as *DreamWeaver* (Macromedia), *GoLive* (Adobe), *FrontPage* (Microsoft), or *Composer* (Netscape) make it very easy for you to do so. These programs function much like a word processing program; however, the output is in the form of a code known as html. Short for "hypertext markup language," html allows a variety of Internet users, regardless of their operating system, to view web pages. Web authoring programs also allow the user to embed links to other web pages, as well as sounds, pictures, and video clips (see Chapter 8 for capturing video clips).

When designing a web site, be sure to follow these steps:
1. Plan - sketch it out on paper
2. Create the text
3. Create and insert the images and sounds
4. Create the links
5. Create the interactive elements
6. Test the site using different browsers
7. Post the site
8. Maintain the site

Once you have created your web site you will need to post your files on a server. You can either use your school's server, server space provided by your Internet Service Provider, or one of the free Web hosting sites. Do be careful when designing your site to follow the Web Site Compliance Tips and Web Design Guidelines in the boxes.

Physical educators can post information related to their curriculum, rules, assessment procedures, the benefits of physical education, homework assignments, and other relevant information for parents. In addition, they can create learning activities (e.g., online quizzes, worksheets) and post them on the web for student use. Coaches can post player information, schedules, scores, statistics, and scholarship information. Physical educators also can create online instruction or courses for their students using additional software such as Web CT (www.webct.com) and Blackboard (www.blackboard.com). These programs include online chat spaces, student progress tracking, grade maintenance and distribution, course calendars, student home pages, and search engine links.

Web Site Compliance

Text equivalents for non-text items
Alternatives for multimedia
Image map - redundant text links
Table - column and row headers
Frames - use a title
Online forms - associated text labels
Flicker rate between 2Hz - 55 Hz (prevent seizures)
Compliance check: http://bobby.watchfire.com/bobby/html/en/index.jsp

Web Design Guidelines

1. Start small and have a plan—for content and appearance.
2. Add material gradually.
3. Create one main folder for your entire site.
4. Create a separate folder inside the main folder for each major category of information.
5. Create one folder named "images" inside your main folder.
6. Keep each level to five to 10 items.
7. Develop a plan for maintenance and updates.
8. Put contact information (name, address, telephone, and fax numbers) on each page.
9. Include an e-mail link on each page.
10. Add new content weekly.
11. Check all links weekly.
12. Use a consistent look and feel.
13. Put navigation devices on each page.
14. Use no more than three images per page.
15. Put no more than two screens of information on each page.
16. If you must use more than two screens of information, provide a menu at the top of the page.
17. Design for 72 dpi, 256 colors, RGB, and 640x480.
18. Load time for a page should not exceed 30 seconds.
19. Test all pages on the two most commonly used browsers Netscape and Explorer—and on both a PC and a Mac.
20. Linked text should not exceed 20 percent of a passage.
** Double check: grammar, spelling, organization, presentation, directions, accuracy, and navigation.

Web Hosting

GeoCities: http://www.geocities.com/
Teacher Web: http://www.teacherweb.com/
Tripod: http://www.tripod.com/
My School Online: http://www.myschoolonline.com/

Web Development Resources

Creating a Web Page	http://www.info.bw/~ledu/create.htm
Fair Use Guidelines	http://www.dartmouth.edu/copyright/ fairuse.html
Cyberbee's	http://www.cyberbee.com/master.html
Design Guidelines	http://www.dreamink.com

Summary

The Internet can provide you with hours of enjoyment as well as the opportunity to secure vast amounts of information. However, it is important to double check information and to ensure that the information you are reading is from a reliable source. A common feature of many Internet sites is "Frequently Asked Questions." This is a list of questions and answers about the site, and it provides a good introduction to the site. For those of you who are ready, try the next step and create your own web page.

Turn on your computer and start surfing, searching, and developing!

Reflection Questions

1. Do you think the benefits of accessing the World Wide Web for physical education-related activities is worth the time, effort, and money invested in Internet access? Explain your answer.
2. Which of the web-based activities would best meet of the needs of your students? Why?

Projects

1. Design a web-based activity for one of your classes. Be sure to align it with the content standards.
2. Create your own web page.

Chapter 11

Using Technology To Improve the Instructional Process

Juan Garcia sits down at his desk and replays the recording of his previous class taken by one of his students. He takes out his handheld computer to collect data on his teaching as he watches. After reviewing his lesson, he has the software analyze his teaching behaviors and produce a print out of areas that need improvement.

In previous chapters, we looked at how technology can be used to improve student learning. In this chapter, we turn our attention to the ways technology can be used to improve teacher effectiveness. Several of the technologies discussed thus far can assist with preservice training as well as with professional development. Physical educators—like students—can use CD-ROMs and the Internet to increase their knowledge, for example. And, just as there are assessment tools for students, there are technology-based assessment tools that teachers can use to improve their performance. Finally, teachers can create "professional portfolios" similar to student portfolios to demonstrate their teaching effectiveness. In fact at many colleges and universities, electronic portfolios are required prior to the student teaching experience.

Information Related to Teaching

There are two categories of information that will be of specific interest to physical educators. The first is current research related to pedagogy and physical education concepts. Some of this information can be accessed from the same sources that students use; other sources are designed specifically for physical educators. The second category is related to lesson planning. It includes instructional materials and student assessment tools. Both types of information are available on CD-ROMs and the Internet.

On the research side, the Sport Information Resource Centre (SIRC) is the largest resource center in the world. It collects and disseminates information in the area of sport, physical education, physical fitness, and sports medicine. Every month, SIRC scans more than 1,200 magazines and journals ranging from the practical *Runner's World* to the scholarly *Research Quarterly for Exercise and Sport* as well as other published material. SIRC then produces the SPORT Data base, which contains bibliographic references to more than 360,000 magazine articles, books, theses, conference papers, and other published research from around the world. More than 235,000 citations also are available. Using the SIRC CD-ROM, you define your search topic by identifying the important words and related terms for each concept. Although this is a very expensive resource (more than $1,000), you may find that your central office, city library, or local university has a copy.

The Internet is an excellent resource for research pertaining to many physical education topics. But, heed the same advice you give your students when conducting research on the Internet: double check all pieces of information and investigate the credentials of the individuals who conducted the research and posted the results. When doing research on the Internet, follow the searching strategies outlined in Chapter 10.

On the lesson plan side, *Movin' On* (available from NASPE) can help physical educators manage elementary physical education activities. The activities in *Movin' On* were collected by experienced physical educators; however, you can personalize the program and add to the activities it contains. The program includes equipment, instructional units, academic skills, and game applications, along with exercises and suggested references. Users can search for lessons by type of equipment, instructional unit (including several thematic units), academic skills, and/or game applications. At the end of the year, the software can provide you with a summary of your lessons. Everything can be printed, so if you want a hard copy of something you can create one.

Preservice Training

Preservice training typically occurs in the college/university setting. And, although there are schools that provide curriculum via the Internet, most still provide the majority of their undergraduate instruction on-site. However, even with on-site courses, technology is often utilized as a means of sharing information, keeping open the lines of communication, and training young professionals to use technology. Let's take a look at each of these areas.

Many professors create their own home pages with hyperlinks to each of the classes they teach. On the main page of each course, they often post the course syllabus, homework assignments, lecture notes, and links to related information. Some instructors have even gone so far as to include sample tests on their web pages; students answer the questions and then receive their scores and other helpful feedback.

Electronic mail has increased communication throughout the educational community, and the interaction between instructor and student at the college level is no exception. Students can use e-mail to ask follow-up questions about lecture material. And, during student teaching, e-mail allows for three-way communication among the student teacher, cooperating teacher, and university supervisor. Student teachers can e-mail their lesson plans simultaneously to both their cooperating teacher and university supervisor. After receiving timely feedback from both advisors, students can adjust lessons before teaching them.

Finally, most undergraduate teacher training programs require some form of instruction on the use of current technologies in education. This often takes the form of a course offered either by the education or physical education department. It typically covers word processing, data bases, spreadsheets, grading software, fitness reporting, instructional software, Internet skills, and the creation of a multimedia project. Helpful resources for the teaching of this course includes this book, along with *Integrating Technology and Pedagogy in Physical Education Teacher Education* (Mitchell & McKethan, 2003). This course is beneficial, but interacting with professors via e-mail, accessing web sites, and using technology in their other coursework also can be very helpful. A few universities require students in the teacher preparation program to purchase and use heart monitors throughout their undergraduate work. This provides an additional experience in using technology in physical education.

Professional Development

Inservice training typically is conducted by local colleges/ universities, professional associations, and/or regional educational institutions (district offices, local educational agencies). These agencies award college credits or salary points for teachers. However, physical educators (especially those with coaching responsibilities) often find it difficult to attend professional development workshops. Today, training can take place via the Internet, allowing educators to learn at their convenience. The number of virtual colleges and training centers on the Internet is growing by leaps and bounds. Virginia Tech (Blacksburg, VA), for example, offers a Masters Degree program in physical education via the Internet.

National Board Certification
http://www.nbpts.org

National Board Certification is a way for the teaching profession to define and recognize highly accomplished practice. A certificate awarded by the National Board for Professional Teaching Standards attests that a teacher has been judged by his or her peers as one who meets high and rigorous professional standards. He or she has demonstrated the ability, in a variety of settings, to make sound professional judgments about students' best interests and to act effectively on those judgments.

The National Board has developed an innovative, two-part assessment process to determine whether a teacher possesses the attributes of accomplished teaching based on the National Board's standards. One component of the assessment is done at a teacher's school. A teacher shows evidence of good teaching practice by preparing a portfolio. The portfolio contains videotapes of classroom teaching, lesson plans, samples of student work, and written commentaries in which the teacher reflects on what he or she is doing and why. The second component of the assessment includes exercises that take place at an assessment center. Candidates spend one day at the assessment center. Exercises are designed around challenging teacher issues and include evaluating other teachers' practice, interviews, and exams in a teacher's field.

In another example, Bonnie's Fitware provides a number of online learning experiences (see Online Course Descriptions box) each year that are designed specifically for physical educators. Information about the courses is distributed nationally through flyers and journal articles. Each course consists of six learning modules (one unit) that can be completed any time between September 1 and December 15 or February 1 and May 15. Class sizes have ranged from 5 to 50 students per course.

Bonnie's Fitware begins each of its online learning opportunities by sending an e-mail message to the participants. The message welcomes students to the course and provides an Internet address that they can click on to get to the course syllabus. The syllabus provides participants with the objectives, a list of the six modules, course assessments, and textbook references. The participants are asked to read the syllabus and then click on Module 1. The first

Sample Online Course Descriptions
http://www.pesoftware.com

Using Technology Devices in Physical Education

This course is designed to introduce physical educators to the use of pedometers, heart monitors, body composition analyzers, blood pressure devices, spirometers, peak flow meters, accelerometers, digital cameras, and digital camcorders in physical education. Participants will design their own standards-based lesson plans using a technology device as a resource. They will learn class management strategies for using technology in the physical education environment.

Using Instructional Software in Physical Education

This course is designed to introduce physical educators to standards-based instructional software. Participants will design their own standards-based lesson plans using a piece of software as a resource. They will learn class management strategies for using technology in the physical education environment. The participants will complete the course with a comprehensive understanding of the software available in physical education.

Designing Web Pages/Activities for Physical Education

This is a beginning web course designed to introduce physical educators to the wide range of instructional possibilities in using the World Wide Web. Participants will explore exemplary web sites, participate in web-based learning activities, and design their own web page.

Fitness Technology for Physical Education

This course is designed to introduce physical educators to the uses of technology in physical education to design electronic fitness reports. Participants will explore each of the fitness reporting software programs available and conduct an analysis and comparison of the various programs. Physical educators will complete the course competent in the use of fitness reporting software.

Record Book for Palm Operating System/Pocket PC

This course is designed to introduce physical educators to standards-based grading/assessment and the use of software to facilitate the grading/assessment process. Participants will design their own standards-base grading system. They will learn to set up and use the *Record Book* software to facilitate the grading process. The participants will complete the course competent in the use of the *Record Book* software.

module introduces participants to online learning and, for those who are interested, how to sign up for college credit. Participants are asked to send an e-mail message that introduces themselves. Participants complete all six modules, including learning activities and assignments, during the time period provided.

Assessing Teacher Performance

Over the years, student teacher and teacher evaluation has shifted from subjective to objective evaluation. Researchers have demonstrated the relationship between increases in student learning and process variables such as time on task, amount and types of feedback, use of class time, and the number of successful completions of a task. These variables can be measured and the feedback provided for use in improving teaching effectiveness. A supervisor can collect these data live or from a videotape of the lesson. Taping lessons facilitates unbiased evaluation and enables both the teacher and supervisor to review the lesson as often as necessary.

There are three methods for recording teaching behaviors during observations: pen-and-paper tallying, portable computers, and palm computers. The use of computers makes the process of recording, storing, analyzing, and printing data more efficient. It also allows for the simultaneous collection of data on a number of different variables. The following sections describe the software that is available.

Observation, Analysis, and Recording System (OARS). OARS is used at the University of Virginia, records frequency and duration data in as many as 10 categories (behaviors or events). You can create an unlimited number of your own categories, and several common categorical systems (e.g., Flanders, Galloway, Blumburg) are predefined and ready to use. Prompts are provided on the screen to label each category being observed and to indicate which categories are active during recording. Comments can be entered at any time during the recording session through the keyboard; they are recorded as part of the session event log. One hundred lines of summary comments also can be entered at the end of each session. The print out includes a graphic summary of all categories across time and a sequential, time-coded log of events. The program is menu driven, user friendly, and complemented by a comprehensive, step-by-step how-to manual available on diskette or in paper format.

Teacher Observation Program 2 (Bonnie's Fitware). This is a Palm OS application designed to record teaching behaviors during physical education classes. It includes tally recording for: positive feedback, corrective feedback, negative feedback, congruent feedback, incongruent feedback, behavior feedback, type of task (inform, refine, extend, repeat, or apply), number of students on task, practice opportunities for three students, and use of time (management, practice, game, lecture, and warm-up). After the class, the data are summarized and available on the handheld computer. They also can be uploaded to a Windows-based machine for storage and printing.

Computer Assisted Systematic Analysis of Instructor and Learner Behavior: Physical Education and Coaching edition (CASAIL-PEC). This is a Windows operating system program created by Daniel Frankle. It was designed to help student teachers, supervisors, teachers, and coaches evaluate instructional efficacy, lesson density, and learner behaviors in an accurate, fast, and relatively effortless manner. It features several data collection formats, such as:

-Academic Learning Time in Physical Education Settings (ALT-PE) variables (e.g., waiting, transition, management, lecture, demonstration).

-Opportunities for response (tallying of successful and unsuccessful learner on-task experiences).

-Feedback (e.g., positive, negative).

-Modeling (e.g., by instructor, student, correct/incorrect).

-Attention to safety issues (e.g., positive/negative).

-Instructional space (e.g., soccer field, basketball court).

Likert scale data collection also is included in *CASAIL-PE*.

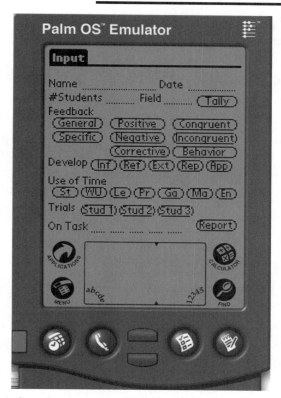

Figure 11.1 Sample screen from Teacher Observation System 2.

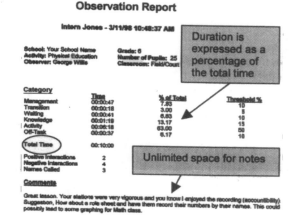

Figure 11.2 Sample screen from Teacher Observation System 2.

Summary

Recent studies have shown that the teacher accounts for 51 percent of the learning that goes on in schools. This chapter has addressed four ways that technology can be used to improve the effectiveness of the teacher. They include software designed to increase teacher understanding of concepts, effective preservice training, inservice professional development designed to maintain teacher effectiveness and to keep teachers abreast of new strategies and techniques, and assessment tools designed to provide teachers with feedback on their instructional effectiveness. So far in this book, we have focused on "what is." In the next chapter we will address "what can be."

Reflection Questions

1. In what other ways can you imagine using technology in teacher preparation programs and teacher inservice programs?
2 What would be the advantage of National Board Certification? Have you considered applying for National Board Certification? Why or why not?
3. Have you ever considered taking a course via the Internet? What would you see as the advantages? What would you see as the disadvantages?
4. Choose a specific teaching behavior and develop a plan to assess the behavior.

Projects

1. Imagine that you are applying for National Board Certification in physical education. Arrange to have yourself videotaped (by an adult or student) during one of your classes. Then, take the time to review the tape and reflect on your teaching practices. Think about what worked, what didn't work, and what you would do differently next time.
2. Select a topic of interest related to pedagogy or physical education content, then conduct an Internet search to bring yourself up-to-date on the topic.

Chapter 12

The Future of Technology in Physical Education

The year is 2020. The place is the gymnasium of Middle School USA, and a physical education class is about to begin. As the students walk across the gym, they turn to face a biometric device that conducts a retina scan and documents their presence. The students begin their warm up and fitness exercises, following a hologram that demonstrates each exercise. The students have been learning tennis for the past several weeks, and today they will focus on the correct technique for the tennis serve. There are five learning stations set up around the gymnasium. The students, working in groups of four, rotate from one station to the next.

At Learning Station 1, students view a hologram of an Olympic athlete demonstrating the correct technique for the serve. The students, racquets in hand, mimic the hologram in order to connect the visual image and kinesthetic feeling to their brains. At Learning Station 2, a computer digitizes the students' images as they replicate the tennis serve and provides them with immediate feedback on their technique. At Learning Station 3, students have the opportunity to hit a "real" ball. A recording device captures their image as they practice serving. Before proceeding to the next station, a computer again provides them with feedback. At Learning Station 4, students have an opportunity to question a tennis pro, via a videoconference, about her serving technique and practice schedule. Learning Station 5 brings together all the skills the students have been working on during the last several weeks. The students use a virtual reality program that provides them with competition customized to their level of experience and ability. At the end of class, the students pause momentarily on their way out of the gym to allow the teacher's computer to upload data (vital signs, calorie expenditure and heart rate data collected during the instructional period, and movement data from the serving activities) from the sensors each student wears. The teacher's computer analyzes the information and forwards a copy of the results to the student's e-mail account and to the teacher for review.

Twenty years ago, most physical educators could not imagine using a computer in any part of their program, and none of us could foresee the role computers would play in our personal and professional lives. As we look to the future and hear wondrous stories of what technology will be like in the next 20 years, we need to remember how far we have come and how far we still have to go.

In this chapter, I will review the 1993, 1998, and 2001 versions of the future (*Using Technology in Physical Education*, Editions 1, 2, and 3) and note how far we have come. Then, I will again attempt to look into the crystal ball and predict the future from the 2004 perspective. However, since it is not only the advancement of the technology but its use by physical educators that will determine the future, I also will examine how these devices may be used in physical education programs tomorrow.

The Future: 1993 Version

In the first edition of this book, I addressed four areas of growth in technology—pen technology/voice recognition, distance learning, student response keypads, and virtual reality. Each area was reviewed along with its application for physical education. Each of the following sections contains a passage from the first edition, followed by information on that technology's current level of sophistication and use in physical education programs.

Pen Technology and Voice Recognition

1993. Typically we use a keyboard, mouse, or touch screen to communicate with our computers. The new pen technology allows us to communicate with our computers by writing on a special surface; the software for pen technology is becoming so sophisticated that it can interpret our handwriting. The next step will be voice recognition—we will communicate with our computers simply by speaking to them. This will be especially convenient for physical educators who are out on the field and want to input information. They will be able to speak into a small microphone and the message will be transmitted to the computer back in the office.

2004. Pen technology in the form of a stylus has become the primary input device for handheld computers. And the age of voice recognition is here. The applications still require time and patience to set up, and there are glitches from time to time. The voice recognition applications haven't yet found their way to the physical education field, but they have been used by persons with disabilities to record information. Although they still require fast computers to work effectively, prices are coming down daily and capability is fast approaching everyday use.

The next step in voice recognition technology will be interpretative telephony. This is the ability of the voice recognition system to translate the language spoken into a second verbal language. This type of system will allow a physical educator to communicate with every child in his/her class in his/her native language. Imagine the instructional and safety implications when working with non-English speaking students. It is projected that portable translation devices for simple conversations will be a reality by 2007. (Just in time for the next edition of this book.)

Distance Learning

1993. Distance education instructors conduct class sessions in front of a video camera. The video is then uplinked to a satellite and downlinked to subscribing schools' satellite dishes. This provides teachers and students in many different geographic areas with the benefits of hearing from an expert on a given subject or seeing a model lesson or demonstration of a skill. You can even call in and ask questions while the program is on the air. If the time is inconvenient for you, you can videotape the program and show it later. This type of staff development will become the norm in the future. It is projected that 3D video conferencing will be available by the year 2015.

2004. This type of professional development is the norm today. The United States Department of Education, along with numerous regional educational agencies and private agencies, commonly conduct distance learning seminars for educators. In addition, Chapters 10 and 11 illustrated how the Internet has become an even more viable option for distance learning—both for teachers and for students. The future for this technology is wide open—the only question that remains is, "Will it, along with the Internet, completely replace regular on-site learning for teachers and students?"

Student Response Keypads

1993. Future students will carry around their own handheld computers. In the meantime, student response keypads (which are about the size of a small television remote control) allow student interaction with the teacher. Up to 255 keypads can be connected to one computer, allowing you to conduct ongoing quizzes during instruction and receive instant feedback on your presentation.

2004. Student response keypads never really infiltrated the K-12 educational setting, and I for one, have never seen their use in physical education. However, we seem to have jumped quickly to the feasibility of the handheld computers. There are schools today where every student carries a handheld computer.

What we are talking about here is miniaturizing computers. And, we are seeing that happen as we watch the size of the computer diminish from laptop, to notebook, to handheld, to watch. Futurists predict that within the first quarter of the new millennium, information storage will be so compact that all the information a well-informed person can consume in a lifetime—all the books, manuals, magazine and newspaper articles, letters, memos, reports, greeting cards, notebooks, diaries, ledgers, bills, pamphlets, brochures, photographs, paintings, posters, movies, TV shows, videos, radio programs, audio records, concerts, lectures, phone calls, etc.—will be stored in an object no bigger than a book and potentially as small as a fat fountain pen (Perelman, 1992).

Virtual Reality

1993. Virtual reality envelops the user in an artificial world. Through special interfaces (such as gloves and a helmet), the user receives from the computer the sensory illusion of being in a very different environment. This artificial world is felt through tactile stimulators in the gloves and seen through a screen mounted in the helmet. The user interacts with this world by gesturing with the gloves or moving the helmeted head, and the computer responds appropriately to those gestures.

2004. This prediction wasn't hard to come by, since virtual reality was a reality by 1985, when a programmer developed such a system so he could learn to juggle. The sophistication of virtual reality systems has increased over time. Currently, there are four categories of virtual reality: desktop systems (navigating through three dimensions on a monitor), partial immersion (navigating through three-dimensional on a monitor with enhancements such as gloves and three dimensions goggles), full-immersion systems (head gear, gloves, and bodysuits), and environmental

Sport Simulators/Virtual Reality

Cyberbike (Frost, 1999), a standard mountain bike that has been modified to allow real-world motion of the bike wheel (using optical sensors) and the steering to determine the speed and direction of movement in the virtual world.

Shut-Out Hockey (Vincent, nd), the user becomes the goaltender, actually defending the net against "virtual" attackers in pass-and-shoot scenarios.

Full Court Slam (Vincent, nd), the user actually plays one-on-one basketball against a "virtual opponent."

Virtual Volleyball (Vincent, nd), the user's video image is placed on a volleyball court to play against a virtual robot named Spike, or against a real person whose image is also projected onto the court.

SmartGolf (Atlantis Cyberspace, 1996), the user drives, chips, and putts real balls using clubs from simulated fairways and greens, including sand and rough areas. A large touch screen is used for projected images from the lie of the ball.

Snowboarding (Vincent, nd), the user moves his or her body to control the direction of the snowboard.

Kayaking (Vincent, nd), the user pilots his or her kayak through different courses, actually learning left or right to avoid objects in the "virtual" water.

White Water Rafting (Patton, nd), an oar-like device that the user manipulates to pilot a virtual raft through different courses.

Hang Gliding (Schroeder, 1996), a simulation where the user's body is suspended in the harness of a hang glider simulation. The crossbar controls the altitude and direction of the glider.

Bobsled (Kelly, et al., 2002), a simulator designed for the United States Olympic Bobsled Team during training. The user shifts his or her body weight to control the direction of the sled.

Virtual Motion's Wind Surfing (Atlantis Cyberspace, 1996), has the user move his or her body to control the board.

systems (externally generated three-dimensional experiences using little or no body paraphernalia).

Partial and full immersion applications that require head gear, gloves, and other external devices are becoming available at prices that are considerably less than the research models. Head gear—including viewers—is becoming lighter and less obtrusive, with even greater resolution and accuracy. Gloves are providing more precision at lower prices. These devices let you play certain VR-compatible games, such as "Virtual Reality Ninja" (http://www.manleytoyquest.com) and those listed in the Sport Simulators/Virtual Reality box. On the flip side, a virtual reality meditation chamber has been designed to monitor and provide biofeedback to users in order to help virtual meditators relax.

Although virtual reality applications have become more common, very few schools use them as instructional tools. However, I believe it is an emerging technology that will have a significant impact on the future of physical education. If you are looking for financial assistance from grants and foundations in order to incorporate technology into your physical education program, then virtual reality is your ticket.

The Future: 1998 Version

In the second edition of this book, I addressed seven areas of growth in technology. Each of the following sections contains a passage from the second edition, followed by information on that technology's current level of sophistication and use in physical education programs.

Identification Units

1998. There are several new biometric identification devices on the market. The Fingerprint Identification Unit scans an image of a fingerprint and saves it in a data base. Then, it matches the print copy against the user's finger as he or she logs in. Other biometric devices scan faces, retinas, voices, and even blood.

Primarily designed for use in security systems, these devices have a place in physical education. They can be used to identify an individual taking a computer-generated test on site or online. No doubt we also will see these devices becoming the attendance takers of the future. I can see students looking into a camera, as described at the beginning of this chapter, or placing their index finger on a pad or screen as they enter the locker room. Eliminating the traditional roll call will provide additional time for instruction.

2004. The sophistication of these devices has continued to develop with an emphasis on fingerprint readers, retina scanners, and facial scanners. Several handheld computers now have built-in software that requires a fingerprint scan for access, and similar external devices are available for desktop and laptop computers. It is projected that by the year 2015, identification cards will have been completely replaced by biometric scanning.

Flat Panel Display

1998. Display monitors are becoming larger, thinner, and better each year. Fujitsu currently sells a 42-inch, gas-plasma flat panel display. The monitor, which can also display computer images, is only four inches thick. Unfortunately the cost, as of 1998, is $17,500.

Flat panel display units will decrease in cost and be used in physical education much like television monitors are used today. However, the quality will be much better and the equipment will take up less space. Panels will display fitness lessons, cognitive concepts, and model demonstrations. An Internet connection will allow an entire class to take electronic or virtual field trips to Olympic training centers or other sporting venues.

2004. The cost is coming down and this technology still holds much promise for the area of physical education. Already, flat-panel displays for computers are a realistic purchase for many. It is projected that holographic television will be the next big step. It should be on the market by 2025.

Three-Dimensional Animation

1998. Three-dimensional animation is finally coming of age. It seems that every month a new three-dimensional product hits the market with a claim to be the best, fastest, and most lifelike. For example, *Biped* (Discreet) is a new plug in program for *3D Studio MAX* (Discreet). It allows the user to create realistic human movement simply by placing footsteps—much like chalking steps on the floor in a dance class. The software automatically generates appropriate walking, running, or jumping movements with the correct foot and leg rotation.

These three-dimensional animation programs allow students to create original routines for dancing, tumbling, and gymnastics. In addition, they can be interactive in real time with on-screen simulations for self-defense and orienteering activities. These programs also provide programmers with the tools to produce higher quality software for use in physical education.

Three-dimensional animation programs also can be used to design new facilities, including playgrounds. Landscape Structures, a playground equipment company, already provides buyers with a two-dimensional working site plan of a new playground that provides a top view layout of the equipment in the proposed site. It includes the actual size and minimum use zones. At this stage, the buyer makes adjustments in the arrangement of the equipment and reconsiders any component choices. Then, the computer generates a high-quality three-dimensional color rendering of the playground, enabling the buyer to verify the design.

2004. Three-dimensional animation programs have continued to develop and improve. Educational programs such as *Poser* (CuriousLabs) and *LifeForms* (Credo Interactive), bring the technology into the hands of students. *Poser* is a figure design and animation tool that allows the user to create lifelike drawings and animations of human figures in action—dancing ballet, climbing a cliff, exercising, etc. You simply create a pose, go to a new position on the time line, change the pose, and let the software generate all the in-between motion.

Life Forms allows you to create three-dimensional animations for choreography, movement planning, and physical education. In addition to its animation feature, *Life Forms* provides you with the tools for applying finishing touches such as textures and colors. You can even export the animations as QuickTime movies or other file formats.

Movement Tracking

1998. As mentioned earlier in this chapter, body suits, or exoskeletons, take virtual reality to another level. Electromagnetic movement tracking technology lets the user move around in three-dimensional space and see the corresponding changes of view while tracking the position of moving objects. For example, *The Gypsy* ($19,995) uses an exoskeleton with potentiometers at the joints. *The Gypsy* can be set up in minutes and it does not require a controlled environment. It requires only one suit and a single analog to digital converter card that connects to a personal computer. Movement of the individual is then monitored on the computer.

Movement trackers have the same potential for physical education as other virtual reality options—skill improvement, strategy sessions, and game play. Although it will be many years before this particular application becomes a reality in physical education, it will revolutionize physical activity as we know it today.

2004. Today we are seeing more and more sensors used for tracking motion. There are even sensors that can be placed in shoes to monitor motion. And, real-time swing analyzers (CyberScan) for golf, baseball, tennis, and hockey are now available at reasonable ($300-500) prices.

Nanotechnology

1998. Nanoparticles—just one one-thousandth of a micron in size—will be 1,000 percent stronger than traditional materials. Nanotechnology—the development of applications using new composite materials made of nanoparticles—will have a wide variety of applications in defense, medicine, sports, and recreational industries.

As mentioned earlier in this chapter, miniaturization is the name of the game. Nanotechnology takes this one step farther. Nanotechnology will help make your clothes "smarter." Future sport fabrics will contain tiny heating and cooling tubes, making a thin jacket as warm as a parka, for example. Nanotechnology also may have a negative impact on physical education: With the development of ultra-tiny micromachines that can travel in the blood vessels of the human body and do repair work, people may become less concerned about preventive health behaviors.

There are now "jackets that grow warmer when the temperature drops, sweat socks that resist bacteria and odors, T-shirts that ward off ultraviolet rays" (Minerd, 2000). This type of clothing allows for safer and more comfortable enjoyment of physical activities. We are even seeing wearable computers that fit into our clothing and jewelry.

2004. Today, nanotechnology also has impacted the three-dimensional fax movement. The nanobox passes plastic back and forth, laying down patterns of molecules much like a regular fax lays down ink on paper. However, the nanobox, using different "toners," can add circuits, antennas, keypads, speakers, microphones, etc., to the product (Port, 1999). Imagine the day when you no longer have to wait for a replacement part to fix a piece of equipment; instead it will be faxed to your nanobox. And, speaking of replacement parts, combining rapid-prototyping techniques with the principles of cell adhesion and smart polymer technologies may allow the manufacturing of custom-made body parts.

Ultra-tiny micromachines for medical purposes are still seen as the number one use of nanotechnology. In fact, it is projected that by 2020, nanobots will be put into toothpaste to attack plaque. And, to that end, President Clinton allocated $500 million dollars for research in the year 2001.

Expert Systems

1998. Expert systems will compress knowledge about a particular topic. It will arrange information in a branching configuration, so that possibilities can be discarded one at a time until a correct answer is found. In other words, this software will lead an individual through a step-by-step problem-solving process.

Expert programs will help teachers and students analyze and improve motor performance, assist coaches with game strategies, help individuals identify health problems and improve health practices, and advise people on the kinds of leisure time experiences they need to balance their lives. Coaches will be able to ask questions such as, "If the defense does this, what should the offense do?" Or, if maximum strength is needed in a given movement pattern, "What exercise program should be applied?"

2004. There are now expert systems that can diagnose human illnesses, make financial forecasts, and schedule routes for delivery vehicles. Some of these expert systems are designed to take the place of human experts, while others are designed to assist them. This area of technology, also known as artificial intelligence, will continue to expand, and much of that expansion will be in the area of education. Halal (2000) also is predicting that virtual assistants will be one of the applications for expert systems. "We envision the virtual assistant as a very smart program stored on your PC or portable device, that monitors all e-mails, faxes, messages, computer files, and phone calls in order to learn all about you and your work. In time, your virtual assistant would gain the knowledge to take over routine tasks, such as writing a letter, retrieving a file, making a phone call, or screening people" (p. 5). Primitive versions are already available in systems such as *Wildfire* and *Portico*. These programs can locate people by phone, take messages, and perform other simple tasks.

Holograms

1998. A hologram is a collection of all possible views of a scene combined into a single plane of light-modulating patterns. A hologram can take the form of an another person or an object. In the future, you will actually experience a sensation when you come in contact with the holographic image, and the image will be capable of reacting to such stimuli.

Holographic images in physical education will be used primarily in model performances. Other uses will include simulations that involve an opponent (e.g., martial arts), and simulations that provide the opportunity to talk with holographic versions of experts. One futurist predicts, "Sometime in the next millennium our grandchildren or great grandchildren will watch a football game by moving aside the coffee table and letting eight-inch-high players run around the living room passing a half-inch football back and forth" (Negroponte, 1995).

2004. The practical application of holograms is still in the future, but the vision and research continue.

The Future: 2001 Version

In the third edition of this book, I addressed two areas of growth in technology. Each of the following sections contains a passage from the third edition, followed by information on that technology's current level of sophistication and use in physical education programs.

Mapping of the Human Genome

2001. On June 26th, 2000, nearly five years ahead of schedule, a "working draft" of the human genome was completed. This draft depicts the layout of 100,000 human genes along with the sequence of the nearly three billion DNA base pairs. This document and the refinement to follow will have a dramatic impact on molecular medicine, microbial genomics, forensics, and agricultural business. Gene therapy may, in fact, improve people's learning abilities and reverse the effects of aging on memory.

Certainly, anything that helps to improve learning and memory has a carry-over effect on physical education. But, the mapping of the human genome also will have an impact on risk assessment. Folks prone to certain illness and disease will have forewarning. This may have a positive impact on physical education as individuals are able to take more responsibility for their own health, or it may have a negative impact as individuals rely more on medical interventions to solve their health issues.

2004. Genetic engineering can now double a worm's life span and mice are living 50 percent longer. Thanks to the human genome project, scientists are closer to identifying ways to decelerate human aging. Questions will arise as to the relative impact of genetics and lifestyle choices in the pursuit of high-quality lives.

Instant Electronic Diagnosis of Illnesses

2001. Small physiological sensors, attached to the body or available at "health" kiosks, will allow for constant monitoring of an individual's health. Smart chips will provide a complete record of patient history from birth to death, replacing the papers that always seem to get lost when transferring between providers (Halal, 2000). Imagine this scenario at a health kiosk in a shopping mall:

Place your arm in a tube on the left side of the chair. The tube and chair are connected to a computer that determines your height, weight, blood pressure, body fat, and blood chemistry. The computer has a floating camera attached, which allows close—even microscopic—inspection of the skin, eyes, mouth, etc. There also is a small mouthpiece for you to blow into; it monitors how your body is handling the air and analyzes a sample of saliva from your lips. When you insert your hand into a glovelike device at the end of the arm tube, it extracts (no needle, just pinpoint suction) two drops of blood from your finger and runs a complete spectrum of tests that once required multiple vials of blood (Wooten, 2000).

Much like the implications for the human genome project, this may have positive or negative effects on physical education. It all depends on whether individuals accept the additional responsibility for their own health or rely more on the medical profession. It is currently being projected that shower body scans will be available by 2015.

2004. Diagnosis of illnesses, along with medical advances to correct those illnesses, is an area that is growing by leaps and bounds. It will continue to do so over the next decade and beyond. Some of these changes will include the instant electronic diagnosis of illnesses as early as 2005, with lifestyle monitoring and insurance linked to medical records projected for 2010. Telepresence is expected to be used extensively in rural settings by the end of 2004, along with the dispensing of smart pills that will adapt to the individual taking the drug shortly thereafter. Again, medical improvements are a double-edge sword for physical education. Some folks will embrace their new found health and lead a more healthy lifestyle, while others will grow to depend on medical support and ignore recommendations for appropriate physical activity and nutrition.

The Future: 2004 Version

Each of the technologies described in the 1993, 1998, and 2001 editions have continued to evolve, and we can project that—like the computer—their growth will double every 18 months. New technologies also have emerged during the last three years, along with their potential applications for physical education. In this section, we will examine three of these new technologies and their potential for physical education.

Body Power

Our bodies actually produce energy in the form of heat. Body power, consists of chips made of silicon about the size of a dime that convert body heat into enough electricity to power a small electronic gadget which would otherwise rely on tiny and expensive batteries. One side of the "thermogenerator" faces the body and the other faces the air. The temperature difference between the two sides actually produces a current. Given a typical temperature difference at the wrist of five degrees C., these devices can generate enough power for a wristwatch.

In physical education, this would be a real money saver for powering heart rate monitors, pedometers, and stop watches. In addition, as this technology improves, the technology will provide power to handheld and notebook computers along with the use of solar power. Batteries will basically be eliminated.

Robots

Robots can take the form of automatic vacuums or more humanoid forms. The "DB" is a million-dollar humanoid robot that has learned to play air hockey by watching its makers play. Using stereo video cameras, it watched the researchers strike the puck with their paddles. Then, using its hydraulically powered arm, the robot imitated the motion. After a few false starts, the DB was able to hit the puck and its movements were surprisingly graceful. This sort of "imitation learning" is yielding smarter, more adaptive robots for physical therapy, search-and-rescue missions, and space applications. Imitation learning combines artificial-intelligence software with cutting-edge neuroscience. The robot uses machine vision algorithms to determine the position and velocity of a person's limbs and maps the information to its hydraulic joints. Comparing its own movement with the original, the robot makes adjustments in real time. It is anticipated that in 10 to 15 years, artificial intelligence will be so sophisticated, you won't be able to tell if you're talking to a real person or a machine.

On a similar note, the Virtual Human Project at Oak Ridge National Laboratory aims to build an entire virtual human, with fully interacting system, within the next 10 years. With a virtual human, researchers could go inside the body and see how various organs respond to medications or procedures. Drug companies could use virtual humans for drug testing, which could speed up the FDA approval process.

Whether it be a robot or virtual human, we may have a new trainer or competitor to practice our motor skills against. The robot or virtual human may even be programmed to provide the appropriate level of instruction or competition based on the needs of the learner.

Wireless (e-books)

Electronic books are becoming a reality with software such as *Palm Reader* (Palm OS) and *Microsoft Reader* (PocketPC). There are many sources on the Internet where books in the public domain have been converted to electronic books and can be downloaded for free or at minimal cost. In addition, we will see more and more books become available in this format, providing students with access to numerous books without having to break their backs carrying them from class to class. The additional benefits for physical education will be embedded video clips in the e-books that will provide students with images of model performances of motor skills.

Teacher With a Vision

I am teaching at a brand new state-of-the art technology school, and have found the use of technology in my curriculum to be the best motivation I have ever had in trying to get students to do "academic" type work in physical education class. My students are using heart rate monitors with computer interface, and using digital cameras—still and video—to do projects based on fitness concepts or skill development. They are using the *Fitness-* and *Activity- Gram* software to track their individual progress. All of this has motivated my students to exercise at home daily, and everyone wants to take physical education all year (it is not a required class at the middle school level in the state of Florida).

I am constantly learning about the newest technology from listservs, other colleagues, and my students. I think the future of education is all about technology, and I hope to be a big part of it.

Daniel Jenkins Academy of Technology is a magnet middle school with a small number of high school students who are on campus every day, but are taking their classes completely online from teachers all over the country. They can take personal fitness or regular physical education from me or online. This is the first school in the country to offer a program such as this. We are being followed by *USA Today* as well as several other news and government agencies to see if this is the type of program that should be offered to everyone.

-Susan Searls,
Daniel Jenkins Academy of Technology, Haines City, Florida

Summary

Each of the advances discussed in this chapter—and more—will have a tremendous impact on society, education, and physical education. We must keep up with these advances to ensure that we find positive applications for them in physical education.

And the journey continues…

Reflection Questions

1. Can you think of other possible applications of cutting-edge technology that might be useful in the future of physical education?

2. What changes related to physical education instruction do you see occurring in the next several years?

3. Given the changes that technology will introduce to the teaching of physical education, what do you see as the role of the physical educator in the future.

Projects

1. Write a one-page letter to an administrator describing why you need a computer (this is an update of the letter you wrote at the end of Chapter 1).

2. Prepare a list of resources (publications, web sites) or activities that can keep you up to date on important developments related to using technology in physical education.

Appendix A

Suggested Vendors

Amateur Athletic Foundation
www.aafla.org

A.D.A.M. Software
770-980-0888
www.adam.com

Adobe Systems, Inc
800-833-6687
www.adobe.com

Agency for Instructional Technology
812-335-7667
www.ait.net

Aladdin
800-732-8881
www.aladdinsys.com

Alfred Higgins Productions
800-766-5353

All-Pro Software
800-776-7859
www.allprosoftware.com

ALVA Access Group
888-318-2582
www.aagi.com

AAHPERD
800-213-7193
www.aahperd.org

American Red Cross
www.redcross.org

Apple Computer
408-996-1010
www.apple.com

Athletic Institute
200 Castlewood Dr.
North Palm Beach, FL 33408

Aurbach & Associates
800-774-7239
www.aurbach.com

Avid Sports
978-275-0200
www.avidsports.com

Baudville
800-728-0888
www.baudville.com

Belkin
800-223-5546
www.belkin.com

Biometric ID
www.biometricid.com/

Biometrics
www.pccoach.com

Blackboard
www.blackboard.com

Broderbund
319-395-9626
www.broderbund.com

Bonnie's Fitware
419-828-2144
www.pesoftware.com

Britannica
800-323-1229/800-621-3900
www.britannica.com

Brown and Benchmark
800-338-5371

Busy Body
1-800-HOME-FIT
www.busybody-fitness.com/

Cable in the Classroom
703-845-1400
www.ciconline.com

Cambridge
888-744-0100
www.cambridgeol.com

Cardiosport
www.cardiosport.com

Casio, Inc.
888-204-7765/800-435-7732
www.casio.com

CDW
http://www.cdw.com

CE Software
800-523-7638
www.cesoft.com

Chalkware Education Solutions
800-838-9058
www.iep.com

Chancery Software Ltd
800-999-9931
www.chancery.com

Chariot Software
www.chariot.com
Chip Taylor
800-876-2447
www.chiptaylor.com

Concept 2 Rower
800-245-5676
www.concept2.com

Conduits
813-907-2562
www.conduits.com

Country Technology, Inc.
608-735-4718
www.fitnessmart.com

Corel
800-772-6735
www.corel.com

Creative Health Products, Inc.
800-742-4478
www.CHPonline.com

Credo Interactive Inc
604-291-6717
www.credo-interactive.com

Crossword Weaver
800-229-3939
crosswordweaver.com

CU See Me Networks
800-241-7463
www.wpine.com

Curious Labs
www.curiouslabs.com

CyberScan
www.cyberscan.com

Dairy Council of California
www.dairycouncilorca.org

Dartfish
888-655-3850
www.dartfish.com

DataViz, Inc.
203-268-0030
www.dataviz.com

Dazzle Multimedia
888-436-4348
www.dazzlemultimedia.com

DDH Software
561-253-2225
www.ddhsoftware.com

DIAMAR Interactive
206-340-5975

DINE Systems
800-688-1848
www.dinesystems.com

Discreet
www.discreet.com

Disney Interacative
800-688-1520
disney.go.com/education

DK Interactive
800-342-5357
www.dk.com

Don Johnston
800-999-4660
www.donjohnston.com

Dragon Systems
800-437-2466
www.dragonsys.com

Dummie Press
800-434-3422
www.dummies.com

Educational Software Institute
800-955-5570
www.edsoft.com

Eovia
866-856-3775
www.eovia.com

ESPN Cable in the Classroom
800-565-0452
www.espn.com

Fetch
866-422-0023
fetchsoftworks.com/

File Maker
617-494-1600
www.filemaker.com

Fitcentric Technologies
800-400-1390
www.fitcentric.com

FSCreations
513-241-3415
www.fscreations.com

Futrex Inc.
800-255-4206
www.futrex.com

Glencoe/McGraw-Hill
800-334-7344
www.glencoe.com

Globalink
www.lhsl.com

Grolier Publishing
800-371-3908
teacherstore.grolie.com

Health Tech
1-800-345-4207
www.healtheTech.com

Health First
800-841-8333
www.healthfirstusa.com

Hi-Ce
734-763-6988
www.hi-ce.org

High Plains Regional
888-TEC-2001
http://hprtec.org/

Human Kinetics
800-747-4457
www.humankinetics.com

IBM Corporation
800-426-4968
www.ibm.com/education

Infogrip
800-397-0921
www.infogrip.com

Inprise
813-431-1000
www.inprise.com

Inspiration Software
800-877-4292
www.inspiration.com

IntelliTools
800-899-6687
www.intellitools.com

Ipswitch
www.ipswitch.com

Jackson Software
800-850-1777
www.jacksoncorp.com

Jay Klein Productions, Inc.
719-599-8786
www.gradebusters.com

JKRB
www.pocketmindmap

K-12 MicroMedia Publishing Inc.
201-529-4500
www.k12mmp.com/

Kendall/Hunt Publishing
800-228-0810
www.kendallhunt.com

Kimbo
800-631-2187
www.kimbo.com

Knowledge Adventure
800-545-7677
www.hyperstudio.com

Lotus Development Corp.
800-343-5414
www.lotus.com

MacIRC
www.macirc.com

Macromedia
415-252-2000
www.macromedia.com

Margi
http://www.margi.com

MGI
www.mgisoft.com

MicroFit
800-822-0405
www.microfit.com

Microsoft
800-426-9400
www.microsoft.com

mIRC
www.mirc.com

Misty City Software
www.mistycity.com

Multimedia Professionals Inc.
www.mmpro.com

Muscle Dynamics
http://www.muscledynamics.com

NASCO
800-558-9595
www.enasco.com

Neat Sports
www.neatsys.com

New Measure
888-881-7979
www.rubrics.com

Newlife Technologies
800-639-5432
www.newlifetech.com

Nordic Software
800-306-6502
www.nordicsoftware.com

Novel Products
800-323-5143
www.novelproductsinc.com

Omron Healthcare, Inc
877 - 216 - 1333
www.omronhealthcare.com

Palm, Inc
www.palm.com

Palm Technology
www.palm-technology.com

Panasonic
800-742-8086
www.panasonic.com

PE-TV
http://www.canamedia.com/
catalogue_agency_04.html

Peachpit Press
800-283-9444
www.peachpit.com

Peak Performance
800-PIK-PEAK
www.peakperform.com

Polar Electro Inc.
800-227-1314
www.polar.fi/index.html

PowerOn Software, Inc.
www.poweronsw.com

Quark, Inc.
www.quark.com

Realviz
www.realviz.com

Reebok
www.reebok.com

SIRS
www.sirs.com

The Skier's Edge Company
800-225-9669
www.skiersedge.com

Slim Goodbody
800-962-7546
http://www.slimgoodbody.com

Sony
800-352-7669
www.sony.com

SoundStep
www.soundstep.com

Sports Illustrated for Kids
800-992-0196
www.sikids.com

Super School Software
800-248-7099
www.superschoolsoftware.com

SyberVision
800-678-0887

Tanita
800-tanita-8
www.tanita.com

Thinking Bytes
www.adessosystems.com

Tom Synder
800-334-0236
www.TeacTSP.com

TurboStats Software Co.
800-607-8287
www.turbostats.com

Turner Multimedia
800-639-7797
learning.turner.com

Ventura Educational Systems
800-336-1022
www.venturaes.com

Vic Braden
www.vicbraden.com

Wagon Wheels
714-846-8169

Walk 4 Life
walk4life.com

WinZip
winzip.com

World Book
www.worldbook.com

APPENDIX B

Television Programmers

ABC
77 W. 66th St., 9th Floor
New York, NY 10023
abc.go.com

CBS
51 West 52nd St.
New York, NY 10019
www.cbs.com

The Disney Channel
3800 West Alameda
Burbank, CA 91505
www.disney.go.com

Discovery Channel
7700 Wisconsin Ave.
Bethesda, MD 20814-3522
school.discovery..com

ESPN/ESPN2
935 Middle St.
Bristol, CT 06010
msn.espn.go.com

The History Channel
235 E. 45th St.
New York, NY 10017
historychannel.com

Lifetime
309 West 49th St.
New York, NY 10019
lifetimetv.com

NBC-TV
30 Rockefeller Plaza, 25th Floor
New York, NY 10112
nbc.com

Nickelodeon
1515 Broadway, 39th Floor
New York, Ny 10036
www.nickjr.com/teachers

Public Broadcasting Service
1320 Braddock Pl.
Alexandria, VA 22314
www.pbs.org

Sci-Fi Channel
1230 Avenue of the Americas
New York, NY 10020
scifi.com

The Learning Channel
7700 Wisconsin Ave.
Bethesda, MD 20814-3522
www.discovery.com

Turner Network Television
1 CNN Center
Atlanta, GA 30348-5366
www.tnt.tv

APPENDIX C

Suggested Journals and Magazines

Camcorder & Computer Video
4880 Market St.
Ventura, CA 93003-7783
805-644-3824

Converge Magazine
100 blue ravine Road
Folsom, CA 95630
916-363-5000
www.convergemag.com

Learning & Leading with Technology
480 Charnelton St.
Eugene, OR 97401
541-346-4414
www.iste.org

MacWorld
P. O. Box 54506
Boulder, CO 80323-4506
303-665-8930
www.macworld.com

Media & Methods
1429 Walnut St - 10th Floor
Philadelphia, PA 19102
215-563-6005
media-methods.com

Mobile Computing
P. O. Box 850901
Braintree, MA 02185-0901
800-274-1218
www.mobilecomputing.com

PC World
501 Second Street
San Francisco, CA 94107
415-243-0500
pcworld.com

Pen Computing
PO Box 408
Plainview, NY 11803-9801
516-349-9333
pencomputing.com

Pocket PC Magazine
110 N Court
Fairfield, IA 52556
800-373-6114
pocketpcmag.com

T.H.E. Journal
17501 17th St, 230
Tustin, CA 92780
714-730-4011
thejournal.com

Technology and Learning
600 Harrison St
San Francisco, CA 94107
techlearning.com

Videomaker
PO Box 3780
Chico, CA 95927-9840
800-284-3226
videomaker.com

Glossary

Address: There are two main types of addresses on the Internet—the Uniform Resource Locator (URL), and the e-mail address.

Alternate text: Descriptive text that can be set to display in place of an image, while the image is downloading or when users place a mouse pointer over an image.

Analog: Refers to an electronic device that uses a system of unlimited variables to measure or represent the flow of data.

Animation: A method for displaying several different frames in rapid succession to give the illusion of movement.

Aperture: The opening at the front of the camera. It determines the amount of light that will pass through the lens to fall on the image sensor, which is used to record an image.

Application : A set of instructions that tell the computer to perform a specific task. Also referred to as a program or software.

ASCII: An acronym for American Standard Code for Information Interchange. It is useful for exchanging information between different kinds of computer equipment and software programs, because it eliminates all program-specific symbols. Sometimes referred to as text.

Aspect ratio: Proportional width and height of a picture on screen.

Attachment: Any file or document that is attached to an e-mail message and sent to another mailbox.

Audio dub: Allows you to replace sound without disturbing the picture.

Audio mixer: Device used to blend multiple sound inputs into a desired composite output.

Authoring systems/languages: Programs used in developing computer-assisted instructional programs. They allow computer-based text, numbers, buttons, graphics, video, and audio to be integrated into an instructional program.

Auto focus: Focuses specifically on a certain object, making it the finest detailed object in the picture.

Avatar: A graphic representation of a real person in cyberspace.

Back up: To make a spare copy of a file or disk.

Bandwidth: A measurement of how much information can be carried over the Internet. The greater the bandwidth, the faster information is transmitted.

Bar code: A set of lines that represents a number.

Bar-code reader: A device that reads and interprets bar codes.

BASIC: Acronym for Beginners All-Purpose Symbolic Instruction Code. One of the more popular languages for personal computers.

Baud: The rate of character transmission speed over asynchronous communication devices such as modems.

Bit: A one (1) or a zero (0) that represents a set or unset switch in machine code. This is the smallest measurement of data.

Bluetooth: A very short-range wireless connection standard that links a wide range of computers, electronics, and telecom devices.

Bookmark: A way of marking an Internet site so that you can easily visit it again.

Boot: To start up a computer.

BPS: Bits per second. The speed at which data are transmitted.

Browser: A program that enables you to navigate the World Wide Web.

Bug: An error in a program.

Button: A graphic element within an interface that represents an embedded action or function.

Byte: A group of eight bits, or one character (letter, digit, symbol).

Cable: Wires or cords used to link various pieces of equipment.

Cable modem: A device used to connect a computer to the cable television network for fast data transfer.

Cache: A high-speed memory area used to store data.

Capacity: The amount of data you can store; the total number of bytes that can be stored in memory or, more likely, on a disk.

Capture: The process of converting analog video to a digital format.

Capture card: A piece of computer hardware that captures digital video and audio from an analog source to a hard drive.

Cardioid: The most common type of unidirectional microphone.

CCD: Light sensitive computer chip in video cameras that converts images into electrical flows.

CD-ROM: A disk that contains graphics, pictures, movies, or text information. It cannot be written to by a personal computer.

CD-R (CD Recordable): A type of compact disc that can record data.

CD-RW (CD Rewritable): Like CD-R, except that it can be erased and rewritten to.

Central processing unit (CPU): Performs the functions as instructed by the program, and controls the transfer of programs, files, and data within the computer system.

Chat: To have a conversation via computer linkups with other computer users.

Chat room: A location on the Internet set up to allow people to converse in real time by typing messages.

Click: To position a pointer on a particular part of the screen, then press and release the mouse button.

Clip art: A drawing that has been saved on a CD-ROM, hard drive, computer program, or floppy disk. The clip art can be imported into another program.

Clock speed: A measure of how fast a computer's microprocessor or brain can think—measured in millions of cycles per second, or megahertz.

Codec: Software that translates video or audio between its uncompressed form and the compressed form in which it is stored.

Color bit depth: Number of different colors a piece of software or hardware can display.

Compact disc (CD): A 4-3/4-inch optical disc that contains programs and files encoded digitally in constant linear velocity format.

Compact flash: Most common type of memory storage for digital cameras.

Compression: A technique for reducing the storage requirements of electronic data.

Computer: The piece of hardware that houses the central processing unit.

Computer system: A complete computer setup, including the computer, monitor, keyboard, disk drive, and other peripherals.

Constant power mode: A feature that allows you to work at a set level of intensity regardless of your pedaling RPM. This means if the user pedals faster or slower the computer will automatically adjust the resistance accordingly.

Continuous-duty horsepower: The continuous power that a treadmill motor can reach and maintain under any load or no-load condition.

Convergence: The merging of all data and all media into a common form.

Cookie: A small piece of text transferred to a Web browser through a server for the purpose of tracking the user.

Courseware: Instructional software and support materials used to deliver a course or instructional module.

Cross talk: An unwanted signal on one channel due to an input on a different channel.

Crosstrainer: Another name for elliptical crosstrainers. A machine similar to steppers, but instead of moving your feet up and down, feet actually move in an elliptical motion. This eliminates the high impact on joints.

Cursor: A blinking underline, rectangle, or other symbol that marks the user's location on the screen.

Data: Information or material that are created on and manipulated by a computer.

Data base: A collection of information stored as a computer file that is set up to allow people to easily retrieve that information.

Data compression: Any method of condensing information so it can be stored in less space and/or transmitted in less time.

Data warehouse: A central database, frequently very large, that can provide authorized users with access to all of a company's information.

Decompression: The decoding of a compressed video data stream to allow playback.

Delimiter: A comma, tab, colon, semicolon, or similar character that separates tabular data in a text file.

Demodulate: To change analog data into digital data.

Desktop publishing: Using software to produce documents with elaborate control of the form and appearance of individual pages.

Desktop videoconferencing: A computer-to-computer form of live action interactive two-way video/audio communication.

Dial-up access: A service that allows the user, with a modem and a personal computer, to create an Internet connection via a phone line.

Digital: The storing of data in a series of numbers.

Digital subscriber line (DSL): Technology used to transmit digital data on regular copper phone lines.

320

Digital video: A technology that displays digital graphics and full-motion video.

Digital zoom: The electronic brain within the camera that zooms in digitally, usually two to three times closer.

Digitizer: Device that imports and converts analog video and/or audio images into digital data.

Directory: A list of the contents on a disk.

Distance learning: Using some means, electronic or otherwise, to connect students with instructors/resources that can help them acquire knowledge and skills.

Document: An electronic file.

Domain name: A IP address expressed in letters instead of numbers, usually reflecting the name of the school or district represented by the web site.

Double click: To position the pointer at a specific location on the screen, then press and release the mouse button twice in quick succession.

Download: To copy something from the Internet and save it to your computer.

Download time: The time it takes to transfer a file to another computer.

Drag: To move something to a new location by positioning the pointer at a specific location on the screen, then pressing and holding the mouse button while moving the mouse.

Driver resource: A program in a system folder or directory that tells the computer how to work with a device (a printer, for example).

DVD: Digital versatile discs or digital video discs. CD-like discs on which you can store massive amounts of data in digital form.

DVD-R: An alternative to a CD-R that will hold up to 10 times more content.

DVD-ROM: An alternative to a CD-ROM that will hold up to 10 times more content.

DVD-RW: An alternative to a CD-RW that will hold up to 10 times more content.

e-book: A flat panel computer display that is designed to resemble a book, but provides interactive graphics and searchable text features.

Electronic gradebook: Software designed to maintain and calculate student grades.

Elevation: The angle of the treadmill deck or elliptical ramp used to simulate walking or running uphill.

e-mail: Electronic mail that is sent via an online service or the Internet.

e-mail address: The Internet equivalent of a mailing address.

Emoticon: A "picture" created with computer keys.

Encoder: A device that translates a video signal into a different format.

Ergonomics: Centers on how the total work environment—including equipment, furnishings, and tasks—affects worker comfort, health, and productivity.

Export: To save all or part of a document in a format other than the one in which it was created.

FAQ: Frequently asked questions about a certain topic.

File: A single, named collection of data—such as a manuscript or a list of addresses—that can be recalled by the computer.

File transfer protocol (FTP): One of several methods of transferring information from one Internet location to another.

Firewall: A combination of hardware and software designed to prevent unauthorized users from entering a company's data infrastructure from the Internet.

Flame: A message that insults or attacks another user.

Focal length: Distance from a camera's lens to a focused image with the lens focused on infinity.

Folder: A holder of programs, files, or other folders on the Macintosh or Windows desktop.

Font: A collection of letters, numbers, punctuation marks, and other typographical symbols with a consistent appearance. Also known as a typeface.

Footer: A line in a document that can be set to repeat automatically at the bottom of each page.

Frame rate: Number of video frames displayed each second.

Freeze-frame: A mode of video replay that stops and holds a video image.

FTP (file transfer protocol): A way of transferring files from one computer to another using common settings and procedures.

Full-motion video: A standard for video playback on a computer (30 frames per second).

Function keys: The keys that contain the letter F and a number. Function keys (or F keys) tell the computer to perform certain functions, depending on the software.

f-stop: Numbers corresponding to variable size of camera's iris opening and the amount of light passing through the lens. The higher the number, the less light that enters.

Generation loss: Degradation in picture and sound quality resulting from duplication of original master video recording.

GIF (graphical interchange format): A compressed graphical file used on the Internet.

Gigabyte (GB): Approximately one billion bytes—specifically, 1,073,741,824 bytes.

GPS: Global Positioning System, uses the government's fleet of 24 satellites to pinpoint a position on the globe to within about 100 yards.

Graphical user interface: A visual metaphor that uses icons to represent actual items that can be selected or manipulated with a pointing device.

Graphics: Computer pictures.

Hard drive: A magnetic disk that stores information.

Hardware: The physical, electronic, and mechanical components of the computer system.

Header: A line in a document that can be set to repeat automatically at the top of each page.

Hertz: The measure of the speed (clock speed) at which the computer processes information.

Hierarchical file system: The feature that uses folders to organize files, programs, and other folders on a disk. Folders (which are analogous to subdirectories in other systems) can be nested in other folders to create as many levels in a hierarchy as necessary.

Hologram: A three-dimensional projection resulting from the interaction of laser beams.

Home page: The main World Wide Web page for an online site; the first screen you see when you connect to a site on the Internet.

http (hypertext transfer protocol): The primary protocol for the World Wide Web; http allows linking between Web sites.

Hyperlinks: Graphic or text elements on a Web page that users click to display another location on the page, another Web page on the same Web site, or a Web page on a different Web site.

Hypermedia: An extension of hypertext that utilizes various types of media. All the various forms of data are organized so that a user can easily move from one to another.

Hypertext: Linking information together through a variety of paths or connections. Hypertext allows users to cross-reference related units of information in a manner similar to the human thinking process.

Icon: A symbolic, pictorial representation of any function, task, program, data, or disk.

IEEE 1394 (Firewire): A specification for a new, high-speed external bus used to connect computer peripherals.

Image map: A graphic that has clickable areas defined on it that when clicked, serve as a link that will take the viewer to another location.

Import: To bring into a document all or part of another document that has been stored in another format.

Incline: The angle of the treadmill deck or elliptical ramp used to simulate walking or running uphill.

Input: Data that are entered into the computer.

Infrared communications: The use of infrared light to move data between two computers.

Interface: Hardware that links the computer to another device, such as a printer.

Internet: A world wide network that allows computers to communicate with one another.

Internet address: An e-mail or other address that specifies a location on the Internet.

Internet appliance: Devices such as WebTV units, Web-ready phones, and hand held devices that give users access to the Internet and e-mail.

Internet Service Provider (ISP): An organization that lets users pay a fee tin order to connect to the Internet.

Interactive heart rate control: A feature on some exercise machines that adjust speed, resistance or incline to keep the user in his/her heart rate training zone. The user must wear a heart rate monitor for this feature to work.

IP (internet protocol): A standard, agreed-upon way of coding and sending data across the Internet.

IP address: Also called an Internet Protocol address. An assigned series of numbers, separated by periods, that designates an address on the Internet.

Jog/Shuttle: Manual control on some videocassette recorders that facilitates viewing and editing precision.

JPEG (joint photographic experts group): A graphic file known for its photographic quality colors.

Keyframe: A complete image used as a reference for subsequent images.

Kilobyte (K): A unit of measurement equal to 1,024 bytes.

Kilohertz (kHz): A measure of audio samples per second. Higher sample rates yield better sound quality and larger file sizes.

Kiosk: A self-contained, stand-alone unit that houses an interactive laser disc system.

Laser: A device that allows light to be amplified and concentrated into a very narrow and concise beam.

Listserv: A subscription mailing list that allows users to send to and receive e-mail messages from other subscribers.

Load: To transfer programs from a storage device into the computer's memory.

Local area network (LAN): A system that connects two or more microcomputers, allowing users to share resources and communications.

Lux: A measurement of light.

Macro: A lens capable of extreme closeup focusing; useful for intimate views of very small objects.

Maintenance-free: A term used by treadmill manufacturers meaning the treadmill deck is laminated and does not have to be maintained or lubricated with wax. Occasional cleaning of dust and debris with silicone spray may still be needed to keep this kind of treadmill operating efficiently.

Megabyte (MB): A unit of measurement equal to approximately one million bytes—specifically, 1,048,576 bytes.

Megahertz (Mhz): One million cycles per second.

Megapixel: One million pixels.

Memory: The amount of space on a storage device in which information can be saved.

Menu: A list of options on the screen.

Menu bar: The horizontal strip at the top of the screen that contains menu titles.

Menu title: A word or phase in the menu bar that designates one menu. Clicking on the menu title causes the title to be highlighted and its menu to appear below it.

Microprocessor: The set of tiny switches (circuitry) that process data in a computer.

Modem: A device that allows a computer to communicate with other computers via telephone lines.

Modulate: To change digital data into analog data.

Monitor: The screen that is used to display the computer's output.

Mouse: An input device that controls a pointer on the screen. By moving the mouse and pressing its button, the user can draw pictures, select from lists, and move things around the screen.

MPEG: A high compression method for video and audio data. MPEG supports the CD playing of full screen/full motion video.

MP3: A method of compressing audio files into one-tenth of their normal size while still keeping near CD-quality sound.

Multimedia: An integration of text, graphics, animation, voice, music, or motion video into a program on a personal computer.

Network: A group of computers joined by data-carrying links.

Newsgroups: Internet discussion groups that focus on specific topics.

Online: Connected to an online service or the Internet.

Online service: A service that enables the user to dial in, connect to the Internet, and send and receive e-mail.

Operating system: Computer system software that facilitates using a computer to create programs and data files. It also controls the transmission and receipt of data to and from peripheral devices connected to the computer.

Optical zoom: The actual lens elements inside the camera move to achieve the desired effect.

Output: The results of a computer operation (data on printed paper or a computer screen, or data stored on some magnetic media).

Pagination: Automatic page numbering done by a word processing or desktop publishing program.

Pan: Horizontal (side to side) camera pivot.

Paste: To clip sections of material from one file and put them into another file.

PC Card: Refers to a credit card-size device that enhances a computer once installed (e.g., flash memory card, a network card, a modem, or even a hard drive).

PCMCIA: Card slots on laptop computers that allow on to use PC cards, printer, or modem.

Peak-duty horsepower: The absolute maximum horsepower a treadmill motor can reach under peak load conditions.

Peripheral device: A piece of computer hardware—such as a disk drive, printer, or modem—that is connected to the computer system.

Photo CD: A compact disc format designed by the Eastman Kodak Company to store and display photographs.

Pixel: A picture element.

Plug in: An application that allows a graphic browser to complete a given task or view a specific file (e.g., Shockwave).

Port: A socket on the back panel of the computer where the cable from a peripheral device, another computer, or a network can be connected.

Portal: A web site that offers a broad array of resources and services, from e-mail to online shopping.

Potentiometers: Sensors that measure changes in joint flexion/extension.

Presentation software: Programs designed to allow people to display pictures and text to support their lectures.

Pre-sets: Used in electronic computer controlled equipment to vary the workout speed, resistance, incline to offer the user a more challenging and variable workout.

Printer: A device that is connected to a computer to allow printed output.

Prosocial skills: Those skills that help partners or groups complete a task and build positive feelings in the participants.

Protocol: A set of rules for using the Internet.

Public domain software: Uncopyrighted programs available for copying and use by the public at no cost.

Push technologies: A system set up to send out information whether or not anyone requests it.

Radio frequency (RF) modulator: A device that transforms a television set into a computer display device.

Random access memory (RAM): Computer memory that temporarily stores programs, files, and data while they are in use.

Read-only memory (ROM): Computer memory that stores permanent information and instructions for the central processing unit.

Rendering time: The time it takes an editing computer to composite source elements so they can be played in full motion.

Resolution: The number of dots (pixels) on the screen.

Royalty free: Graphics that you can purchase and use in your published Web pages without have to pay a royalty to the company that created them.

San-serif fonts: Block style characters used frequently for headings, sub-headings, and Web pages.

Save: To store data.

Search engine: A software program that helps the user find information on the Internet.

Serial interface (RS -232): Transmits information one bit at a time.

Serif fonts: Fonts with small extra strokes at the top and bottom of the characters; used frequently for paragraph text in printed materials.

Shareware: Uncopyrighted software that anyone may use; each user is asked to pay a voluntary fee to the designer.

Simulation: A resemblance to the actual, without being the actual activity.

Snail mail: Regular postal service mail, as opposed to e-mail.

Software piracy: Illegally copying and using a copyrighted software package without buying it.

Spamming: Flooding a mailbox or a listserv with unsolicited messages (usually advertisements).

Speech synthesizer: An electronic device, usually a computer chip, that passes words and sentences through a speaker.

Spreadsheet: A computer accounting program that organizes financial data by placing it in categories in a series of columns and rows.

Streaming: Movie or audio data that are visible in real time while they are downloading.

Superimposing: Titles or graphics appearing over an existing video picture.

System file: The program the computer uses to start up.

Terabyte: Approximately 1,000,000,000,000 bytes.

Test generator: Software designed to help teachers prepare and/or administer tests.

Tilde (~): A squiggly character sometimes used in Internet addresses.

Tilt: Vertical (up and down) camera pivot.

Touch screen: Type of input device designed to allow users to make selections by touching the monitor.

Treadmill horsepower: The amount of horsepower a motor can reach under intermitten load conditions.

Uniform Resource Locator (URL): Connects the user to a specific place on the Internet; a web page address.

Upload: To save something from your computer to the Internet.

URL: The acronym for Uniform Resource Locator. A URL is the address for a Web page that can be typed in the address box in a browser to open a Web page.

USB: A computer port to which peripherals can be connected.

User name: The name used to log on to a network.

Vector-based graphics: Graphics based on mathematical formulas rather than pixels.

Video authoring software: An application that's designed to save and transfer edited video to a finished format, such as DVD.

Video card: A circuit board in a computer that controls display factors such as resolution, colors displayed, and speed of images displayed.

Video compression: Reducing the digital data in a file, by throwing away information that the eye can't see.

Video dub: Insert edit that records video without disturbing the existing audio.

Video editing software: A program used to capture, edit, save, and output video clips.

Virtual reality: A computer-generated environment designed to provide a lifelike simulation of actual settings.

Virus: A program written with the purpose of doing harm or mischief to programs, data, and/or hardware components of a computer system.

Voice recognition: The capability provided by a computer and program to respond predictably to speech commands.

Wearable systems: Computer components worn on one's body or clothing.

Web site: The place where a home page and its associated files are located.

Word wraparound: The automatic continuation of text from the end of one line to the beginning of the next.

World Wide Web (www): The collection of "pages" available to the millions of computers connected to the Internet.

Zoom lens: A specific type of lens in a digital camera that is able to change its focal length to close in on a subject to a certain degree, with the effect of enlarging the subject in the image.

References

Anglin, G. A. (Ed.). (1995). *Instructional technology: Past, present, and future*, 2nd ed. Englewood, CO: Libraries Unlimited.

Barrett, H. C. (2000). Create your own electronic portfolio. *Learning and Leading with Technology, 27(7):*14-21.

Bass, S. (2003). Maximum google. *PC World,* June 2003: 121-126.

Bassett, D. R., Ainsworth, B. E., Swartz, A. M., Strath, S. J., O'Brien, W. L., & King, G. A. (2000). Validity of four motion sensors in measuring moderate intensity physical activity. *Medicine and Science in Sports and Exercise,32:* S471-S480.

Bassett, D. R., Ainsworth, B. E., Leggett, S. R., Mathien, C. A., Main, J. A., Hunter, D. C., & Duncan, G. E. (1996). Accuracy of five electronic pedometers for measuring distance walked. *Medicine and Science in Sports and Exercise, 28:* 1071-1077.

Baumgartner, T. A., & Cicciarella, C. F. (1987). *Directory of computer software with application to sport science, health, and dance II.* Reston, VA: AAHPERD Research Consortium.

Beighle, A., Pangrazi, R. P. & Vincent, S. D. (2001). Pedometers, physical activity, and accountability. *Journal of Physical Education, Recreation, and Dance, 72:*16-19, 36.

Blackall, B. (1992). *Australian physical education, book 1.* South Melbourne: MacMillan Company of Autralia.

Blackall, B., & Davis, D. (1992). *Australian physical education, book 2.* South Melbourne: MacMillan Company of Australia.

Bouten, C. V., Sauren, A. A. H. J., Verduin, M., & Janssen, J. D. (1997). Effects of placement and orientation of body-fixed accelerometers on the assessment of energy expenditure during walking. *Medical and Biological Engineering and Computing, 35:*50-56.

Briggs, J. C. (2002). Virtual reality is getting real: Prepare to meet your clone. *The Futurist,* May-June 2002.

Buck, M. M. (2002). *Assessing heart rate in physical education.* Reston, VA: NASPE.

Burkett, L. N. (1994). A comparison of three methods to measure percent body fat on mentally retarded adults. *Physical Educator, 51(2):* 67-73.

Campbell, K. L., Crocker, P. R. E., & McKenzie, D. C. (2002). Field evaluation of energy expenditure in women using Tritrac accelerometers. *Medicine and Science in Sports and Exercise, 34(10):*1667-1674.

Cassady, S. L., Nielsen, D. H., Janz, K. F., Wu, Y. T., Cook, J. S., & Hansen, J. R. (1993). Validity of near infrared body composition analysis in children and adolescents. *Medicine and Science in Sports and Exercise, 25(10):* 1185-1191.

Coleman, K. J., Saelens, B. E., Wiedrich-Smith, M. D., Finn, J. D., & Epstein, L. H. (1997). Relationship between TriTrac-R3D vectors, heart rate, and self report in obese children. *Medicine and Science in Sport and Exercise, 29:* 1535-1542.

Corbin, C. B., & Lindsey, R. (2002). *Fitness for life, 4th edition.* Champaign, IL: Human Kinetics.

References

Corbin, C. B. & Pangrazi, R. P. (1998). *Physical activity for children: A statement of guidelines.* Reston, VA: NASPE.

Council for Physical Education for Children. (1998). *Physical activity for children: A statement of guidelines.* Reston, VA: NASPE.

Crouter, S. E., Schneider, P. L., Karabulut, M., & Bassett, D. R. (2003). Pedometer reliability. *Medicine and Science in Sports and Exercise, 35*(8): 1455-1460.

Dale, D., Corbin, C. B., & Dale, K. S. (2000). Restricting opportunities to be active during school time. *Research Quarterly for Exercise and Sport, 71*(3): 240-248.

Darden, G. (1999). Videotape feedback or student learning and performance: A learning-stages approach. *Journal of Physical Education, Recreation, and Dance, 70*(9): 40-45.

Darden, G. & Shimon, J. (2000). Revisit an "Old" technology: Videotape feedback for motor skill learning and performance. *Strategies, 13*(4): 17-21.

Davis, D., Kimmet, T., & Auty, M. (1986). *Physical education: Theory and practice.* South Melbourne: MacMillan Company of Australia.

Doering, N. (2000). Measuring student understanding with a videotape performance assessment. *Journal of Physical Education, Recreation, and Dance, 71*(7): 47-52.

Dougherty, N. J. IV (Ed.). (2002). *Physical activity and sport for the secondary school student,* 3rd ed. Reston, VA: AAHPERD.

Epstein, L., Paluch, R., Coleman, K., Vito, D., & Anderson, K. (1996). Determinants of physical activity in obese children assessed by accelerometer and self-report. *Medicine and Science in Sports and Exercise, 28:* 1157-1164.

Ernst, M. P. (2000). Examination of research supported physical activity measurement techniques. *CAHPERD Journal/Times, 63*(2): 20-23.

Eston, R. G., Crug, A., Fu, F., & Fung, L. M. (1993). Fat-free mass estimation by bioelectrical impedance and anthropometric techniques in Chinese children. *Journal of Sports Science, 11:*241-247.

Eston, R. E., Rowlands, A.V., & Ingledew, D. K. (1998). Validity of heart rate, pedometry, and accelerometry for predicting the energy cost of children's activities. *Journal of Applied Physiology, 84:* 362-371.

Freedson, P. (1991). Electronic motion sensors and heart rate as measures of physical activity in children. *Journal of School Health, 61:* 220-223.

Freedson, P. (1989). Field monitoring of physical activity in children. *Pediatric Exercise Science, 1:* 8-18.

Freedson, P. S., & Miller, K. (2000). Objective monitoring of physical activity using motion sensors. *Research Quarterly for Exercise and Sport, 71*(2): 21-29.

Gibbs-Smith, C. (1978). *The inventions of Leonardo da Vinci.* London: Phaidon Press.

Goran, M. I., Kaskoun, M. C., Carpenter, W. H., Poehlman, E. T., Ravussin, E., & Fontvieille, A. M. (1993). Estimating body composition of young children by using bioelectrical resistance. *Journal of Applied Physiology, 75:*1776-1780.

Gu, W. (1996). The experiment of researching the teaching method of fundamental volleyball skills with an optimized combination of multimedia. *Journal of Guanghous Physical Education Institute, 16*(2):73-78.

Haggerty, T. R. (1999). *The use and abuse of computer-based information technologies for teaching, learning, and performing in sport and physical education.* World congress on information technology in physical education. National Taiwan College of Physical Education. Taipei, Taiwan.

Halal, W. E. (2000). The top 10 emerging technologies. *The Futurist 2000 Special Report.*

Hendleman, D., Miller, K., Bagget, C., Debold, E., & Freedson, P. (2000). Validity of accelerometry for the assessment of moderate intensity physical activity in the field. *Medicine and Science in Sports and Exercise, 32*: S442-S449.

Houtkooper, L. B., Lohman, T. G., Going, S. B., & Hall, M. C. (1989). Validity of bioelectrical impedance for body composition assessment in children. *Journal of Applied Physiology, 66*: 814-821.

Jakicic, J. M., Winters, C., Lagally, K., Ho, J., Robertson, R. J., & Wing, R. R. (1999). The accuracy of the Tritrac-R3D accelerometer to estimate energy expenditure. *Medicine and Science in Sports and Exercise, 31*: 747-754.

Janz, K. F. (1994). Validation of the CSA accelerometer for assessing children's physical activity. *Medicine and Science in Sports and Exercise, 26*: 369-375.

Janz, K., Golden, J., Hansen, G. & Mahony, L. (1992). Heart rate monitoring of physical activity in children and adolescents: The Muscatine study. *Pediatrics, 89*: 256-261.

Janz, K., Witt, J., & Mahoney, L. (1995). The stability of children's physical activity as measured by accelerometery and self-report. *Medicine and Science in Sports and Exercise, 27*: 1326-1332.

Karvonen, J., Chwalbinska-Moneta, J., & Saynajakangas, S. (1984). Comparison of heart rates measured by ECG and microcomputer. *Physician and Sportsmedicine, 12*:65-69.

Knudson, D. V. & Morrison, C. S. (1997). *Qualitative analysis of human movement.* Champaign, IL: Human Kinetics.

Kromhout, O. & Butzin, S. (1993). Integrating computers into the elementary school curriculum: An evaluation of nine project CHILD model schools. *Journal of Research on Computing in Education, 26*(1): 55-69.

Kulik, J. A. (1994). Meta-analytic studies of findings on computer-based instruction. In E. Baker & H. O'Neil (Eds.). *Technology assessment in education and training.* Hillsdale, NJ: Lawrence Erlbaum Associates.

Lee, T. D., Swinnen, S. P. & Serrrien, D. J. (1994). Cognitive effort and motor learning, *Quest 46*: 328-344.

Levin, H. M., & Meister, G. (1986). Is CAI cost-effective? *Phi Delta Kappan, 67*, 745-749.

Macfarlane, D. J., Fogarty, B. A., Hopkins, W. G. (1989). The accuracy and variability of commercially available heart rate monitors. *New Zealand Journal of Sports Medicine, 17*(4): 51-53.

Meijer, G. A., Klass, R., Westerterp, H. K., & Foppe, T. H. (1989). Assessment of energy expenditure by recording heart rate and body acceleration. *Medicine and Science in Sport and Exercise, 21*: 343-347.

Minerd, J. (2000). High-tech clothes. *The Futurist, 34*(1): 12.

Mitchell, M. & McKethan, R. (2003). *Integrating technology and pedagogy in physical education teacher education.* Cerritos, CA: Bonnie's Fitware.

Mitchell, M., McKethan, R. & Mohnsen, B. S. (2004). *Integrating technology and physical education: Standards-based K-12 lessons.* Cerritos, CA: Bonnie's Fitware.

Mohnsen, B. S. (Ed.). (2003a). *Concepts and principles of physical education: What every student needs to know,* 2nd ed. Reston, VA: NASPE.

Mohnsen, B. S. (2003b). *Teaching middle school physical education,* 2nd ed. Champaign, IL: Human Kinetics.

Mohnsen, B. S. (Ed.). (1999). *The new leadership paradigm in physical education: What we need to lead.* Reston, VA: NASPE.

Mohnsen, B. (1998a). Professional development: When you want it and where you want it. *Journal of Physical Education, Recreation, and Dance, 69*(2): 14-17.

Mohnsen, B. (1998b). Search the web for personal and professional needs. *Teaching Elementary Physical Education, 9*(2): 29-30.

Mohnsen, B. (1998). California physical education web site. *CAHPERD Journal/Timesc, 60*(6): 11.

Mohnsen, B. (1998d). Technology and special events. *Teaching Elementary Physical Education, 9*(1): 27-29.

Mohnsen, B. (1997a). What's the ideal system? *Teaching Elementary Physical Education, 8(4)*: 14-15.

Mohnsen, B. (1997b). Authentic assessment in physical education. *Learning and Leading with Technology, 24*(7): 30-33.

Mohnsen, B. (1997c). Exercise physiology software. *Teaching Secondary Physical Education, 3*(6): 24-25.

Mohnsen, B. (1997d). Exercise physiology software. *Teaching Elementary Physical Education 8*(6): 22-24.

Mohnsen, B. (1997e). Social skills and technology: What's the connection? *Teaching Elementary Physical Education, 8*(5): 20-22.

Mohnsen, B. (1997f). Social skills and technology: What's the connection? *Teaching Secondary Physical Education, 3*(5): 20-22.

Mohnsen, B. (1997g).Stretching bodies and minds through technology. *Educational Leadership, 55*(3): 46-48.

Mohnsen, B. (1997h) What's the ideal system? *Teaching Secondary Physical Education, 3*(4): 10-11.

Mohnsen, B. S. & Mendon, K. (1997). Electronic portfolios in physical education. *Strategies, 11*(2): 13-16.

Mohnsen, B. S. & Schiemer, S. (1997). Handheld technology: Practical application of the Newton message pad. *Strategies, 10*(5): 11-14.

Mohnsen, B. S. & Thompson, C. (1997). Using video technology in physical education. *Strategies,* 10(6): 8-11.

Mohnsen, B. S., Chesnutt, C. B., & Burke, D. K. (1997). Multimedia projects for physical education, *Strategies, 11*(1): 10-13.

Mohnsen, B. S., Thompson, C., & Mendon, K. (1996). Effective ways to use technology. *Teaching Secondary Physical Education, 2* (1): 14-17.

Montoye, H. J., Kemper, H. C. G., Saris, W. H. M., & Washburn, R. A. (1996). *Measuring physical activity and energy expenditure.* Champaign, IL: Human Kinetics.

Moursund, D. (1998). Project-based learning in an information-technology environment. *Learning & Leading with Technology, 25*(8): 4, 55.

National Association for Sport and Physical Education. (2004). *Moving into the future: National physical education standards,* 2nd ed. St Louis: Mosby.

Negroponte, N. (1995). *Being digital.* New York: Knopf.

Nichols, J. F., Morgan, C. G., Chabot, L. E., Sallis, J. F., & Calfas, K. J. (2000). Assessment of physical activity with the Computer Science and Applications, Inc., Accelerometer: Laboratory versus field validation. *Research Quarterly for Exercise and Sport, 71*(1): 36-43.

Niemiec, R. P., Blackwell, M. C., & Walberg, H. J. (1986). CAI can be doubly effective. *Phi Delta Kappan, 67*:751.

Normal, D. (1993). *Things that make us smart: Defending human attributes in the age of the machine.* Reading, MA: Addison-Wesley.

Nunez, C., Gallagher, D., Visser, M., Pi-Sunyer, F. X., Wang, Z., & Heymsfield, S. B. (1997). Bioimpedance analysis: Evaluation of leg-to-leg system based on pressure contact footpad electrodes. *Medicine and Science in Sports and Exercise, 29*(4): 524-531.

Pambianco, G., Wing, R. R., Robertson, R. (1990). Accuracy and reliability of the Caltrac accelerometer for estimating energy expenditure. *Medicine and Science in Sport and Exercise, 22*: 858-862.

Perelman, L. J. (1992). *School's out: Hyperlearning, the new technology, and the end of education.* New York: Morrow.

Port, O. (1999). 21 Bright Ideas for the 21st Century. Business Week Online. http://www.businessweek.com/1999/99_35/b3644007.htm (30 August 1999).

Rainey, D. L. & Murray, T. D. (1997). *Foundations of personal fitness.* Minneapolis/St.Paul: West Publishing.

Rothstein, A. L. (1981). Using feedback to enhance learning and performance with emphasis on videotape replay. *Sport Psychology*, 22-30.

Rowland, T. W. (1996). *Developmental exercise physiology.* Champaign, IL: Huamn Kinetics.

Sallis, J. F., Buono, M. J., Roby, J. J., Carlson, D., & Nelson, J. A. (1990). The Caltrac accelerometer as a physical activity monitor for school-age children. *Medicine and Science in Sport and Exercise, 22*: 698-703.

Sallis, J., Condon, A., Goggin, K., Roby, J., Kolody, B., & Alcaraz, J. (1993). The development of self-administered physical activity surveys for 4th grade students. *Research Quarterly for Exercise and Sport, 64*: 25-31.

Simons-Morton, B. G., Taylor, W. C., & Huang, I. W. (1994). Validity of the physical activity interview and Caltrac with preadolescent children. *Research Quarterly for Exercise and Sport, 65*: 84-89.

Simpson, C. (2002). Copyright 101. *Educational Leadership,* January 2002, Spindt, G. B., Monti, W. H., & Hennessy, B. (1991). *Moving for life.* Dubuque, IA: Kendall/Hunt.

Spindt, G. B., Monti, W. H., Hennessy, B., Holyoak, C., & Weinberg, H. (1992). *Middle school physical education textbook series.* Dubuque, IA: Kendall/Hunt.

Stokes, R., & Schultz, S. L. (2002). *Personal fitness and you,* 2nd. Winston-Salem, NC: Hunter Textbooks.

Stokes, R., Schultz, S. L., & Polansky, B. C. (1997). *Lifetime personal fitness.* Winston-Salem, NC: Hunter Textbooks.

Thornburg, D. D. (1992). *Edutrends 2010: Restructuring, technology, and the future of education.* San Francisco, CA: Starson Publications.

Torp, L. T. & Sage, S. M. (1998). *Problems as possibilities: Problem-based learning for K-12 education.* Alexandria. VA: Association for Supervision and Curriculum Development.

Treiber, F. A., Musante, L., Hartdagan, S., Davis, H., Levy, M., & Strong, W. B. (1989). Validation of a heart rate monitor with children in laboratory and field settings. *Medicine and Science in Sports and Exercise, 21*:338-342.

Trost, S. G., Ward, D. S., & Burke, J. R. (1998). Validity of the computer science and application (CSA) activity monitor in children. *Medicine and Science in Sports and Exercise, 30*: 629-633.

Wajciechowski, J. A., Gayle R. C., Andrews, R. L., & Dintiman, G.B. (1991). Polar electro radio telemetry heart rate compared to ECG measurements. *Clinical Kinesiology, 45*(2):9-12.

Weiss, P. & Jessel, A. S. (1998). Virtual reality applications to work. *Work, 11*(3): 227-293.

Welk, G. J. (Ed.). (2002a). *Physical activity assessments for health-related research.* Champaign, IL: Human Kinetics.

Welk, G. J., Blair, S. N., Wood, K., Jones, S., & Thompson, R. (2000). A comparative evaluation of three accelerometry-based physical activity monitors. *Medicine and Science in Sports and Exercise, 32*: S489-S497.

Welk, G. J. & Corbin, C. B. (1995).The validity of the Tritrac-R3D activity monitor for the assessment of physical activity in children. *Research Quarterly for Exercise and Sport, 66*: 202-209.

Wilkinson, C., Pennington, T. R. & Padfield, G. (2000). Student perceptions of using skills software in physical education. *Journal of Physical Education, Recreation, and Dance, 71*(6): 37-40, 53.

Williams, C. S., Harageones, E. G., Johnson, D. J., & Smith, C. D. (2000). *Personal fitness: Looking good, feeling good.* Dubuque, IA: Kendall/Hunt.

Wooten, J. O. (2000). Health care in 2025: A patient's encounter. *The Futurist.* July-August 2000, 18-22.

Zeni, A. I., Hoffman, M. D., & Clifford, P. S. (1996). Energy expenditure with indoor exercise machines. *JAMA, 275* (18): 1424-1430.

Index

About the Author

Bonnie S. Mohnsen is the C.E.O. of Bonnie's Fitware Inc. She develops software, presents online training, writes books, provides presentations, and serves as an expert witness. Bonnie is a former physical educator with experience at the elementary, middle school, high school, and college levels.

Bonnie received her PhD in physical education administration from the University of Southern California in 1984. In 1990, she established the California Physical Education Electronic Bulletin Board which served as a model for physical education web pages. Dr. Mohnsen has received grants for using computers in education, including a $100,000 IBM Partnership Grant for using technology to teach biomechanic concepts in physical education.

Bonnie is a member of the American Alliance for Health, Physical Education, Recreation, and Dance and the International Society for Technology in Education. Her favorite leisure-time activities include skiing, jogging, hiking, swimming, boating, reading, and playing with her computer.

Other Books from Bonnie's Fitware Inc.
Available at: www.pesoftware.com

Integrating Technolgy and
Physical Education
Melanie Mitchell
Robert McKethan
Bonnie Mohnsen

Integrating Technology and Physical Education

Over 60 lesson plans (primary, elementary, middle school, and high school) addressing both the NASPE physical education content standards and ISTE technology standards. The must have book for K-12 physical educators.

Using Technology in Physical Education
Bonnie Mohnsen, Ph.D.

Using Technology in Physical Education

The fourth edition of the most popular and comprehensive book on using technology in physical educaiton. Used both as a college textbook and a handy resource for current physical educators.

Integrating Technology &Pedagogy in Physical Education Teacher Education

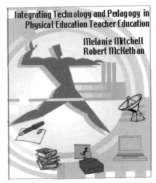

Integrating Technology and Pedagogy in
Physical Education Teacher Education
Melanie Mitchell
Robert McKethan

A valuable resource for college instructors and professional developers. This text shows the alignment between NASPE Beginning Teacher Standards and ISTE technology standards. THese standards are directed to minimum acceptable teaching competencies for beginning teachers. Lesson plan examples are provided for each standard.